An Altar of Roses

The Memoir of a Young Lady's Marriage to and Life with a Commander and Martyr of the Revolutionary Guards of the Islamic Republic of Iran

The Memoirs of Zahrā Panāhī-Ravā
As related to Bahrām Zarabī-Zādeh

Translated and Annotated
by Blake Archer Williams

Copyright © 2020 by Blake Archer Williams

All rights reserved. No part of this publication may be reproduced, distributed, or transmitted in any form or by any means, including photocopying, recording, or other electronic or mechanical methods, without the prior written permission of the publisher, except in the case of brief quotations embodied in critical reviews and certain other noncommercial uses permitted by copyright law. For permission requests, write to the publisher, addressed "Attention: - Permissions [An Altar of Roses]," at the email address below.

Lantern Publications
info@lanternpublications.com
www.lanternpublications.com

Ordering Information:
Quantity sales. Special discounts are available on quantity purchases by corporations, associations, and others. For details, contact the distributor at the address below.

Shia Books Australia
www.shiabooks.com.au
info@shiabooks.com.au

ISBN- 978-0-6489869-1-1

First Edition

In the Name of God,
the Most Compassionate, the Most Merciful

The martyr, Commander **Ali Chītsāzīān**; and his wife, Mrs. **Zahrā Panāhī-Ravā**, the author of the present book.

Contents

My Memories get played like a Movie Reel 9

A Suitor with Blue Eyes 79

Love Letters 133

A Second Honeymoon 153

My Beloved Flower 181

The Eleventh Rose Garden 183

Would that we had not Gone 209

Pink and Purple Curtains 223

Pink Lady 249

A Solution of Tears 265

Knitting 273

Split Pomegranates 275

Living with a Real Man for One Night 285

Father's Star 319

The Parent Student 325

Behind the Row of Trees 327

A Miraculous Sign 331

Translator's Preface

After the triumph of the Islamic Revolution of Iran, which was, among other things, an uprising against colonialism and its accommodationist regime, Iran's erstwhile master, the United States, attempted to execute various means of regaining what it considered to be a lost territory in its sphere of influence. When all other options (such as a failed coup d'état attempt and a botched-up military incursion) proved to be unsuccessful, a war was imposed on Iran by Saddam Hosayn's Bathist regime in Iraq. This was a war of manifestly unprovoked aggression on the part of Iraq which was nevertheless supported by *both* superpowers of the day, the United States and the Soviet Union, both of whom provided Saddam Hussein with advanced armaments. The US also provided Iraq with maps and satellite intelligence regarding Iran's troop and materiel positions and movements. The lesser European powers such as Britain, France, and Germany, also contributed to the war effort against Iran. France, for example, provided Saddam Hussein not only with its most sophisticated Mirage fighter jets, but it also provided the pilots to fly them and to drop bombs and missiles on Iran. Germany and Britain, for their part, provided Iraq with the chemical weapons with which it waged chemical warfare against Iran.[1] All of this was financed

---

[1] According to Iraqi documents, assistance in developing chemical weapons was obtained from firms in many countries, including the United States, West Germany, the Netherlands, the United Kingdom, and France. A report stated that Dutch, Australian, Italian, French and both West and East German companies were involved in the export of raw materials to Iraqi chemical weapons factories. Declassified CIA

by funds from Iraq's Arab neighbors, such as Saudi Arabia, Kuwait, and the UAE,[2] and was carried out with the full knowledge and support of the United States. According to Foreign Policy, the "Iraqis used mustard gas and sarin prior to four major offensives in early 1988 that relied on U.S. satellite imagery, maps, and other intelligence... According to recently declassified CIA documents and interviews with former intelligence officials like Francona, the U.S. had firm evidence of Iraqi chemical attacks beginning in 1983".[3]

Iran ultimately prevailed in this war, whose purpose was to nip the burgeoning anti-colonialist values and ideals of the revolution in the bud and whose imposition was an ongoing outrage against justice and decency, by surviving it and pushing the invading forces back to the international borders. But it did

---

documents show that the United States was providing reconnaissance intelligence to Iraq around 1987–88 which was then used to launch chemical weapon attacks on Iranian troops and that the CIA fully knew that chemical weapons would be deployed and sarin and cyclosarin attacks followed.

[2] Iraq's main financial backers were the oil-rich Persian Gulf states, most notably Saudi Arabia ($30.9 billion), Kuwait ($8.2 billion), and the United Arab Emirates ($8 billion); (Pike, John, ed. *Iraq debt: Non-Paris Club Creditors*). In all, Iraq received $35 billion in loans from the West and between $30 and $40 billion from the Persian Gulf states during the 1980s; ("Annex D: Iraq Economic Data (1989–2003)". Comprehensive Report of the Special Advisor to the DCI [Director of Central Intelligence] on Iraq's WMD. 1 of 3. Central Intelligence Agency. 27 April 2007).

[3] "Exclusive: CIA Files Prove America Helped Saddam as He Gassed Iran". Foreign Policy. 26 August 2013.

not do so without paying a great price in human suffering and loss of life. The war lasted eight years (1980 – 1988) and its casualties on Iran's side included half a million dead soldiers and civilians and as many wounded.

The incredible sacrifices and courage that was shown on the part of Iranian soldiers and the Iranian nation more generally for the war effort and in defense of their country and the values of their nascent revolution gave rise to a genre of literature which goes by the name of the Sacred Defense (*defā-e moqaddas*) in Iran. The present memoir is a prominent example of a literary work in this fascinating yet almost completely unknown genre.

Blake Archer Williams
November 2020

My Memories get played like a Movie Reel

We were passing by Bū-Alī Hospital and I said, "Ali, a few months from now, our child will be born here."

"Here?" He asked, surprised.

"Well," I said, "because this is a private hospital. It's the best hospital in Hamedān."

Ali slowed the car down and said, "No. We will be going to a hospital that is frequented by the poor; this is where rich people go. Not everyone can afford to come here."

I was in my eighth month of pregnancy and I was not feeling at all well. It was a Thursday evening; December 24th, 1987. The pain would come and go and there was no telling when it would be back again. I had told everyone about Ali Agha's situation. In those days, my mother-in-law's house was full of guests and there was always someone coming or going. Mother was there too. As soon as I told her I was not feeling well, she called a cab and took me to the Fātemīeh Hospital, which was a public hospital. As soon as we stepped foot into the hospital, the news sounded everywhere as if a bomb had gone off: "Shahīd[4] Chītsāzīān's child is about to be born!"

The hospital workers were all excited, and suddenly I found myself surrounded by doctors and nurses. The news had spread in town like lightning. People would call the hospital and inquire about my health and that of the baby's. Mother, who was always by my side, would have to go and respond to these inquiries every once in a while. And although the doctors had said there were no signs of birth pangs, the head of the hospital had given instructions that I be admitted anyway.

I didn't have any pain that night, but the pains started on the following morning. Once again, a big group of doctors and nurses gathered around me in a circle. After a few hours, they repeated the same verdict: "It's nothing. Don't worry; there are no signs of a possible premature birth."

I insisted that I be allowed to go back home, but they would not release me. A few hours later the pain came back, and this time it was unbearable. Mother became very concerned. This

---

[4] Shahīd means martyr in Persian. The word has been left untranslated when it is used as an appellation of honor and is thus a title.

cycle repeated itself several times; and each time, several nurses would gather round and examine me, after which they would repeat the same words with dejection.

It was now Friday evening, December 25th, 1987; the birthday of His Eminence the Christ Jesus, son of Lady Mary, unto both of whom be God's peace and blessings. The unbearable pains had returned, and I was suffering them in long stretches. I thought I was going to die. I don't know why, but I was scared, and felt embarrassed. I thought that perhaps there was some issue, and that I might not be able to give birth to my child or something!

My heart was heavy and full of sorrow. I had still not been able to reconcile myself with the pain of Ali Agha's absence. His loss still seared everyone's heart, but it seared mine especially. It was a depressing evening. My mind was turned inward and I wept gently as I carried on a conversation with Ali in my heart. During these thirty-seven days I had become accustomed to talk to him every time his loss became too much to bear and overwhelmed me. I said to him, "Help me, my beloved Ali! I pray that nothing untoward has befallen the baby, God forbid! I feel ashamed before the doctors and nurses. And the people are waiting for news of the baby's birth. Pray do something so that if the baby is due to be born, that his birth is quick and painless. I don't want to put people out like this!"

After the evening *azān* or call to prayer, the pain got worse. I got out of bed and made my ablutions and evening devotions with difficulty. At first the pains would come about every hour; then they came every half hour. Mother was still at my bedside. I said, "I don't feel well!"

Like the other times, she didn't know what to do with herself. She ran to the nurses' station. It was not long before the nurses had formed a ring around me again, and this time the nurse who examined me said, "He will be born tonight, God willing."

The doctor came and told the nurses to make the preparations, and with the help of the orderlies, I was dressed for the operating room, and taken over to the delivery room. Mother was weeping uncontrollably. I stretched my hand out to her with concern. She was walking fast behind me, trying to keep up, with tears running down her face. The lady doctor who was leading the way told the nurses to provide Mother with clothing appropriate for the delivery room.

A little later, Mother came and stood beside me, dressed in one of those mild green frocks that surgeons wear. In those painful moments, my prayers were only for the baby's wellbeing. Like every other mother, I too was concerned for my baby's health. I had cried so much during these thirty-seven days and shed so many silent tears that I thought that I would be giving birth to a small and underweight baby. In those days, having sonograms done was not as common as it is today. Friends and neighbors would guess at whether the baby was going to be a girl or a boy using their intuition, the size of the mother's swelling, and so on. The consensus among most of the womenfolk was that my baby was going to be a girl.

My Memories get played like a Movie Reel

I was in the third month of my pregnancy when Ali's brother Amīr was martyred. What hard days those were! I passed the hours with grief and tears and much bawling. Shortly after that, Ali Agha was also martyred. After Ali Agha's martyrdom, I lost my appetite and took in nothing but water for a week. I had lost a lot of weight; I didn't look like a pregnant woman at all. There were many who simply couldn't believe that I was expecting.

Pain was coursing throughout my body like blood. I didn't want to yell out in pain, so I would bite my lip and squeeze my mother's hand as hard as I could. Mother's face was soaked with her tears. The intensity of the pain brought tears to my eyes as well. Mother had brought my hand up to her lips and kept kissing it in quick succession, so that it was all wet. I cried out in pain for Ali Agha, begging for his aid and succor from beyond the veil of this world.

I held my left hand in front of my face. My wedding ring had Ali Agha's aura about it. I kissed it. All of a sudden, I saw him appear before me. He was standing in front of me and was smiling. The sight of him made me forget my pain. I couldn't believe it! Ali Agha was there, right in front of me! He had a big smile on his face and was giving me strength and courage. I said to him, "Ali Agha, my love. Help me. Help me to be strong and not to yell out in pain. I don't want anyone to hear my voice. Please help me!"

I would bite my lips and squeeze my mother's hand. Mother could not stand to see me in such pain. She was sitting on the floor by my bed, praying. I was whispering the "Yā Alī" invocation under my breath. I was deaf to the outside world; it was as if I had been cut off from it completely. Ali Agha was still standing there with a smile on his face. He was speaking, but I could not hear or understand what he was saying.

When I heard the baby's cry, my body relaxed and I felt lighter. What a beautiful feeling! I was exhausted and wanted to go to sleep. I could hear the sound of *salawāts*.[5] I raised myself up onto my elbows. The doctors and the nurses were smiling. One of the nurses beamed, "It's a boy. God willing, he will live to be a hundred and make up for his father's early demise."

Everyone was congratulating me. The lady doctor raised the baby up in the air and said, "Take a look at your little boy. What a little prince he is!"

My baby boy was small but rosy and chubby-cheeked with hair as black as a raven's feathers.

Ali Agha was still standing there. He was so close to me that I could smell the fragrance of his body all around me. He was smiling. The moment was as beatific and luminous as our last farewell. I whispered under my lips, "Thank you, my love."

They placed the baby on the table next to the bed and weighed him. I heard them say he weighed five and a half pounds. A few nurses had gathered round the baby. Mother bowed down and kissed my face. She was still shedding tears, but her face now had a big smile on it. She whispered in my ear, "Fereshteh, praise be unto God, he is [as luminous as] a prophet!"

---

[5] The invocation of blessings on the Prophet Mohammad and on the purified and immaculate members of his Family. A highly recommended practice.

I looked in front of me to where Ali Agha was standing. He was still there, and he still had a smile on his lips. I missed him like I missed him during the past thirty-seven days. I wanted him to descend from Heaven, take his baby boy in his arms and say, "My dearly beloved Fereshteh, thank you; what a handsome son you delivered for me."

Mother left to call my mother-in-law and give her the good news. The lady doctor left, and the nurses left, taking my son with them. It wasn't too long before some orderlies came to wheel me back to the maternity ward. My body was weak and exhausted, and I was in pain. I looked back to where Ali Agha had been standing, and turned to him with tears in my eyes and said, "Thank you, my love. I can't believe how quickly I was able to deliver the baby and find relief. Come along with me too, please. Don't leave me alone! I miss you so much!"

I was taken out of the delivery room, and did not feel Ali Agha's presence by my side anymore. Tears welled up in my eyes, blurring my vision. I said, "Ali Agha, my love. I persevered and endured this long after your passing and held back my tears so that your only memento would be born healthily. So, in consideration of my having done my duty well, do not leave me alone. Don't go! Take me with you! I want to go with you, Ali Agha. I have already grown weary of this world, and can't stand being away from you any longer. Would that you were not as good as you were! Would that you had bothered me, even a little bit!"

I remember when I wanted to go to Dezfūl with him, he had said, "It is the war front there. It is being bombed night and day. I won't be able to be with you all the time. Will you be able to endure that?"

And I had happily said, "Yes! At least there, I will see you more frequently."

If it can be said that there were sweet moments in the entirety of my life, they would without doubt be those five and a half months which I spent with Ali Agha in Dezful.

It was the December of 1986, the peak of the bombing sorties and rocket fire in Dezful. Ali Agha asked, "Will you come with me?"

I said without a moment's hesitation, "You mean I can??"

We packed the bare necessities of our belongings together that same night; the sewing machine, the iron, the pots and pans, the crockery and kitchen utensils, a suitcase of clothes, and some other knick-knacks.

On the morning of the next day, we loaded everything into the back of the dull mustard-colored Jeep which he had been given the use of, and headed toward Dezful. I have thought about those days a lot in these last twenty-seven years. It's to the point that every time I miss Ali Agha and want to be near him, I unconsciously think of Dezful and the December of 1986. In truth, all of Ali Agha's and my life together were those days we spent in Dezful together. The pleasure of seeing the orange trees and orange blossoms in bloom, of smelling the scent of the leaves of lemon trees and eucalyptus trees, and the mild winter weather of that year, are still with me today, all these years later, as I relate these memories.

My Memories get played like a Movie Reel

In fact, in the first months after Ali Agha's martyrdom, this is what I did every day and every night. I would pull a blanket over my face and would play and replay my memories of those days over and over again in my mind like a movie, without falling asleep. And if this movie was interrupted by someone's arrival or for any other reason, I would take it up exactly where I had left it off, and in the same prone position in the following hour or at the first opportunity that availed itself. Like that night in the Fātemīeh Hospital in Hamedān where I was in a twilight state between waking and sleep as a result of the sedatives which they had injected me with… I wanted Ali Agha to be by my side. Just like all birthing mothers-to-be, I yearned for the presence of my husband at my side. I wanted him to be alive and there with me. I missed him indescribably. That same night, because I missed him so much, I took the threadbare hospital blanket which smelled of Betadine and alcohol swabs and medicine, and pulled it over my head and started the ritual of recalling my memories of our entering the city of Dezfūl.

I love this part of my memories – it was the night of the 26th of December of 1986 when we arrived at Dezfūl – despite the fact that the house we arrived at was not the one which I had imagined in my mind on the way from Hamedān. It was a one and a half story building which had been built recently but which did not have any of the basic necessities, and which was located in a new development on the outskirts of Dezfūl called Pānsad

An Altar of Roses

Dastgāh. Ali Agha's friend, Mr. Hādī Fazlī,[6] had arrived there before us with his wife and little girl, Zeynab.

We were so tired on that night of our arrival. I can't imagine how we managed to unpack and spread our bedding so that we could go to sleep.

We were up early the following morning thanks to the ruckus that Ali Agha was making. He had gone and bought some fresh bread after the dawn prayers. He went about his business noisily, hoping to get us to wake up with the ruckus that he was making. We were sleeping in the den and Hādī Fazlī and his family were in the living room. I got up and quickly gathered the bedding and put them to one side, and Hādī helped Ali Agha to spread the tablecloth and to lay the breakfast things out on it. Zeynab was still asleep. After breakfast, Ali Agha and Hādī put on their *Sepāh*[7] uniforms. When saying out farewells, I asked, "When will you be back?"

Ali Agha spoke with a heavy Hamedānī accent. He said, "It is uncertain. But a soldier will stop by the house every day. If you need anything, let him know."

It was only after Ali Agha and Hādī left and closed the door behind them that I realized how out of place and alone I was in that house. I started to look around the house, half out of curiosity, and half out of a want of something better to do.

---

[6] Mr. Fazlī was martyred less than a year and a half later in Operation Mersād on the 29th of July, 1988.
[7] The *Sepāh* is short for *Sepāh-e Pāsdārān-e Enqelāb-e Islāmī*, i.e. the Guardians of the Islamic Revolution, or the "Revolutionary Guards" for short.

My Memories get played like a Movie Reel

The toilet and bathroom were outside in the yard. To the left, there was a small garden of about sixty or seventy square yards. The mason had only recently finished his work on the walls and on the brick building. The sharp glare of the sun was hard on the eyes. I strolled around in the front yard and then climbed the four or five steps up to the narrow portico which led to the house. The house had a relatively large entry hall, which led to a living room of about thirty square feet. The kitchen was bare. No cabinets had been installed, nor had it even been tiled. But the dust and debris that was all over the floor and walls made up for that in spades. At the end of the entry hall there was a flight of thirteen or fourteen steps which led down to two dark and dank [subterranean] rooms: the larger one had a small window, and the smaller one was square and had a small window almost at ceiling level which opened onto a small enclosed light well with high walls and a window which opened onto the front yard. There was an ugly bare hundred-watt bulb which struggled to illuminate the room – a task it was only just able to accomplish, thanks to the light that came in from the window. A few days later, this room became Ali Agha's and my room. The house had not yet been finished, properly speaking. Fātemeh's daughter Zeynab was a year and a half old then, and she was still asleep. So Fātemeh and I decided to start cleaning the house while she was still asleep. We set our *chādors*[8] aside, pushed our head

---

[8] The full head to toe covering that veils a woman's body and which is considered the appropriate outer garment for a Moslem woman to wear when in the company of those who are not *mahram*. *Mahram* is a category of people in the sacred law of Islam (the *sharī'a*) who are related

19

scarves back so that they hung around our necks like a kerchief that rested on the shoulders, and cleared the tablecloth of the breakfast fixings. We were looking for a broom when the loud thumping sound of the anti-aircraft batteries started. Fātemeh ran toward Zeynab, picked her up, and the three of us headed toward the basement. Zeynab was looking at us through her groggy eyes to see if she could find an explanation of what was happening, and when she saw that this was not forthcoming, she started wailing. There was nothing that we could do to get her to stop. The noise got louder, shaking the whole house. We were sitting on what was left of the construction dust and debris. Zeynab was screaming out of freight, and because we did not know what was happening outside, we were frightened as well. More than a half hour had passed by now, and although Zeynab had stopped her screaming, she was restless and fussy because she needed to be fed. When the noise died down a little, we went back upstairs. Fātemeh was washing Zeynab's milk bottle and I

---

to each other by blood or marriage such that they are not allowed to marry one another. For example, a mother and son, or a father and daughter or daughter in law, or brothers and sisters. As there is such a close familial bond between them that no sexual intercourse can ever take place between them, the females within the *mahram* circle are not obligated to veil their hair with head covering when they are in the company of males (such as their father or brothers) who are within their *mahram* circle and not in public. *Mahram* is contrasted with *nāmahram*, which is a category of people who are strangers and whose gaze, therefore, is not licit according to the sacred law of God. Men must lower their gaze when in the company of *nāmahram* women.

was in the middle of lighting the stove under the kettle when the sound of the anti-aircraft batteries started again. This time we were not as scared as the first time, but we still ran for shelter in the basement.

Another half hour passed. There was no sign of the soldier who Ali Agha had said would stop by. This time we did not wait for the noise to die down and climbed up the stairs. Fātemeh prepared Zeynab's milk bottle. We put on our *chādors* and went out into the street. We were surprised to see the people going about their business as if nothing had happened. It was incredible for us to think that these people could go about living life normally with all of the incredible ruckus of the air defense systems going off to counter a threat from the air. We walked ahead and a little further up the street, there were a few people lined up at a *lavāsh*[9] baker's, waiting their turn for fresh bread to come out of the oven. The baker was a tall and gaunt man with a tanned complexion who worked the balls of dough into sheets which were ready to be slapped into the oven; a task which he accomplished with skill. He moved rhythmically from one foot to the other and back again as he spread the dough out, and up and down, and when the dough was spread out and ready, he would jump and slap it to the roof of the clay oven and then come back and take another ball of dough and start the whole process over again.

There was a dairy opposite the *lavāsh* baker's shop which sold locally produced milk and yoghurt and butter. The sight of

---

[9] A type of flatbread popular throughout Western Asia.

the dairy made Fātemeh happy, and the sight of an *āsh*[10] sellers at the head of the street made me happy. I said to Fātemeh, "Let's have *āsh* for breakfast tomorrow; my treat."

❖

Some nurses entered the room and drew the blanket away from my face. I opened my eyes. The nurse who was standing before the others asked, "How are you feeling?"

I looked at her with bewilderment. It was as if I had been flung onto the hospital bed from another world. Another nurse came forward and pushed up the sleeve of the thin pink gown which they had had me put on.

"Any problems?"

I didn't know what I was supposed to say. When the nurse saw that I was unresponsive, she took the cuff of the blood pressure gauge and fastened the Velcro around my right arm, placed the gauge on the crook of my arm and started pumping the bulb, monitoring the rise in the level of the mercury. A little later, she took off the stethoscope and, facing the senior nurse, said, "Her systolic pressure is 80."

The senior nurse looked at me in surprise and said, "So where is your IV drip?"

I didn't understand why they asked me these things. I didn't answer. The senior nurse left and returned a little later with

---

[10] A local thick soup that is like a stew in some ways; there are different varieties, but most of them have different kinds of pulses and beans, aromatic herbs, some rice or noodles, and some meat.

a trolley full of medicines and medical supplies, and started preparing the IV drip. The second nurse picked up my medical chart which was enclosed in an aluminum case which was suspended from the foot of my bed and said, "Have you not been seen by the doctor yet?"

As the senior nurse was inserting the needle of the IV drip into my hand, she smiled and said, "The birth of your son has made everyone here so happy that we plain forgot about his mother!"

I made an effort at a smile.

When the nurse was finished with attaching the IV drip, she injected some phials of medicine into the saline solution. The ampules reminded me of one of Ali Agha's paintings [which he had drawn] when he was bedridden in Sāsān Hospital. It was a painting of a butterfly whose wing had been shot through with an arrow and was bleeding.

I asked, "How is the baby doing?"

The nurse put her hand on my shoulder and with a smile which put my mind at ease said, "Good! He's full of energy; he's got the whole hospital staff coming and going. Your mother went into the nursery and held him up so that everyone could see him from behind the glass."

The nurse gathered her gear and, placing them on the trolley, said: "Your IV drip will take about an hour. I added some pain killers and sedatives to it, so you should be dozing off before too long."

It was only after the nurse left that I started to look around the room. There was a round white clock on the opposite wall that showed the time as being half past one. I felt like getting up and switching the overhead florescent lamps off. I realized that no matter how much I tried, I did not have the strength to get up. I was restless. Where was Mother? Why wasn't she here? Why can't I go to sleep? I was staring at the steady drip of the saline solution which was gradually entering my veins through the tube and IV needle attached to the back of my hand. Everything was so quiet and peaceful. I looked at the empty bed to my left. If Ali Agha was here, I wondered, would he have come to visit me tonight when he got off work. Would he sleep on that bed? Or would he be at the warfront? I wanted so much to be able to turn back the clock. What times we had in Dezfūl!

Around ten o'clock in the morning, someone rang the doorbell. We thought it might be that soldier that Ali Agha had talked about. I put on my *chādor* and went out to the front door. I asked, "Who is it?"

The voice was unfamiliar. It said, "It's me, Sa'īd Sedāqatī. Master Ali's assistant."

Even today, when I think of those days and remember the events, I tell myself, 'I wish that we had not gone with him to Ahvāz. Would that we were not even home, or would not have opened the door for him. Then our lives would have unfolded differently.' But unfortunately, I opened the door. Even though, even then I thought that I should have resisted. But I don't know why I didn't resist. I don't know why we went with Sa'īd Sedāqatī, even though in my heart of hearts I didn't want to.

❖

A nurse was standing over me. She would look at me and smile. She turned the valve of the IV drip so that the remnants of the solution made their way to the tube quickly. She pulled the blanket aside, locked the fingers of her hands together, and pressed down hard on my belly. A terrible pain coursed through my body. Ignoring my pain, the nurse repeated the process, pressing down on my belly with both hands, as if she was reviving a patient who had had a cardiac arrest. I screamed out in pain spontaneously. The nurse pulled the blanket back onto my chest and said, "Finished. I'm sorry; it's something that had to be done."

I shook my head slightly. She pulled the IV needle out of my hand and disposed of it. Mother entered the room carrying a bouquet of flowers. She put the flowers on the side-table which stood between the two beds and said, "Are you doing alright, Fereshteh Jān?"

My belly was screaming in pain, but I said, "I'm OK."

Mother busied herself with straightening out the blanket and my headscarf and seeing to my general appearances. She was very happy and said, "Such a handsome boy! Praise the Lord! People are constantly calling to ask how you are doing, from the office of the Friday Congressional Prayer Leader to the Governor's Office, to everywhere else!"

I looked at Mother with sadness. I wished Ali Agha was alive and would call too. If only he were here to share this moment with me. It was all I could do to prevent myself from crying. I wanted Mother to turn the lights out and leave me to sleep, so that I could dream of Ali Agha; or so that I could close my eyes and recount my memories with him.

Mother picked up the flowers from the bedside stand. They were white gladiolas. She held them in front of me and said, "Smell them!"

I remembered the day of Ali Agha's funeral. His casket was full of flowers. The Bāq-e Behesht cemetery was full of gladiola arrangements. Ali Agha flew like a butterfly among all those flowers.

Mother opened the door of the small fridge which was in the room and said, "If there was a pitcher of water or something, I could put the flowers in them. They'll wilt by morning."

I asked, "Is it snowing?"

Mother took the flowers to the window and looked out.

"No. But its snowy weather. If it doesn't snow tonight, it will definitely be snowing by the morning."

I thought of last year's heavy snow. I said, "Do you remember the third of Bahman (January / February) last year, Mother? It was a Friday. Ali Agha's friends had brought him from Esfahān. What a bad day that was."

The flowers were no longer in her hands. I don't know what she ended up doing with them. She came and laid down on the bed next to mine. She asked, "Are you not able to sleep?"

My Memories get played like a Movie Reel

"Mother!" I said, upset.

She became aware of how upset I was.

"Yes, dear. What is it, my love?"

"Do you remember?"

"Of course I remember, my love. Of course I remember, my beautiful child. A heavy snow had fallen. Everything was frozen solid. His friends brought him right over to our house. I laid out his bedding right next to the heater so that he would not catch a cold. I made chicken soup for him. He ate it and said, 'Lady Vajīheh, it is delicious. May God reward you'."

Tears began to run down my cheeks uncontrollably.

I said, "Ali Agha suffered a lot, Mother. In those days, I would not mention such things to you so that you would not get upset. But it was very difficult for me."

Mother laid her head on the pillow over her right hand, facing me, and said, "May your reward be [your being resurrected in] the company of Imam Hosayn. May your reward be [your being resurrected in] the company of the Lord of the Age, God willing."

I gazed up at the ceiling and at the fluorescent light that was above my bed. I thought about how fast everything happened; all these events. I looked at Mother. She had fallen asleep on her right hand, without a blanket. I felt sorry for her. I got myself out of bed with difficulty and pulled a blanket over her. Like always, I kissed her below her throat. She smelled so good. I switched the overhead lights off. It had started to snow, ever so gently. It was light out and there was a pink hue to the sky.

When I awoke the next morning, I first noticed my mother's empty bed. Then I saw the bedsheet which she had spread on the floor of the room. There she was, busy with her morning devotions and prayers. I gently said, "*Salām*. Good morning."

After completing her ritual devotions and prayers, Mother stood up. She was holding a *tasbīh*[11] in her hand. She came over and held my hand and said, "*Salām*. Good morning, my dear. Are you well this morning?"

"I'm well, praise the Lord."

Mother's face was weary and morose. I thought maybe it was because of her headdress and the black manteaux she was wearing and the fact that she had not been able to see to herself in the mirror, or that perhaps something was bothering her. I asked, "Mother, how is the baby? Is he OK?"
That put a smile on her face.

"He's doing just fine! I went to see him first thing. He was sleeping like an angel. How about yourself? Are you not well?"

I shook my head and said, "No, I'm fine." I asked, "How is Father, and Royā and Nafīseh?" These are my sisters.

She smiled. "They're all well. I'll call them in an hour or two and you can talk to them." And then, as if it was an afterthought, she said, "We have a telephone now, thank God. It makes things so much easier".

---

[11] A Moslem rosary.

When we were in Dezfūl, whenever I longed for the company of my family, I would go to the post office and put a call through to Mrs. Sakīneh Rowghanī's house, who was one of our neighbors whose house was seven or eight doors down from ours. It would take a long time before Mother or someone else would come to the phone. Lately I had learned to ask the Rowghanīs to call my mother first, and then I would hang up and call back in a half hour.

Mother sat on her bed and started to recite the ritual invocations using her *tasbīh*. I said, "Do you remember when I used to call Mrs. Sakīneh Rowghanī's house? Once we were almost martyred on account of having to go out to make those calls."

The *tasbīh* stopped moving in Mother's hands. She looked at me with grave concern in her eyes. I smiled, making light of it.

"Don't worry. I said *almost* martyred!"

Mother resumed her *zekr* (ritual invocation of divine blessings or grace) and shook her head reproachfully. "You little rascal! You always said everything was fine there, and you were having the time of your life, and that you were always going out partying with friends!"

"I wasn't fibbing, Mother. We went out partying too, but there was this other aspect as well."

My belly ached like it was never going to let up. It had been a week since Ali Agha had left. One morning I woke up with a belly ache and suffered through the pain all day. Poor Fātemeh did whatever she could think of. It was the middle of the week, and so I did not hold out hope of seeing Ali Agha anytime soon. At nightfall I thought, 'What am I to do if it gets worse in the middle of the night?' I wished that it was the weekend so that Ali Agha would come. As God is my witness, Mother, right then I heard the sound of Ali Agha's car from the street. I think it was 2:30 in the afternoon. When Ali Agha stepped into the house and saw the state I was in, he was taken aback; even though he was not faring any better than me himself. He was covered with dust, and was tired, and his face and eyes were all puffed up and inflamed, as if he hadn't slept in a week. He asked, "What's going on?"

I said, "I don't know why, but I've had a bellyache since this morning." Ali Agha's driver had already left, so Ali Agha turned right around and went to our neighbor's, Mr. Seddīq, to borrow his car. Fātemeh and I got in and he drove us to the hospital. When we got to the hospital he said, "Fereshteh, I am very tired. Can you manage to go in by yourself?" He switched the car off and rested his head on the steering wheel and said, "Come and get me if you run into any problems." The doctor on duty examined me and said, "It seems it might be appendicitis." He wrote up some tests and told me to be sure to get them done without delay. When I brought the results back to him, he said, "Thank God, it is nothing serious." He prescribed a bunch of pills and potions. The whole thing took about two or three hours, after which I exited the hospital with the medicines in hand. And would you believe it, Mother? I found Ali Agha just as I had left him, with his head resting on the steering wheel, fast asleep. I woke him up and we started off. And because I had just started to feel better, I was seeing the streets for the first time. It was the 14th of Shaʿbān;[12] and while the city was not crowded, those who were still there had gone all out to decorate the streets and to celebrate the birth anniversary of their beloved Imam. They had lined the middle of the streets with flower pots. People would offer us confectionaries and sweets and pastries in freshly packed flat boxes when we stopped for a traffic light. Streamers of light could be seen hanging from the branches of the trees that lined the streets. I was so excited. I kept pointing different scenes out to Ali Agha, saying, "Look at this! Look at that! That's so beautiful!" When Ali Agha saw how happy the decorations and celebrations made me, he cruised the streets some more, even though he was very tired. We eventually made our way back home and saw Hādī standing at the head of our street. Apparently Zeynab had been fussing and had not let him rest.

Mother stood up and began gathering up her impromptu "prayer mat". I was hungry. I felt as if my whole body was quivering from want of sustenance. I set the blanket aside with difficulty and sat up. The room started to whirl around my head, like a spell of vertigo. I was trying to find the pair of slippers which were resting on the step at my bedside. I felt my heart was no longer beating, and as I started to black out, I managed to say with difficulty, "Mother…"

---

[12] The birthday of the *Imām az-Zamān* or the Lord of the Age, the title given to the Twelfth Imam by the Shīʿa.

Mother ran over to me immediately and held me by my arm. "What is it, Fereshteh? You look like you've seen a ghost! What's the matter?"

My whole body was numb. I couldn't see or hear anything. Mother laid me back down on the bed and ran out to get help. A little later, I regained my senses. There were some nurses around the bed. I heard Mother saying, "Open your mouth, Fereshteh Jān."

I opened my mouth and tasted a sweet fruit juice, which I sipped slowly. As it went down my throat, it was as if it gave new life to my arms and legs. I then drank it voraciously. A nurse told Mother, "Her blood pressure is very low. It's not serious. She's weak, is all. Let her take her breakfast now."

Mother drew up the table which was at the foot of the bed and put a morsel of bread and jam in my mouth. My lips and mouth quivered like a famine victim's. It was as if it had been years since I had had anything to eat. Mother put a second morsel in my mouth, and continued to feed me. She held up a glass of milk to my mouth. I smelled the aroma of hot milk, freshly brought to the boil.

"I sweetened it."

Mother's hands were shaking as she held up the glass of milk to my mouth. I grabbed the glass with both hands. Both of my hands were trembling and shaking the glass and knocking it against my teeth. Mother held the glass steady and helped me sip the milk slowly.

Mother said, "I forgot to tell you. Last night, Fātemeh, Shahīd Fazlī's wife, called asking after you."

I am always reminded of Dezfūl when I hear Fātemeh's name. Even though we were constantly being bombarded and there was gunfire all around us, those were the best days of our lives.

Mother patiently put another morsel of bread and butter with jam in my mouth and asked, "Are you feeling better? Are you feeling stronger?"

I still felt that my whole body was trembling. I could not utter any words. I just wanted to wolf down all the food that was on the breakfast table! Mother didn't say anything and continued to make little mouthfuls of bread, butter and jam for me to eat.

A smile came to my face and Mother asked, "What is it? Why are you smiling?"

I said, "I remembered Dezfūl and how much fun we used to have."

As she continued to feed me these bite-sized morsels, Mother said, "Just another one of your embellishments!"

I said, "No, honest to God, it's the truth!"

Mother smiled and said, "Ok, no need to take an oath. I'll take your word for it. Dezfūl is a wonderful town! And certainly, when we came to visit you and Ali Agha, we had a great time."

I chewed my food. "Ah yes, those were the days, Mother. It was so good of you to come. We had such a good time. Fātemeh and I were sitting on the steps of the patio anxiously awaiting you and thinking what we should prepare for dinner."

Mother said, "You had made baked beans."

"Well, it's a dish that I like. And Fātemeh had said that it was too rich for dinner, but I said, that's ok."

"And my, how Ali Agha loved baked beans!"

"I tossed in a big bowlful of beans into the stewpot. I was smiling to myself, saying that if Ali Agha shows up tonight too, I'm in trouble. Not only did he not like baked beans, he disliked anything that did not sit well with his digestion and caused gas! Cherish the memory; Fātemeh peeled three or four large onions and chopped them up. They brought tears to our eyes. We were shedding tears and talking. She fried the onions and I fried up the ground beef, each of us on our own camper stoves. When I took the lid off the pot, I saw that the beans had swelled up and become two or three times their original size! I said, 'Fātemeh, I guess this means that you and I have to eat all these beans!' Some noise could be heard coming from the street. It seemed the neighbors had guests. Fātemeh said with melancholy, 'I wish we had guests too.' We were in the planning stage of how we were to go about stealing our neighbors' guests when you arrived."

Mother said, "The power had been cut off [for security reasons]. We came in your father's car. It was the tenth day of the New Year. It was something that we decided to do on the spur of the moment. Your uncle came with us. Nafiseh and Royā and I were seated in the back. We didn't know our way around and searched around for a long time before we found the Pānsad Dastgāh development. We found the Fat'h ol-Mobīn roundabout, but for the life of us we could not find the Eleventh Rose Garden. We kept going around in circles in the dark and would ask everyone we saw where the Eleventh Rose Garden was, number 215. It was dark all around; we could barely see one another. Your father dared not turn the car's headlights on [for fear of the Iraqi fighter jets]. Suddenly we saw a car coming up behind us with its headlights on. When your father pulled aside, we saw that it was Ali Agha."

"We were sitting in the yard. We heard you talking, but still couldn't believe it!"

"Those were the days!" Mother said.

"When I opened the door, it actually sunk in that you had come. It was as if someone had given me the whole world. And I was also happy that we were going to have help eating all those baked beans!"

"Yes, but I couldn't just sit there, so I rolled my sleeves up and started making some proper food for my groom."
As Mother was putting the breakfast stuff away, she said, "The following morning, your father and uncle and Ali Agha went to the war zone and we made a pilgrimage to the shrine of Imām-Zādeh[13] Zabzeh-Qobā."[14]

I let out a sigh. "When you went back home on the thirteenth, it was as if all of the sorrows of the world had been piled on my shoulders. I was so despondent that Ali Agha stayed behind to comfort me rather than returning to the warfront. He kept me company and comforted me for as long as it took for you to arrive back at Hamedān. At nightfall, Ali Agha said, "I think your parents must have arrived by now. Go and call Lady Sakīneh's house and talk for as long as you want."

---

[13] Imāmzādeh: the shrine and pilgrimage destination of a saint who is a son or daughter of one of the Twelve Imams.
[14] The brother of Imam Rezā, the Eighth Imam of the Shī'a.

Mother picked up the breakfast tray and left the room. I was feeling better. I looked out the window. It was snowing, and it was beautiful out. It was morning and I wanted to go and see my baby boy. I whispered, "Ali Agha, did you see our son?"

I was broken hearted. As soon as I recalled that Ali was no longer with me and my son did not have a father, tears would well up inside me and my body would tremble. How was I supposed to be able to raise him on my own?? I felt sorry for my son. I saw Ali Agha appear in the room once again. And he was smiling again. Wherever I turned my head, there he was: by Mother's bedside, by the window, at the foot of my own bed, and even behind the window, under the beautiful snowfall. It was as if he had been multiplied so that there were as many of him as there were flakes of the snow that was coming down. The snow was coming down steadily and had settled on the window sill. There was a good scent in the room, something like lemon verbena. The room smelled of spring. Like the fragrance of Ali Agha's body. I said, "You have to watch out for the two of us, Ali Agha. I can't do it on my own."

I felt as if Ali Agha was smiling his usual smile and saying, "I will, my love; I will."

And so, this thought gave me an inner peace and contentment. I felt lighter, and happy.

It was 11:30 in the morning. I couldn't believe I had fallen asleep and slept all morning. The gladiolas were in a plastic pitcher on top of the refrigerator. It had stopped snowing; but the sky was still overcast. The purple curtains of the room were filled with little orange and yellow flowers, and they had been

My Memories get played like a Movie Reel

bunched up to either side of the window very tastefully. The room was clean and tidy and smelled nice. I raised myself up and sat on the bed. I felt good. I no longer felt tired and the pain had left me. I looked at the window and the beautiful curtains which framed it. They seemed so familiar to me. Cherish the memory! They were like the curtains of the Dezfūl house.

I hopped down from the bed and went to the window. I held the curtains in my hands and brought them to my nose. They smelled of Dezfūl! I turned around and stood in the doorway. The hospital corridor was long and clean and desolate. Mother was speaking on the phone at the nurse's station. When she saw me, she smiled and waved at me. The pink hospital frock that I was wearing dragged on the floor. Mother placed the phone handle on its receiver and came toward me. When she got to where I was, she said, "Did you sleep well, Fereshteh Jān?"

I smiled and said, "I slept a lot!"

Mother took my hand in hers and said, "I've been taking calls all morning long. I told them that you are sleeping and not to put any calls through to the room."

Surprised, I said, "Is something wrong?"

Mother accompanied me up to the bathroom. "Wash up. It'll make you feel better. Have you washed up already?"

I hadn't. Mother opened the bathroom door. Everything was white and sparkled with cleanliness. I turned the faucet on. Mother said, "Everyone is calling, be they friends and family, or people who we don't even know, asking about your health. And extended family too, of course."

I looked at myself in the mirror. I looked drab and lifeless. There were two half-moons puffed up under my eyes. When I washed my face, I got the feeling that it had been a lifetime since I had been in touch with anyone. I left the bathroom.

"Who were you talking to just now?" I asked.

"To Vahīd, your cousin Vahīd."

Hearing his name, I spontaneously whispered, "It was Vahīd. Poor thing."

I sat down. I recalled the night Ali Agha brought Vahīd to Dezfūl. Mother took my hand and said, "Lie down, Fereshteh."

I asked, "How long will I be here? Why haven't they brought the baby to me?"

Mother said, "They'll do that tomorrow morning."

I got concerned. I asked, "Is he ok? Is there something wrong with him? Tell me the truth!"

Mother pulled the blanket over my chest. "Don't be silly. That's the God's honest truth. You want me to lie to you?"

I closed my eyes. Mother dried my face with a hand towel and straightened my headscarf and my sleeves. I hugged her and kissed her under her throat. What a wonderful fragrance she had!

"You'll have some visitors in the afternoon."

Mother busied herself straightening the bedding out. It was so difficult seeing her do this. I never thought I would be in this prone position without Ali Agha being by my side. Every time I looked ahead to what I had in store, Ali Agha was always a part of those thoughts. What happy times I imagined we would have. I never once imagined that everyone would be in mourning and in tears at the time I gave birth to my baby. I mean to say, are there times that are even more difficult than these? Mother said, "Are you up, Fereshteh?"

I missed Ali Agha so much. How I needed to feel the comfort of his warm hands. I needed to let out all the tears that had pent up inside me. Mother said, "You fell asleep so soon?"

I didn't open my eyes. I didn't even respond to her. Even though my eyes were closed, I realized Mother was sitting on her bed. I heard her opening the zipper of her purse. From the time that I became a mother, my love and affection for Mother had increased. I felt sorry for her. I didn't want to upset her, even for a single moment.

I opened my eyes just a bit, enough to see out of, but not so much that others would know I was awake, and looked at her. Even though I could only see her in profile, I could see that she was looking at a picture which she held in her hand and her shoulders were trembling. She had placed her purse on her chest, and it was as if she was whispering something to herself. I thought it must be a picture of Ali Agha. I missed him so much. I had a strange, heavy foreboding; it was as if I could no longer stand his absence, even for a minute. I felt that if I didn't see him right away, I would die. I wanted to take his picture away from Mother at all costs. I asked, "Mother, what are you doing?"

Mother stirred and quickly tucked her purse under her arm.

I said, "Was it a picture of Ali Agha? Let me see it too."

Mother didn't respond and quickly wiped away her tears. Holding back my tears I said, "I swear to God, Mother; I miss him too."

   Mother turned around and made light of the situation: "Picture? What picture?"

   Her eyes were red. She always had a mobile gallery in her wallet. Pictures of Royā and Nafiseh and me and Father and her brother and mother and father. And it had been about a year since Ali Agha's picture had been added to the gallery.

   I said, "Please, Mother. Let me see it."

   I think she felt sorry for me then. She reluctantly let her purse out from under her arm and held it out towards me. I saw Ali Agha smiling from behind his dirty blond beard and mustache. It was the picture where he was standing next to his fellow soldiers and everyone had a black shawl on their shoulders. Mother had trimmed the picture so that only Ali Agha's image remained. She had then pasted it onto a picture of me, next to me. I said, "He took this picture last year. It was February. During the Fātemīeh[15] period; when the Karbalā 5 Operations were taking place. That evening, Ali Agha had come home carrying a bolt of black cloth and asked, "Fereshteh, do you know how to sew shawls?" I took the bolt of cloth from him. It was the kind of "wash and wear" cloth that didn't need ironing. I asked with surprise, "All this cloth for shawls?" He said, "All of the boys in my unit resolved that we would wear black shawls this year, to

---

[15] The time of year when the Shī'a faithful mourn the death of Her Eminence Lady Fātemeh, the beloved daughter of our Prophet.

My Memories get played like a Movie Reel

honor the memory of Lady Fātemaᵗ oz-Zahrā (the Luminous One)." I opened the bolt and said, "You determine the size." We cut the first couple of shawls together. Hādī and Fātemeh joined us too. They would cut the cloth and I would tuck the edges in and sow the seams. We were up almost until dawn that night. The following morning Fātemeh and I took turns behind the sewing machine once Ali Agha and Agha Hādī left. The spool of thread ran out before we had finished. We looked for a spool of black thread all over, but nowhere was one to be found. I was forced to buy a thread that was only suitable for hand stitching, so that it kept on coming apart, or the sewing machine's needle would get stuck or would break off. We finally finished the task of making the shawls, but with great difficulty. When Ali Agha came back that evening and saw that they were ready, it made him very happy. He took one and wrapped it around Hādī's neck."

I shed tears as I recalled the story for Mother. Mother wiped away her tears with her fingers. I was staring at the picture, transfixed, as I was lying down in bed. Mother said, "That's enough, Fereshteh!"

I put the picture on my breast and said, "I promise not to cry."

I was not able to honor my promise even for a minute. Mother took back the picture.

A nurse entered the room with a food trolley. She turned in sympathy and said, "How are you feeling, Mrs. Panāhī?"

I wiped my tears away quickly. She looked at me and asked, "Is something wrong?"

As she was putting her wallet back in her purse, Mother turned to the nurse and said, "May it please God, kindly tell this young lady how bad mother's milk which has been stained with the taint of her tears is for her baby."

The nurse looked at me reproachfully and said, "It prevents the baby from growing to be strong and healthy."

She then put her hand on my shoulder and said, "Mrs. Panāhī, now you are responsible for two people!"

I said, "It's nothing. I'm just a little depressed, that's all."

I wiped away my tears and put on a brave face. The nurse put the meal, which was rice with lamb kabāb and soup, on the table by the bed and said, "Now eat your meal heartily and rest, as from two o'clock on it is visiting hours. I am sure that will change your mood for the better."

It was the second of February and I was looking at the clock on the wall in front of me. I wanted it to be two o'clock already. I felt like seeing everyone, and I had missed their company since the previous night.

Mansūreh Khānūm and Agha Nāser, my in-laws, entered the room carrying a bouquet of flowers. They smiled when they saw me, but their eyes were red and swollen. I knew how hard it must be for them to see their granddaughter in Ali Agha's absence. Seeing them made me want to cry, and it was as if this urge was stuck like a lump in my throat; it would neither come out, nor would it go back down.

I felt sorry for Mansūreh Khānūm and Agha Nāser. They still wore the black clothes of mourning. The pain of the loss of their son Amīr was still fresh for them. And Ali Agha's loss still tore at their hearts. My heart went out to them; and I knew that their seeing me in this state without him would refresh their pain. They showed such forbearance in the face of adversity. It had not yet been a full day since my son was born, and I missed him already. How did Mansūreh Khānūm and Agha Nāser show such forbearance and longanimity?!

They sat on the plastic chairs next to the bed. Before too long, Agha Nāser regained his good spirits and said, "We went and saw our son. He looks like Ali Agha when he was young. A genuine facsimile!"

Mansūreh Khānūm was concerned that the baby not go hungry. She said, "I told them to bring him, Fereshteh Jān, so that you can feed him. Be sure not to waste the first milk, Fereshteh Jān. Make him take it, if need be, so that he will grow up strong-boned like his father."

A little later, the room was brimming with visitors, such that there was no room to sit and some of the visitors sat on Mother's bed. Everyone asked how I was doing, and then invariably asked how the baby was. They would spend a few minutes in the room, and then would leave to go and see the baby. Mother and Father and Royā offered pastries and tea to the visitors. For her part, Nafīseh, who had fallen in love with the baby, refused to leave the window of the nursery.

The table and the top of the fridge had become filled to overflowing with bouquets of flowers and boxes of pastry and cartons of fruit juice which the visitors had brought for me. Many of the visitors would come back after having visited the nursery and report on what they saw from behind the glass of the nursery partition.

Hearing what they had to say, I wanted to see my baby all the more. At four o'clock there was an announcement over the PA system that visiting hours were now over. One by one, our guests slowly took their leave. Only Mansūreh Khānūm and Agha Nāser remained, together with Father and Mother. Agha Nāser had the gift of the gab and a good sense of humor. He was recounting the story of their trip to Dezfūl to Father. He was such a good storyteller that everyone was mesmerized by his narrative.

He said, "We had an appointment at the hospital to operate the cataract of my eye. From the break of dawn to the time we went to sleep, Mansūreh Khānūm would nag and complain that Fereshteh has gotten herself stuck in the crossfire of the enemy's bombs and rockets. 'Agha Nāser', she would say, 'Fereshteh is given to us in trust; go and get her!' Nag, nag, nag. She nagged so much that instead of making our hospital appointment, before I knew what was happening, I found myself in the heart of Dezfūl! No matter how much I pleaded with her that I can't see anything with these cataracts, that I'm going blind, that I'm losing what little sight I had left – none of this made the least bit of difference to her. My eyes were standing on ceremony and were pretending to have a modicum of vision, I told her, otherwise I was legally and certifiably as blind as a bat. All to no avail, of course. And so, what is a blind man to do but to say 'Yā Ali!'? And that is how we ended up in Dezfūl. It was nightfall before we arrived. My eyes couldn't see a blessed thing. It was Ali Agha's friends who saw us in the street and took us to his house. So I rang the buzzer and none other than this here angel ('Fereshteh') opened the door for us and greeted us. I said, "Who are you?" She said, "What do you mean, sir. It's me, Fereshteh; your bride!" I asked, "If it is as you say it is and you are my bride, what in God's name are you doing here?" She said, "But this is your son's home. This is where Ali Agha lives!" So I said, "What nonsense! This is no place for my son to make a home! Come on, let's go. We're from Hamedān. Come on, get up and pack your things and let us take you back to Hamedān." I don't know how this Miss Fereshteh tricked me into setting foot into that house and what magical words she used to bewitch me again into staying for dinner, but that is *exactly* what she did. And so it was that it came time for us to sleep. And I said to myself, well, home it ain't, but what the heck. A man's gotta sleep. So I said, "Ven is vinter, I es-sleep *out*-saayd, cause is too hot *in*-saayd." And what did my bride say? "It is not safe out, as it is possible for the bombs and the rockets to start falling in the middle of the night." And I said, "No meeses, bomb no fall on *me*. Allah he protect me. Me fall on bomb!" And so we went back and forth, the two of us, arguing about where we were going to sleep, and so when she saw that there was no logic to her position and that I had won the argument based on rational proofs, and that she was going to have to broom out the porch and wash it down to make it ready for my bedding, she resorted to guerilla tactics. She said, "But sir, you don't understand. There are scorpions in these parts!" And so I said, "Vaat? You tink I scare off coupel es-scorpion?? I kill many es-scorpion in my *es*-sleep!" Anyway, to make a long story short, we slept over and I was up at the crack of dawn, and after offering my devotions to the good Lord, I went and bought some fresh cream from the creamery at the head of the street, together with some fresh bread. As soon as I set foot in the yard, I saw Miss Fereshteh with a sandal in her raised hand, as if she was getting ready to swat a fly. "Sir," she shouted excitedly, "A scorpion! A scorpion! Didn't I tell you this region was no place to sleep outdoors? Look at the size of the critter!" So I said, "Don't vaary, meeses. Dees creecher are *bandeye-khodaa*. Dey are God creecher! Vaan no good kill God creecher." In any event, the long and short of it is that not only were we not able to return our bride to Hamedān, but she got us to stay over a spell to boot."

❖

Then a nurse came in and restated that visiting hours were over, and so Mansūreh Khānūm and Agha Nāser and Father slowly made their way out, while Agha Nāser was still chatting up a storm.

The room was filled with the scent of all of the flowers that everyone had brought. Everywhere I looked there were beautiful bouquets of gladiolas and roses and tee-roses and freesias.

That night, I slept easier than the previous night. The following morning, after breakfast, Mother helped me put on my

My Memories get played like a Movie Reel

head dress and *manteaux* and *chador*.[16] She said, "Your father is here too, and is waiting in the waiting area. There were two nurses standing next to me with a bouquet of flowers, a gift-wrapped box, and a copy of the Noble Quran. The head of the hospital had ordered them to accompany us all the way home as a sign of respect and as his way of expressing his congratulations. I sat in the wheelchair they had provided and they pushed me into the waiting area. Father came forward to greet me. Mother had gone to get the baby. I had dressed warmly, but this notwithstanding, I felt very cold as soon as we stepped outside the hospital doors. There was snow and ice everywhere and there was a nasty chill in the air. The two nurses helped me out of the wheelchair and helped me to climb into a van which had the insignia of the Fātemīeh Hospital on its side panels. Having been seated in the van, I saw Mother holding a well-wrapped newborn baby making her way carefully down the hospital steps from behind one of the glass panels of the van. The driver waited for my father to start his car and to take the lead, and then drove off after him.

It was as if they had painted the trees and rooftops and sidewalks and roundabouts of the town with a big can of white spray paint. We went past the Abbās-Ābād bus station and entered Mīrzādeh Eshqī Street. Icicles had formed and were

---

[16] A *chador* is an outer garment or open cloak made of light cloth that is worn over the head and which comes all the way down to the ankles, which women wrap around their bodies to act as a full-body veil. It is considered the appropriate form of veiling by the clergy and practicing Moslems in Iran.

hanging from the eaves and gutters of the buildings. People were walking carefully on the frozen sidewalks. When we passed through Mīrzādeh Eshqī Street, I spontaneously looked back on our house. The van passed by the street rapidly and bypassed the intersection where the city jail was located as well. I enjoyed the sound of the wheels of the cars as they ran over the slush.

We entered Dībāj Street and passed by the Dībāj Arts Center. My father's car made it into the parking area of the Arts Center's residential apartment complex with difficulty, as the snow of the alley leading to it had not yet been ploughed. He stopped his car in front of Building No. 6, got out and came towards us. The neighbors were standing outside my father-in-law's apartment building in the cold, waiting. There was a sheep whose head was being held steady by the hands of a butcher, and it was making the baa, baa sounds that sheep make. [He was about to be slaughtered as a sacrifice;] I felt sorry for the sheep and my heart went out to him. Two banners had been attached, one on the left and the other to the right of the entryway of the apartment building, each with a picture of Ali Agha and his ever-present smile. One of the neighbors was busy burning wild rue on a censer. The fragrant smoke gently wafted up in the cold air. The womenfolk among the neighbors came forward and embraced me. One of them started to weep upon seeing me. The bleating of the sheep could no longer be heard. I looked over and saw a red trail of blood in the snow from which steam was rising.

My father in law's apartment was on the fourth floor. I was thinking about how I was going to be able to climb all those stairs. One of the nurses held me by the arm. The neighbors were sending *salawāts*.¹⁷ There was a poster announcing the fortieth day of Ali Agha's passing posted on the wall at the first landing. I stopped and read it: "Monday January 4th, 1988, from 8 AM to 11:30 AM, at the Medina Mosque. Note that a special women's commemoration will be held in the women's section of the mosque."

At the bottom of the announcement it was written: "The Intelligence Unit of the Lashgar-e Ansār ol-Hosayn Operations, Hamedān Province; and the Families of the Martyrs Amīr and Alī Chītsāzīān."

I managed to climb the stairs slowly with the help of the nurses. Everyone else followed slowly behind us. I had the expectation that Ali Agha would run down the stairs, smiling, and say, "Zahra, my love! My love... my love... my love..."

I loved him addressing me in such terms of endearment. Thinking of it made me want to cry, and it was as if this urge was stuck like a lump in my throat; it would neither come out, nor would it go back down. Mother overtook me and went up the stairs quickly with the baby. The stairwell was cold. The neighbors, who wanted to see the baby, followed in pursuit. I asked the nurse, "What floor are we on?"

"The second," she answered.

On the half-landing of the second floor, the walls were again filled with posters announcing the fortieth day of Ali Agha's passing; and again, he could be seen with that smile of his

---

¹⁷ An invocation of blessings on the Prophet Mohammad (PBUH) and on the purified and immaculate members of his house.

hidden behind his heavy light brown beard. My legs were quivering. I couldn't continue the climb any further. When we got to the third half-landing, I stopped. One of the third-floor neighbors opened her door.

"Come in, Lady Fereshteh, Fereshteh *Khānūm*, please. Come and rest your feet a little, and then we can make the rest of the way up together," she said.

One of the nurses answered for me: "Thank you; we are almost there. There's only one more flight, and we will make it up there, one way or another."

I could hear people sending *salawāts* from the fourth floor. The scent of *esfand* or wild rue smoke had filled the stairwell. My legs were quivering from exhaustion. Would the climb never end? Could it be that this climb will eventually be over and that I will be able to enter into the living room and sit down? When we reached the fourth-floor landing, it was as if all of my wishes had been granted.

The apartment was warm and bright. The curtains had been drawn and the weak light of the winter sun was reflected off the carpet. There was a bed on the floor up against the radiator. The nurse helped me settle in it. My baby was already lying next to the bed. I pulled the blanket away from his face. It was rosy. He was sleeping peacefully without a single worry in the world. I laid down in the bed. What a good feeling. The two nurses and all of the neighbors sat all around the room.

There was a picture of Amīr and Alī in a picture frame. I thought to myself, "Uncle Amīr, did you see our baby? Did you see how handsome he is?"

I felt like crying again, but I overcame the urge and willed my tears back down.

Mansūreh Khānūm loved her children. She loved Amīr and Alī and Ḥājj Sādeq and Maryam.

She had affixed two gladiola flowers to each picture frame. I knew it was she who had done this, as she loved flowers as well. Maryam came out with a tray full of tea and offered tea to all of the guests. Monīreh Khānūm, Ḥājj Sādeq's wife, placed the side plates next to each guest and then held out a confectionary platter before each of them in turn. This home had been witness to great trials over the last few months; it kept being filled with the tears and wailing of mourners.

The day Amīr was martyred, Mansūreh Khānūm collapsed into the arms of Ali Agha in this very kitchen. She was crying while kissing him and taking in his scent, asking him if he had seen his brother. Ali Agha, for his part, was weeping silently. I'll never forget the way he cried.

The nurses bid their farewells and left. Then the neighbors had their tea and pastries, came forward one by one and congratulated me, and they too left. I was tired. I felt dizzy. My body was weak. I was in pain. I lied down on the bed. For the first time, the baby let out a cry. Mother ran over and took him in her arms.

"He's hungry. See how he's moving his mouth? He's looking for a breast to suckle."

Mother uttered these words and sat down next to me. She took a pastry from my plate and put it in my mouth. It tasted sweet. I felt the energy which had left me returning to my arms and legs.

Mansūreh Khānūm brought over a sweet tonic and stood next to me.

"Drink it so it will sweeten your breastmilk."

Mother took the glass of sweet tonic and fed it to me sip by sip. I felt better. I picked up my boy. He was searching for something with his mouth. He seemed smaller and rosier all wrapped up as he was. He was so small that I was afraid to hold him. When he started suckling, everyone gathered round and watched him with glee. He had curled his little bony hands into round balls. I opened his fist gently. He had pink, elongated nails.

Mansūreh Khānūm said, "It is as God has willed: he takes from his father, poor thing. Ali Agha was just like him when he was a baby."

I was sitting with my back to the kitchen wall, facing the picture frame with Ali Agha and Amīr's picture. My baby was very hungry. He suckled with gusto. I stroked his white cap and looked at the picture. There was a sentence beneath the picture from Ali Agha, written in red ink:

> "It is only those who have been able to circumvent the barbed wires of their own lower desires and have not been ensnared by them who are able to breach the barbed wires of the enemy."

The baby started coughing. Mother took him from my arms. The milk had gone down the wrong tube. Mother placed her index finger between the baby's eyebrows and pressed down. I was looking on anxiously. The baby had turned a redder shade of pink. Mother gently tapped the baby's back and put him to bed in his cot. The baby went to sleep quietly. His hands were rolled up into little balls which he held above his head. The smell of fried flour filled the house. Mother stood up and went to the kitchen. Everyone was busy doing something.

A week before his parting, my belly started to ache. It was the twenty-seventh or twenty-eighth of Ābān. Mansūreh Khānūm had made me some *kāchī*[18]; she was sitting right here. Around noon, when Ali Agha had returned, she said to Ali Agha, "Give me a bowl of *qeymāq*, dear. It might be that when my nephew is born, I will no longer be around."

Mother came and sat next to me carrying a porcelain bowl on a steel serving tray. The smell of the clarified butter was sharp. I said, "No thank you. I don't have an appetite for it."

That upset Mother. "What's that supposed to mean?"

It was just the two of us in the room. I broke out wailing loudly. The baby stirred in his sleep, clearly upset. The lines of a frown could be seen on his forehead. He moved his fists back and forth several times. Mother asked with concern, "What is it now?"

Mansūreh Khānūm rushed into the room. One of her hands held a spoon, and the other one was covered with a red and white kitchen glove which I had sewn for her myself. She was

---

[18] A traditional Iranian desert made from wheat flour, butter, sugar, rose water, and saffron.

looking at me with great concern, and so I could not bring myself to tell her what memory had triggered my tears and what was burning me up inside.

Mansūreh Khānūm sat next to me, holding the spoon and glove away from me in the air. I saw that tears were welling up in her eyes too. She looked at the picture frame of her two boys. Mansūreh Khānūm said, "If you don't have an appetite for *qeymāq*, you should still have some. It is good for you, my dear. It is full of nutrition. Cherish his memory, Ali loved my *qeymāq*.

Mother, who wanted to calm the two of us down, said, "Send *salawāts*."

Through my tears, I said, "Mother, I will not forget Ali Agha, even after forty years. I will burn inside for his loss like this until the Day of Resurrection."

Mansūreh Khānūm moaned and let out a sigh. She had gone pale and yellow, and her eyes had lost their sparkle and become lifeless.

Mother asked, "Mansūreh Khānūm, are you feeling OK?"

Mansūreh Khānūm shook her head. It was clear that she was suffering inwardly. Mother placed the spoon in the *qeymāq*. There were a few stamens of brilliant saffron in it. She said, "Will you help yourself or should I spoon feed it to you?"

I had no appetite. The smell of the fried flower and saffron which had filled the house made me want to retch. I remembered the halva that was served at Amīr and Ali's wakes, and I was disquieted. "I miss Ali Agha," I sobbed.

Mansūreh Khānūm quietly stood up and left. Mother said, "Fereshteh, my dear, I thought we had agreed that we were not going to cry in public. You have to stay strong. Tomorrow is Ali Agha's *chehelom*.[19] There might be some *monāfeqīn*[20] among the guests. If you continue to carry on like this, it will gladden the hearts of the enemy. You have to be like a man. Have you forgotten how Ali Agha was when Amīr was martyred? That's what you need to be like. Your son is not an orphan; he is the son of a *shahīd*, a martyr. And you are the wife of a *shahīd*. If I see you crying and showing weakness, *halālet nemīkonam*, I will take my complaint against you to God on Judgment Day. We chose this path ourselves. Have you forgotten when we came asking your family for your hand in marriage, you said you would only marry someone who was a warrior in the path of Islam; someone who did not demure from going to the warfront? Remember how you

---

[19] The fortieth day after someone's passing. The third, seventh, and fortieth days of the first year are commemorated formally; as are the anniversaries, of course.

[20] Literally, hypocrites. In the moral hierarchy within Islam, hypocrites are even lower than unbelievers and infidels. However, *monāfeqīn* can also refer to any member of the terrorist group, the Mojāhedīn-e Khalq Organization (MKO), who refer to themselves as the Mojāhedīn, but who everyone in Iran refers to as the Monāfeqīn, because this terrorist organization is responsible for the murder and assassination of over 17,000 Iranian citizens in the years since the Islamic Revolution of 1979. They are also hated because they fought along Saddām Hussein's army against Iran during the eight-year Iran-Iraq war that was imposed on Iran by the Saddām Bathist regime.

said you wanted to do your part for the revolution? Do you not want to do your duty for your religion? Well, now is the time. Do your part! Did you not say that you wanted your husband to be brave and to have faith in God? Well, was Ali Agha not courageous? Did he not have faith? Now it's your turn! You have to have courage and you have to have faith. No more tears. Tears are a sign of weakness. And a Moslem is not weak; especially not my adorable Fereshteh."

I said, "Mother, I know all these things. But what can I do? My heart is broken. I can't pretend that it isn't."

Monīreh Khānūm called Mother from the kitchen. Mother got up and said, "Eat it and I'll go and come back. When you are feeling better, we will go to the Golzār-e Shohadā (the Martyr's Cemetery). You'll be able to be with Ali Agha there."

I pulled the tray forward. The curtain had been pulled back from the window. It was snowing gently. Outside the window, everything was quiet and tranquil. White flakes of snow made their way gently from the heavens to the ground in a way that was pleasing to behold. I thought that by now Ali Agha and Amīr's gravestones must be covered with a white blanket of snow. I thought about my diary and felt the need to write, as it had been several days since I had written anything. I wanted to write Ali Agha a letter and say, "Beloved Ali, your son was born. Should I name him Mosayyeb or Amīr?" I started to cry again. I moaned, "Oh God! I miss Ali Agha! What can I do, dear God, I miss him so much!" I had become just like a child. I started crying out loud.

When evening came, they gathered all of the bedding from in front of the radiator in the living room and took them to the bedroom. It was going to be crowded before too long, as the morrow was Ali Agha's *chehellom* or "fortieth" commemoration. There were going to be a lot of people to come to see if there was anything, they could do to help out for the big day tomorrow.

And so, it was that my son and I became residents in the bedroom. And everyone would tell me not to be so sad and not to cry; but I thought, "How is it possible for me to live in a room with all of those memories and not be sad and be able to surmount my urge to cry?" Only God knew and understood why I was so torn and why I was hurting and cried so much. Because only He fully understood what kind of a person I had been deprived of. Ali Agha's picture album was still in the room's closet.

The first time I entered this room, the wall to wall closet on the left drew my attention. It had taken up the whole wall. To its left and right, there were places where clothes could be hung, and the middle was taken up by a decorative series of drawers and cupboards. The cupboards were filled with Ali Agha's books and picture album and personal belongings. He loved that album; it was full of pictures of his friends who had been martyred. When he had some free time, he would say, "Fereshteh, will you go and fetch that album so that we can leaf through it together?" The doors of the two wardrobes to either side of the wall to wall closet, as well as the walls on either side of it, were filled with pictures of his friends who had been martyred, together with their headbands, ID tags, and hand written mementos. I had been surprised at the fact that Ali Agha had so many friends who had been martyred. I let out a sigh and thought, "You finally did what you had to do and made your way up to the wall of fame."

Agha Nāser came into the room and asked, "Lady Fereshteh, did you decide what you are going to name the young master?"

I said, "I don't know, sir. Whatever you determine is right."

In his usual humorous way he said, "Ali has stipulated everything to me, from the imperative of having lots of clarified butter and milk and honey, down to how the child is supposed to be clothed. But he forgot to instruct me concerning the main thing."

Lowering my head down in shame, I said, "But he did tell me, sir."

Agha Nāser got excited and asked with a big smile on his face, "He did? What did he say?"

He always used to say, "If it's a girl, it should be Zeynab, and if it's a boy, Mosayyeb."[21]

A frown appeared on Agha Nāser's brows. "Nah, that's what he said when Mosayyeb was recently martyred and he and Amīr were still alive."

I didn't say anything. Agha Nāser let out a groan. Then he said, "Ali liked Mosayyeb a lot. It was as if they were brothers."

---

[21] Mosayyeb Majīdī was a friend of Ali's whose friendship went back to their childhood days. He was martyred in the operation to take Faw Island in Iraq on the 17th of March, 1986.

Agha Nāser went and stood in front of Mosayyeb's picture and said, "May God have mercy on your soul, Mosayyeb. My son ended up following in your footsteps."

He turned and looked at me, then turned back and looked at the picture again and let out another groan. "Aaaaaaaah! You *told* him that the way of martyrdom was a vale of tears!"

Agha Nāser came and sat by my side. "After Mosayyeb's martyrdom," he said, "my son's eyes were always red."

I looked at Amīr's picture. His picture, too, was among the pictures of the martyrs. Agha Nāser bent over the baby's face and said, "I named my sons myself: Sādeq, and Alī, and Amīr. Amīr was short for Mohammad Amīr; and Ali was born on the 13th of Rajab, the birthday of His Eminence Imam Ali."

I didn't say anything. Mansūreh Khānum entered the room. It was as if she had heard everything. She said, "Agha Nāser; come and let us do something to keep Ali's name alive."

Mansūreh Khānum looked at Amīr and Ali Agha's picture and let out a sigh. "I say we name him Mohammad Ali. In honor of Mohammad Amīr and Ali Agha. How's that?"

I said, "Mohammad Ali? It's good. It's very good, *Mādar* (Mother)."

Agha Nāser was gladdened by this and bent and kissed Mohammad Ali's forehead. Mohammad Ali's eyes were open but he was not fussing. Agha Nāser picked him up and said, "Come now, little one. Let the two of us go together like two men. How much longer do you want to keep on sleeping?"

I ran my hands over the pictures. Ali Agha had thumb-tacked these pictures to the walls with such affection. I could still see his fingerprints on some of the full-gloss pictures. It was only his and Amīr's picture that had been framed.

I placed my forehead on the glass of the picture frame. The frame carried the scent of Ali Agha's hands. He had hung it on the wall himself. I said, "Well, our son's name became Mohammad Ali, but I will call him Ali in your memory; my beloved Ali."

With this thought I could no longer hold back my tears. All of the pictures carried the scent of Ali Agha's hands. The whole room smelled of his scent. I tried hard to recall the shape of those pale warm hands, his tall stature, his light brown full beard, his blue eyes, the lines on his forehead, and his disheveled light brown hair and eyebrows.

That night, he slept in this same room. But no; we were in Hājj Sādeq's room. He wasn't feeling well. He was supposed to leave at two thirty in the morning. He said, "Fereshteh, if I go to sleep, will you wake me up?"

"Yes," I said.

Would that I hadn't woken him! Would that I had gone to sleep too, so that the two of us would have slept through that fateful hour. At the bottom of my heart, I knew that he wouldn't be coming back this time. How did I know? There was an inner voice that kept telling me, "Fereshteh, take a good look at him. Take him in well. You will need to remember his visage, his hair, and his brows, and his countenance, for a whole lifetime. The sounds of his footfalls..." He had a habit of walking on the balls of his feet.

Ali was always in a hurry. He was always restless, ready to move on to the next thing. Those blue eyes would never fall into a full sleep. It was as if he slept with one eye open. But that night, he fell into a deep sleep. He breathed deeply in his sleep. I reproach myself: "Fereshteh, why did you wake him? Why did you not lie next to him and go to sleep as well? Did you not hear that inner voice whispering in your ear and telling you, 'This will be the last time that you will see him. This is your last farewell. Your last chance to see him before he goes. The last goodbye...'? You heard, but you did not listen!"

When you went to sleep, I came back into the living room. Why did I come back? Why didn't I stand there and look at you to my heart's content? Did I not know that I would not be able to see you again until the Day of Resurrection?

I could hear Mother calling me. "Fereshteh... Fereshteh Jān, do you want me to bring your dinner over there, or will you come here?"

I wiped my tears away quickly. I looked at myself in the reflection in the glass of Ali's picture frame. The tip of my nose and my eyes were red. Even though I had no appetite, I went into the living room. There was a large tablecloth spread on the floor. There were no strangers; it was just us: Maryam, with her husband and daughter; Hājj Sādeq, with his wife and kids; Grandfather and Mansūreh Khānūm, and Father and Mother and Mother's brother, Uncle Mohammad, who had lived abroad, but had left his family there a few years already and was living with his parents. I was filled with melancholy. What a big happy family we were. If Ali and Amīr were present, that would have completed us and made us whole. There would be the telling of stories and jokes and laughter and merriment and mirth. Why, pray, had we become like this all of a sudden?

What a dull and lifeless gathering. Mansūreh Khānūm was not feeling well. Earlier in the evening her kidneys had been giving her trouble again, and Hājj Sādeq had taken her to the doctor's. Everyone was sitting around the table-spread silently, not uttering a single word. Agha Jān (Fereshteh's father in law) was still in high spirits. He said, "This son of yours will be the end of me, Lady Fereshteh; I haven't heard him cry even once!"

Nafīseh said, "Fereshteh dear, instead of wailing, his face goes all red."

There was *gheymeh* (meat and yellow split pea stew) with rice for dinner. Maryam passed by me carrying a dish. The smell of sun-dried limes wafted under my nose.

I sat down next to Mansūreh Khānūm. I said, "Are you feeling better now? What did the doctor have to say?"

Mansūreh Khānūm was looking pale and lifeless, and the discoloration under her eyes was more pronounced. She said, "The cyst on my kidney has grown larger. The doctor says that I need an operation."

She looked at me sadly and said, "How can one not be affected by such a prospect?"

Agha Nāser was still holding Mohammad Ali. He said, "Come and take this boy of yours, my lady bride. What kind of boy is this? No matter what I did, he didn't cry out. I pinched him, and slapped him around a little; I even bit him – all to no avail. No matter what I did, I couldn't make him cry!"

With mock outrage, I said, "Sir! You didn't!"

Mansūreh Khānūm said weakly, "Would that God gives to him whatever good that was Ali's due, Agha Nāser; he takes after his father. Ali was the same way: he would get sick, he would suffer pain, but you would never hear him say anything."

Agha Nāser smiled. He said, "He made up for all the taciturnity of his infancy once he entered into his childhood proper. Then he became a real firebrand and troublemaker."

Mansūreh Khānūm spoke with difficulty. "Who? *My* son? Have you forgotten the time before his martyrdom when he had contracted the flu? Not once did he say that he was ill! We only found out because of his appearance; he had become as white as a ghost!"

It seemed as if Agha Nāser's memory had been jogged. He said quietly, "One's appearance betrays one's inner state. You are right. He had just come back from the warfront and was not feeling at all well, but he didn't utter a word about his being ill.

I said, "What is it, my son?"

He said, "Nothing."

I asked, "Have you caught a cold?"

He said, "I think so."

I said, "Shall we go to the doctor's?"

He said, "No, Fereshteh will get me some medicine."

I went and fetched him some Adult Cold and acetaminophen tablets from the fridge, which he took with some water. Hājj Sādeq finally convinced him with some difficulty to let him take him to the doctor's, where they gave him some injections. I made a bed for him when he got back home. He got under the blankets and slept the whole day through. He got up in the middle of the night and went into the kitchen. I followed him.

I asked, "Are you not feeling well?"

He said, "No; I'm hungry."

Mansūreh Khānūm said, "Their voices got me up, so I went to the kitchen to find my Ali sitting on the floor of the kitchen eating some eggs he had fried up. It was past midnight, and he kept on eating and kept on saying how delicious they taste! I later found out that he hadn't eaten for several days, the poor thing."

Father said, "That's true, Ali's tolerance for pain was very high. His friends related that no one heard a peep out of him during any of the seven times he was injured in the war."

Father looked at me and said, "Do you remember, a few days after the wedding celebrations, we had invited them to our place. Earlier in the afternoon of that day, he had sprained his ankle. After they arrived, I saw Ali moving around the dinner spread as if something was bothering him. His face had turned red, but he didn't say anything. I didn't know what had happened."

Mother shook her head a little and said, "It was the seventh of Khordād (May/June), last year. I remember it well. It was Fereshteh's birthday, so I wanted to buy a cake; but Fereshteh wouldn't let me. She said she didn't want to put anyone to any trouble on her account, so I agreed to her wishes.

Father is right. At dinner time I noticed that Ali Agha kept moving about and fidgeting. He had become all red in the face. He had crouched down in some corner, and I thought it was because of his shyness."

Mother then turned to me and asked, "Fereshteh, should I serve you some *gheymeh* and rice, or some *qeymāq*?

I felt like crying again. I wanted to go back into the room and let it all out. I said with a lump in my throat, "Rice, but only a very little, please."

Monday, January 4th, 1988 was Ali Agha's *chehellom* or the "fortieth" of his martyrdom, which was commemorated in the Mahdīyeh[22] Mosque in Hamedān. I stayed home. A few neighbors came to keep me company so that I would not be alone. The ceremonies were scheduled to be from 9:30 to 11:00 AM, but it was past one when everyone came back home. They said that there were between sixty and seventy commemorative ceremonies held in Hamadān province for Ali Agha's *chehellom*, in the cities and townships, down to small villages. A large crowd had showed up at the Mahdīyeh Mosque as well. The mosque was completely full from the start of the ceremonies until the end. We had a large number of guests for lunch. Hājj Sādeq had seen to the catering in advance.

---

[22] A Mahdīyeh is a Hosaynīyeh that is dedicated to Imam Mahdi. A Hosaynīyeh is a congregation hall for Shi'a commemoration ceremonies and rites, especially those associated with mourning in the month of Moharram.

In the mosque, friends and family had asked after me, and those who had not known already, realized that Mohammad Ali had been born. In the afternoon, the womenfolk of the family and among our friends and acquaintances came to see me. Most of them had obliged me and, in addition to having taken the time out of their schedules to come over, had brought gifts for me and my son as a way of welcoming the newborn into the world. The gifts ranged from blankets and sets of baby clothing, to toys such as cars and airplanes. A few among my close family also brought lengths of cloth and blouses and colorful headscarves, advising me out of the kindness of their hearts that the time had come to put aside my black mourning attire and to start wearing colorful clothing again (and thereby to come out of my state of mourning). some of them even insisted that I give them permission to make an appointment for me at the hairdressers. Among the guests there was a lady who was about the same age as me. She was light-skinned, with light-colored eyes and light brown eyebrows. She was seated next to me the whole time and expressed affection for me. No matter how hard I thought about who she could be, I could not place her. I thought that she is perhaps the wife of one of Ali Agha's fellow soldiers. Eventually she spoke up and said, "Mrs. Panāhī, do you not remember me?"

I said, "I'm sorry, but no. I haven't been able to place you, no matter how hard I've tried."

She said, "You have every right not to know me. But everyone knows who *you* are. Because you are the wife of Mr. Ali Chitsāzīān; and who is there, in the whole of Hamedān, who doesn't know who *he* is."

My Memories get played like a Movie Reel

I whispered, "You are too kind. Thank you kindly."

She then said, "Of course, after New Year's last year, we had some firearms training as part of a group from the Mahdīyeh Mosque. Do you recall that? Your attention was elsewhere, but all of us women use to point you out to each other 'with our eyes and eyebrows', as they say. You had just gotten married. The womenfolk would say out of your earshot, 'This tall lady is Mr. Ali Chītsāzīān's wife. I don't know why I had the idea that because you are the wife of a commander, your aim should be better than all of the rest of us!"

The lady smiled and continued, "But when it came time for the practice session, your aim missed the target altogether." That brought a smile to my face.

Maryam leaning forward holding a large tray full of glasses of tea and was going around the room offering the guests tea. And Nafīseh followed her with a sugar bowl full of cube sugar. The lady said, "Mrs. Panāhī, the ladies who are part of the resistance force of the Mahdīyeh Mosque are also involved in some literary and publication activities. I came to pay my respects today, but I was also hoping to ask if you were willing to share any interesting memories that you had with Commander Chītsāzīān, so that we could publish them in our journal."

She then opened her purse and took out a notepad and pen.

I started thinking: memoirs! Memoirs from Ali Agha! Nothing came to mind at that moment in time, so I said, "Well, it is not as if I was on the front lines with Ali Agha. And he had a habit of not talking about what took place in the war or on the war front at home."

The woman asked with surprise, "You mean to say that he never talked to you about any of the operations, or about any of his friends who were martyred or wounded in action??"

I said, "No, nothing. And if I know of certain events, it is because I heard about them from those around him and from his friends. And he was especially reticent when it came to talking about himself personally."

The woman continued to look at me with surprise, then asked, "Excuse me, but if I may, when did you marry?"

"In the March of 1986."

The woman started counting on the fingers of both her hands, and then said, "You lived with each other for approximately one year and nine months, is that right?"

"Yes."

"I am sure that during this time you must have accumulated many stories to relate. Would you be so kind as to tell us one? An interesting one?"

I started thinking. Which memory was I supposed to relate? The memories of our living in Dezfūl? Or our pilgrimage to Mashhad and Qom? The memory of our wedding? Or Sāsān's hospitalization? I asked, "Excuse me, but what is the purpose of this interview?"

"Well, I just think people would like to know what kind of people the commanders of the war are; especially in their private lives, in terms of how they relate to their wives and families."

I smiled and said, "I think people know Ali Agha better than they know me or his family. Ali Agha is famous for his courage; for the love that he had for Imam [Khomeini], and to the attention he paid and the importance he gave to the Imam's words and speeches. In every one of his speeches, Ali Agha would beseech his audience not to let the words of Imam Khomeini be forgotten. And he was a very genial and sociable person as well."

The woman looked at me dejectedly, put her pen inside her notebook and closed it. "You mean to tell me you don't have a single story to tell us?"

I had many remembrances from Ali Agha; from the first day when he came to ask for my hand in marriage, to the day of our last farewell. As a matter of fact, I had recorded all of them in my diaries for the years 1986 and 1987. I was especially fond of recording some of the events and occurrences of my life. And if I didn't have time, I would jot down the important events just with a single word or a short reminder of what occurred in those same datebooks and mark them. And I would collect all sorts of different things as mementos. I kept all of his letter, for example. And everything that he had ever given me: from the cake of clay from Karbalā which was used to place my forehead on when in the position of prostration in offering the ritual devotions to the Lord, to the prayer mat and the *tasbīh* or Moslem rosary, and the piece of cloth which had the *tabarrok*[23] of His Eminence the Imam, to the small bottles of scent whose fragrance he used to

---

[23] The property of a relic or some mundane object which has been blessed or charged in some other way with sacral properties.

rub on the back of his ears before offering his prayers. But I thought, "What possible use can my reminiscences be to the general public?"

When the woman saw that I had fallen silent and did not say anything more, she asked again, "Do you really not have any memories to share with us?"

I smiled a little and said, "I'm sorry; none occur to me under these circumstances."

The poor soul did not insist any further. She put her pen and notepad back in her purse, had her tea and sweet pastry, and got me to agree to see her at another time for another interview, said her goodbyes, and made her way out.

That night, when the guests and visitors left, we were back to the familiar circle of the extended family. Mansūreh Khānum was still not feeling well. And she was using Maryam, who needed to pack her things as she was leaving for Tehran with her husband first thing in the morning, as an excuse. Nāser and the others were sitting all quiet in a corner. Mother was changing Mohammad Ali's diapers. She said, "Fereshteh, why don't you pack your things too and come with us tomorrow? Your father is feeling lonely. And the kids have school. I don't know what they've been up to these last few days."

Mother put Mohammad Ali into his cot. The room smelled of the baby: of soap, baby powder, and milk. I got up and folded my clothes and that of the baby's and packed them in a bag; the diapers, the milk bottle, and the flask. I packed everything up so that I would not forget anything in the morning. Mohammad Ali was awake. He was still rosy, but his swelling had gone down and he seemed thinner. He looked at the ceiling with his grey eyes and fussed.

My gaze fell on Ali Agha's picture frame, where he was looking at me gloomily. I said, "What is it, my love? Why are you gloomy? All of a woman's honor depends on her husband. And now that you are not here, I feel different. I feel that I might be something extra, and that I don't quite fit in."

I was leaving and it would perhaps be a long time before I returned. I was leaving that room of memories, the room to which Ali Agha came when he came back home from the war front. The room which smelled of Ali Agha's scent and had something about him in it. The room in whose wardrobes hung his clothes. The room whose bookshelves held his books and his manuscripts. And the picture album of pictures of which he was inordinately fond. I was leaving. I thought that it would be best if I took his framed picture with me. I stood up to take it off the wall, but my hand got stuck on the picture frame. No matter how I tried, I could not separate my hand from the picture frame. I heard Agha Nāser's voice behind me.

"Fereshteh Khānūm, what are you doing?"

The frame let go of my hand. "Sir, I want to go to my mother's house tomorrow. With your permission, I would like to take Ali Agha's picture with me."

Agha Nāser said with surprise, "You want to leave?" Then he turned to the door and said, "Mansūreh? Mansūreh Khānūm, come and see what Fereshteh Khānūm is saying. She wants to leave!"

A little later, Mansūreh Khānūm and Mother and Hājj Bābā and Khānūm Jān came into the room. As soon as Mansūreh Khānūm saw that I had packed up my things, she got upset and started to cry. Maryam took her into her arms in order to calm her down, but instead broke down herself. The atmosphere was such that anyone who now entered the room and saw the scene started to cry. I knew that everyone had been trying not to shed tears in public during these few days [that led up to Ali's "fortieth"] so as not to give comfort to any enemy that might have hidden themselves in the crowds, and in order not to give any excuses to the hypocrites...

The only person who was not crying at this point was Agha Nāser. He said, "Amīr and Ali's spirits are here with us now. Send a loud *salawāt* in order to please their spirits."

Everyone sent a loud *salawāt*. Uncle Mohammad was sitting next to Mohammad Ali and was playing with him. Agha Nāser said again, "I am sure Amīr and Ali's spirits are watching over us, so for the love of the *Mowlā*[24] [= the master, i.e. Imam Ali], stop crying!"

---

[24] Mowlā means master. It is a title the Shī'a reserve for Imam Ali, based on a report of a saying of the Prophet on his farewell sermon where he entrusted his ministry to Imam Ali by raising his hand and declaring: "O People! Almighty God is my lord and master [*mowlā*], and I am your lord and master. Of whomsoever I have [hitherto] been lord and master [*mowlā*], [so too] this [here] Ali shall [henceforth similarly] be his lord and master." The Prophet then raised his hands in supplication and prayed, "Almighty God, Be Thou a friend to whoever is a friend of Ali, and an enemy of whoever is his enemy; be Thou a supporter of

My Memories get played like a Movie Reel

When Agha Nāser uttered these words, his voice was quivering. He was like a cracked bottle that was ready to fall apart at the slightest impact.

Mansūreh Khānūm and Mother and Maryam quieted down. Agha Nāser turned to me and said, "Now tell me, Fereshteh Jān; bless your heart. Have you grown weary of us? Did someone say something to upset you? Was there some unpleasantness or something?"

I quickly replied, "No sir! As God is my witness, no! There is nothing that anyone said and there was certainly no unpleasantness or anything else."

Mansūreh Khānūm started crying again. "So then why do you want to go?"

I said, "Well, because I have been enough of a burden. My staying would just cause you more hardship."

I looked over at Mother. "And Mother wants to go back to her home, and my father and sister are on their own."

Mansūreh Khānūm picked Mohammad Ali up and held him close to her breast and said in a plaintiff tone, "Where do you want to take my handsome grandson? My beloved Amīr, my beloved Ali, where are you headed?"

Agha Nāser's voice was quivering. He said, "No, dearest. Don't say such things. That kind of talk is for strangers. You are [no different to us than] our daughter. And Mohammad Ali is

---

whoever supports Ali, and oppose whoever opposes him; be a friend of anyone who is a friend of Ali and be wrathful to whoever subjects Ali to his wrath." This hadith report is reported in many of the Sunni books of hadith, including Bokhārī and Moslem's *sahīhayn*.

[no different to us than] our son. What do you mean, you'll be a burden to us? This is your home!" He then raised his hands heavenward and said, "Praise be to God! Praise be to God! If both my sons were martyred, it is because they were worthy of martyrdom, and You accepted them [and entered them into this exalted spiritual station]. Praise God that my sons did not turn out to be the cause of our dishonor and shame. Praise God that my sons are a cause of our honor and respect and pride. A thousand praises, O Lord, for the good that You gave us. And a hundred thousand praises, O Lord, for the good way in which You took them away."

A little later, in order to change the mood, Agha Nāser began to spoof and said, "Just take this baby of yours. What kind of baby is it anyway that doesn't cry or complain? My fingernails have become all black and blue from pinching him so much, and he still won't let out a peep. Where are the good old days when you could hear a baby's screams a mile away?"

Mohammad Ali had finished his second month. We would at times go to Hājj Sādeq's home for family gatherings, and at other times we would go to my Mother's house; but my main base had been Agha Nāser's home.

Mansūreh Khānūm was not well. The cysts on her kidneys had grown larger and had disrupted her whole biological system. And so, Agha Nāser had decided to take her to Tehran for a while to get second opinions and in order to get better medical treatment. And that is how, after two months, Mohammad Ali and I, together with a few bags and suitcases, headed for my mother's home. We determined right there that when they returned, we would have an arrangement such that we would stay with Mother on the week days, but would stay in Agha Nāser's house on the weekends (on Thursdays and Fridays).

My condition changed when I went to Mother's house. I had become lonelier. Father would go to attend to his shop every morning. He was a barber, and in those days, his Do Hezār barber shop at the Sharīatī intersection was famous and had its own special clientele in abundance. Mother would go to the sewing workshop every morning and afternoon, where a number of women worked without wages and in order to seek God's good pleasure sewing army uniforms and fatigues. The workshop was on the second floor of a store on Bābā Tāher Street, adjacent to the Mīrzā Dāvūd Mosque.

Both of my sisters were students and went to school. And so every morning the house would become empty of its residents other than Mohammad Ali and myself, who would be left on our own. Mohammad Ali was a quiet baby who didn't give me any trouble.

Those were difficult times for me. They were lonely days, and days where I felt isolated, and where I became more introspective. I spent most of my time either writing down my memories or by recalling them by reading my datebooks for the years 1986 and 1987.

Mother was the only person who attempted to relieve me of my isolation. She would usually go to the sewing workshop to make sure everything was in order, and would then come back as soon as she could. Occasionally she would cancel her afternoon shift. And she would organize a *rowzeh*[25] or take me along to ones she had been invited to. At other times, she would place father under 'house arrest', as it were, and make him babysit Mohammad Ali, and thus create the opportunity for the two of us to go out, even if at times this was only for half an hour. She would buy me something and we would stroll through the bazaar, and then make our way back home. I spent most of my weekends in Mansūreh Khānūm's home. Loneliness and missing Ali Agha's company were the hardest factors of my life. During the day, I would look at the entry door in the hope that someone would step through it. But very few people did so. Everyone was preoccupied with their own lives. It seemed that with Ali Agha's martyrdom, I, too, had been erased from people's memories.

---

[25] *Rowzeh:* a religious ceremony and mourning ritual where people gather to hear a popular religious authority (a *rowzeh-khūn*) discuss social or moral issues, which usually ends with an elegiac eulogy of one of the Imams or members of the house of the Prophet who died as a martyr in the cause of Islam. Such ceremonies are usually but not always centered around the martyrdom of Imam Hosayn and his entourage at the Plain of Karbalā; or they are dedicated to one of the Imams on the anniversary of his martyrdom; or are dedicated to commemorating Lady Fātema the Luminous (*az-Zahrā*), the blessed daughter of the Prophet of Islam.

My Memories get played like a Movie Reel

Those days, and the days which followed them, had many hardships and travails which I could perhaps not have been able to endure if it were not for my love for Imam [Khomeini], for the [values and ideals of] the [Islamic] Revolution, and if it had not been for my being steadfast and faithful to my [creedal] principles and [religious] objectives. I had entered a difficult phase of my life, and was faced with greater and more difficult decisions. Ali had followed his ideals and objectives, and left me to discover my ideals and objectives on my own.

The following year, the war came to an end and the soldiers returned to the cities and towns from the war front, and became engaged in leading normal lives, and gradually many things changed.

With my mother's encouragement and insistence, I enrolled in the Tahzīb community college and started studying the second year of childcare for the third time. The first years of being without Ali Agha were probably the most trying times of my life; but given my diaries and my memories of him with which I lived, he had an extraordinary and tangible presence in my life during those years. I still have those diaries, and by looking at them and at certain key words or phrases which I wrote as mnemonic reminders of larger memories, I am able to bring back to life all of my memories of Ali Agha, from the first day when he asked for my hand in marriage, through to the day of his martyrdom, and beyond.

A Suitor with Blue Eyes

1 It was the February of 1986. I was looking at the dry and bare trees that lined the sidewalk, and at the soot-stained snow that was slowly melting, from behind the window of a bus. The sky was blue and cloudless, and occasionally a flock of birds could be seen flying overhead. The bus came to a halt and the driver looked in his back mirror and shouted the name of the stop: "Honarestān!"

A pale-complexioned girl with a round face and beautiful green eyes got off the bus. I thought that she was the most attractive girl on the bus. She always used to sit in the back of the bus and chatter away with her friends. I knew that, like me, she was in her second year at the college. Her name was Maryam. I had learned that from her friends; we were not classmates. The bus had stopped at the Martyrs of Dībāj community college bus stop. She arranged her *chādor* over her head, gathered it around her firmly and got off. She waved goodbye to her friends inside the bus for the nth time. Most of the commuters on the bus were students at Tahzīb Community College. The bus passed Mīrzādeh Eshqī Street, where our house is located. I used to get off the bus every day at the Imam Khomeini Hospital stop. At that time, the name of our street was Mehregān Street, which was opposite Qāzīān Street. I crossed the street. When I entered our own street, I saw that there was a truck parked outside our house. A few men entered the yard and a little later they came back out carrying a few large containers, which they placed in the back of a truck.

Our front yard was small; it was filled with different kinds of scents. Small clusters of women were sitting or standing in the corners and along the sides of the yard, busy doing different things. Some were gathered around a gas burner and were cooking jam in a large pot. Others were busy pouring chilled oxymel into pitchers. There were a few women sitting on a large carpet packing mixed nuts from a large tray that was positioned in the center of the carpet into small plastic packets, and sealing the packs with small green ribbons.

I greeted Mrs. Hamīd-Zādeh as I passed her. She was a friend of my mothers who did volunteer work in my mother's sewing workshop. She greeted me with a smile and then turned and whispered something to the woman who was sitting next to her. I felt embarrassed and felt my cheeks tingle; and quickly made my way into the house.

A Suitor with Blue Eyes

There were about seven or eight women sitting in a circle in the living room. There was a large white spread laid out on the carpet with a large mound of jagged pieces of cube sugar piled up in the middle of it. I breathed in the sugar dust that had become airborne as a result of the breaking down of the solid bolts of sugar, and made my way quietly to the kitchen. My mother was stirring a large pot which she had on the stove. The smell of vinegar rasped at my throat. I greeted my mother and asked her how she was doing. I wanted to open the door of the fridge, but I saw that Mrs. Hamīd-Zādeh had followed me into the kitchen and was quietly saying something to my mother.

A little bird told me what was cooking, so I hurried out of the kitchen on the pretext of changing out of my outside clothes into my house clothes, and went into my room and stayed there. Nafīseh who was five years old at the time was there, sleeping.

Mother called me a little later. I pulled my blouse over my trousers and came out. Mrs. Hamīd-Zādeh and the lady who was seated next to her in the yard were waiting in a corner of the living room, seated behind the women who were breaking up the solid bolts of sugar into bite-sized cubes. Mother told me to straighten my hair, which reminded me that I hadn't brushed my hair. Mother hinted subtly that I should offer them some tea.

By now I had realized why Mrs. Hamīd-Zādeh's friend was looking at me with such a keen interest. I poured tea in the glasses which were reserved for guests. I filled the sugar bowl with sugar cubes and placed it in the middle of the tray. I took a couple of steps back in order to inspect the color of the tea and to see how everything was arranged on the tray. The tea's color was good, and steam could be seen rising from the small glasses. I looked at myself in the polished steel of the samovar and straightened my hair out, and came into the living room. Mrs. Hamīd-Zādeh's friend was of a medium height and build. She was fair-complexioned and had light-colored eye brows. Her clothes were immaculate and stylish. When I bent forward to offer her tea from the tray, she smiled and said in a motherly tone, "Thank you, my dear; may God grant you good fortune."

I held out the tray of tea with trembling arms in front of Mrs. Hamīd-Zādeh and my mother, and then took the tray and the sugar-cube bowl back into the kitchen, and went back and closed myself off in my room. I took out my datebook from my purse and marked March 7th, 1986 with a small x, and wrote, "Matrimonial suit" (*khāstegārī*).

As the following day was a break between two exam days, I went back to bed and slept until 9:30 after offering my morning ritual devotions and prayers. When I got up to go to the bathroom to brush my teeth, I was taken aback with surprise to see Mrs. Hamīd-Zādeh and her stylish friend talking to my mother in the front yard.

I went and hid in the kitchen. They left after a little while, and my mother came and said, "Fereshteh, it was Mansūreh Khānūm, Mrs. Hamīd-Zādeh's friend. The same lady who was here yesterday. You have met with her approval. Mrs. Hamīd-Zādeh has spoken very well of them; she says they are a good and reputable family, and that Mansūreh Khānūm's son is a friend of Mrs. Hamīd-Zādeh's son, and that they are in the army together."

I said with annoyance, "Don't start again, Mom! How many times do I have to say that I don't plan on marrying right now? I want to go to university and study."

Mother said, "Calm down! It's not as if these things are going to happen overnight. I have already stipulated these things on your behalf to them, as well as many other things besides. Mansūreh Khānūm said she was taken by your nobility of character and gentility. She said that her son wants a girl like you. She said that he has no problems with your wanting to continue your studies. This way, if you want to, you can continue to study after the marriage. She said that her own daughter has 'tied the wedding knot' even though she is a student."

I lowered my head and didn't say anything more. Mother smiled and said with a certain glee in her voice, "They seem to be a respectable family; her son is a *pāsdār*, a member of the Guardians of the Revolution or of the "Revolutionary Guards".

Mother knew that one of my criteria for a suitor is that he needed to be a *pāsdār*. I considered *pāsdārs* to be perfect and flawless persons who were true believes (*mo'men*) who believed in the values and ideals of Islam and of the revolution (*mo'taqed*). For me, they had the same exalted status and high code of moral conduct as the *rowhānīat* or clergy. Mother said, "Mansūreh Khānūm said that her son has been on the war front from the very beginning of the war all the way up to now."

I got the feeling that Mother approved of this marriage, because she was recounting my criteria for marriage. Another one of my criteria was that my husband should be a soldier. I had told my mother that I wanted to do my part for the Islamic Revolution. I didn't want to be a burden on society. My goal was to serve my country and the objectives of the Revolution by marrying one who was engaged in the armed struggle for their survival.

When Mother saw that I did not say anything, she did not pursue the line of conversation further.

The following day, when I came back from school, Mother had made the house spic and span and had put everything in order. The sidewalk in front of the house had been swept and watered down. The patio had been washed. She had cleaned the windows to a sparkle. The rooms had been vacuumed and dusted, and everything had been put in its proper place and beautifully arranged. There was no longer any sign of the disheveled state that the house was in as a result of the preparations of the fruit preserves and vegetable pickles and mixed nuts packets which were being prepared for distribution at the war front.

The house smelled like flowers. My heart went out to my mother on account of her having done all this work on her own in the four or five hours of our absence. Mother whispered in my ear that Mansūreh Khānūm and her son were going to show up later that night. Upon hearing this news, it was as if my arms and legs had become frozen stiff, and my heart began beating fast. After lunch, Royā and I completed the task of cleaning the house, while I was overtaken by anxiety about the impending visit by my suitor.

A Suitor with Blue Eyes

Night had fallen. Mother was preparing dinner. It was 8:30 when the doorbell rang. Father opened the door; it was Mansūreh Khānūm and her son. My sisters and I had taken refuge in our own room. But Mother and Father showed the guests to the living room. I didn't know what I was supposed to do. I had become more anxious; so much so that I could hardly breathe. Not having anything else to do, I started looking through my datebook. I opened it and made a small mark on the page for Monday, the 18th of Esfand (February/ March).

There was an Aladdin Blue Flame heater in the middle of the room, on top of which was a kettle which was giving off steam from its spout and lid. Even though the room was warm, I was cold and shivering, and my teeth were chattering uncontrollably. I felt that I was in the middle of a process of slowly turning into a block of ice from within.

After a few minutes had passed, Mother came into the room and gently said, "Come, Fereshteh. Your father has given his consent for you to talk to the bridegroom."

I felt as if my heart was bursting through my ribcage. I had lost control of the movement of my arms and legs. Mother had taken the lead. As soon as I stepped into the living room, I felt very faint. Mansūreh Khānūm and her son arose and greeted me genially. Father and Mother stepped out of the room together with Mansūreh Khānūm.

The suitor was standing at the head of the room. He seemed tall to me. Right then the thought occurred to me that I would match his height with a pair of ten-centimeter platform shoes. His head was bowed down. I took advantage of the opportunity and examined him closely. He was wearing army-issue trousers; the ones with eight pockets; with a brown shirt and a tan overcoat. His hair was light brown, and his beard and mustache were light brown with some strands of red mixed in. I did not see his eyes, because he did not raise his head even for a single moment throughout. I didn't know what I was supposed to do. I held my *chādor* tightly around my face, in a way that only my nose showed. There was a box of sweet pastries and a bouquet of flowers on the floor in the middle of the room. The pleasing scent of the flowers had filled the room. He was now seated at the head of the living room next to a window which opened up onto the street, and I was seated on the right with my back to the wall. A few minutes passed in silence. But in the end, it was he who started the conversation.

"In the name of God, the Munificent, the Merciful. My name is Ali Chītsāzīān. I am a *Basījī*.[26] A *Basījī* who follows the line of Imam Khomeinī. I am a moment away from death. [I beseech you to] Pray that I be granted [the exalted station of] martyrdom [by Almighty God]. It is entirely possible that I become martyred, or injured, or taken prisoner at any moment

---

[26] The *Basīj*, whose full name (*Sāzmān-e Basīj-e Mostaʿzafīn*) can be rendered as something like "The Organization for the Mustering of the Forces of the Oppressed", is one of the five forces of the Islamic Revolutionary Guard Corps. A paramilitary peoples' militia established in Iran in 1979 by order of Imam Khomeini, the leader of the Iranian Revolution, the organization originally consisted of civilian volunteers who defended the country against the Iraqi aggressors in the Iran-Iraq war (1980 - 1988).

[while the war lasts]. It is a common occurrence that my duties keep me at the warfront so that I cannot return to Hamedān for months at a time."

He paused. He was perhaps waiting to see if I was going to say anything. When he saw that I remained silent, he continued.

"I only went to school up to the tenth grade, because of [my volunteering to fight in] the war. In my life, the war [effort] is the first priority because Imam [Khomeini] has stated that it is our religious duty not to abandon the warfronts. [Therefore,] I will stay and fight, even if the war lasts twenty years, in order to defend my faith and way of life and [the values of] the [Islamic] Revolution. I studied electrical engineering in Dībāj community college. And I have nothing in terms of the riches of this lower world or realm [of existence] (the *donyā*). Neither a car, or any money; nothing."

He paused again, to give me an opportunity to say something. He then went on, "Of course, I am whole physically, praise God. I am an athlete. I practice the martial arts. Although, if these conditions are not to your liking, then everything can change. In other words, if my future wife is not content with my being on the front lines, I can easily return to Hamedān and find a way to make a living here."

I was taken aback by these words. I said, "No. Actually, one of my criteria and conditions for marriage is that my husband-to-be must definitely be a soldier who fights on the warfront."

He smiled. He held a *tasbīh* or Moslem rosary in his hand which he was twirling around rapidly. His hand suddenly stopped moving. A big smile covered his whole face. I felt that I had aced my first exam.

He said with satisfaction, "Thank God! Because I have dedicated myself to the warfront, as in a religious endowment (*waqf*). When someone gives a carpet or some crockery to the mosque as a religious endowment, that carpet or crockery can never be taken out of the mosque, unless the carpet wears thin or the crockery breaks, so that they no longer serve a useful purpose. But even then, the carpet can be taken out to be patched, after which it will be returned to the mosque or *masjed*."

He then asked, "What about you? What is your aim in life and in marriage?"

I said, "I am passionate about helping the cause of the Revolution. I help my mother in supporting the war effort. I believe that I should be doing a lot more than what I do; but I don't know how. Maybe if my future husband is a soldier, then perhaps he can help me in this regard. That having been said, I should also add that one's religion and creed and faith are very important for me; my husband's being a true Moslem and a true believer are very important."

I could not express myself properly under those conditions. I would utter two or three sentences, and then would stop speaking. The truth is that I strove to speak in a formal and sophisticated style. And it was evident that Ali was also trying to be bookish and formal too.

A Suitor with Blue Eyes

He asked, "So you don't have a problem with my becoming martyred or wounded and taken prisoner?"

I became discomposed, and I don't know how this thought came to my mind, but I answered hastily, "Well, it is not as if, God forbid, anyone is going to become martyred and get wounded and taken prisoner all at the same time!"

He smiled. I began to get concerned that I had perhaps said something superficial and flippant, so I moved to recover the situation, and said, "Your mother said that you have been at the warfront from the beginning of the war. Nothing has happened so far, praise God. God willing, nothing untoward will happen in the future either."

He didn't say anything. His head was bowed forward, and he was repeating his *zekr* (ritual invocation of divine blessings or grace) using his *tasbīh*. Suddenly I remembered my main question, which I had practiced since the day before. I asked, "Excuse me but, what is your aim in marriage?"

Without having to think about it he said, "The perfection of [living my life in accordance with the tenets of] my religion[27]; conforming to the exemplary model set by the Apostle of God." He paused, and then continued, "When one is posted to the warfront, vacations are cancelled when there is an operation under way. When this happens, the soldiers who are married say that Ali has no worries, because he doesn't have a family. I want to understand their situation. I think it is better if

---

[27] Marriage is a *duty* in Islam that is incumbent on all men who have the financial wherewithal to form a family.

everyone was operating under the same conditions. Of course, this is only a secondary consideration."

I was surprised at hearing this response also. At the same time, I liked his sincerity and frankness. I stole a peek at him. His head was still bowed down [in a posture of humility and ocular chastity], and he was repeating his *zekr*.

When the silence between us became extended, I said, "By the way, my name is Zahrā. At least that is how it appears in my birth certificate; but everyone calls me Fereshteh.[28]

He smiled and said, "Zahrā Khānūm. How wonderful! We love the Members of the Household of the Prophet, the *Ahl al-Bayt*; and we are devoted to Her Eminence Lady Zahrā [the august and immaculate daughter of the Prophet]. One must be worthy even to be able to utter her blessed name."

I stood up and left the room. Father was seated in front of the door to the living room in the den. As soon as he saw me, he asked with a nod and a wink, "How's it going?"

I said bashfully, "Nothing. Whatever you think is best…"

Father smiled and said, "Congratulations!"

Father turned to Mother and Mansūreh Khānūm who were both busy talking, and asked them to accompany him back into the living room. I wanted to go back to the room and be with my sisters, but Mother took hold of my arm and we went back into the living room together. Father sat next to Ali and started talking about work and asking about the warfront and how the war was going. And Mother was busy telling Mansūreh Khānūm

---

[28] Fereshteh means angel in Persian.

about all of the things that her workshop did to help the war effort and the soldiers on the front lines; about the tailoring of uniforms and other such support activities.

I suddenly realized that Father was already talking about the details of the wedding, and that he had broached the subject of the *mahrīyeh* or bride-dower. Father said, "I do not have anything specific in mind; [it should be set at] whatever you had in mind and believe to be for the best."

Mansūreh Khānūm looked at me contentedly and said, "In honor of the Fourteen Immaculates,[29] we shall set the bride dower at fourteen gold coins for the lady bride."

I whispered in Mother's ear, "That's very high!"

Mansūreh Khānūm heard what I said. "No, my child," She said, "It is not too high. You are more worthy than these sorts of [material] considerations. But, it's a tradition…"

My father said, "For us, material possessions are not important in the least. God Himself is witness to the fact that we have not even carried out any sort of inquiry into your family. Praise God, Ali is a good and pure young man who is a true believer in the faith. The fact that he has been at the warfront from the beginning of the war is sufficient [testimony of his character] for us. I entrust my daughter to his hands with pride. Ali is a pious and God-fearing man who acts with courage to

---

[29] The Apostle of God, his august daughter Her Eminence Lady Fātemaᵗ oz-Zahrā, and the Twelve Imams, unto all of whom be God's peace and blessings.

defend the honor and values of his religion. He is a *Hezbollāhī*[30] who upholds the principles of the Revolution. These are things which have more value than anything else. Upon my word of honor before Almighty God, if I knew that were you to marry today and be martyred on the morrow, I would still give the hand of my daughter to you in sacred matrimony."

Ali had turned red. In response to my father he said, "We feel the same way about your family. Upon my word before God, we would not have been upset with you even if we had been turned down. Praise God, yours is also a *basījī* family and one which upholds the values [of Islam and of the Revolution]. And it is an honor for us also to make a matrimonial bond with a family of faith such as yours, who has shown so much self-sacrifice for the war effort." He then paused and continued in a lower tone, "Although when I stepped foot in this household, I was sure that I would not leave it with my hopes dashed."

The following morning we went to my grandmother's house in order to invite them to our home after dinner that night, where the groom's family had been invited; and also in order to see my Uncle Mahmoud. Uncle Mahmoud had just returned from the warfront. He was talking about different things and nothing in particular.

---

[30] *Hezbollāhī*: Literally, belonging to the 'Party of God'. Hezbollāh is a Quranic expression which refers to those who have self-surrendered (*Islām*) their will to the will of God and to His Providential Lordship (*rubūbīat*) and are hence aligned with His Party. *Hezbollāhīs* are contrasted with *Hezb osh-Shaytān* or *Hezb ot-Tāghut*, the Party of Satan or the Party of any usurping illegitimate authority and/ or false idol.

A Suitor with Blue Eyes

Mother said, "Mahmoud Jān, Fereshteh has a suitor."

Uncle Mahmoud smiled mischievously and winked at me and said, "*Mobārak!* Congratulations, dear!"

I held my head down bashfully and started to play with the fringe of my black *chador*.

Uncle Mahmoud asked, "So what is the good groom's profession?"

Mother said, "He is a *Pāsdār* like yourself, a member of the Revolutionary Guards. His name is Ali Chītsāzīān."

Uncle Mahmoud was sipping his tea, and upon hearing this, it was as if the tea had gotten lodged in his throat. His eyes widened in surprise.

"Ali Agha?!"

Mother said, "Do you know him?"

Mother smiled and turned to me in triumph and said, "Didn't I tell you that if we told Uncle Mahmoud, he would know him?"

As soon as Uncle Mahmoud recovered from his coughing fit, he said, "You mean you don't know Ali Agha? Man, Ali Agha is our Commanding Officer! He is unique in the whole Ansār ol-Hosayn legion in which he serves. He is a man of courage who is utterly fearless. He is the Commander of Operations Intelligence. The boys tell tales of his scouting operations and ventures, both true and legendary; but we believe the legends to be true too. It is said that he penetrates enemy lines and stands in line in their chow halls, listening. There are a lot of stories circulating about his exploits. But when all is said and done, because he is so fearless, he is a great asset for the Operations Intelligence of the Ansār. May God preserve him."

Mother looked at me and said with surprise, "They never mentioned that he was a commander; neither himself nor his mother."

Uncle Mahmoud said, "Ali Agha is one of those unique people who is devout and God-fearing. If he were to become Vajīheh Khānūm's son-in-law, it would be her good fortune. The most important thing is that he is not one for pretense and lies; he neither lies to God, nor to any of His creatures. When he talks to us, he starts with a *hadīth*[31] report from Imam Ali, unto whom be God's peace, to the effect that, '[The court of] one's conscience is the only court which does not stand in need of a judge.' Use that sentence as your starting point, and go forward from there."

Uncle Mahmoud then took on a more serious tone and said, "But dear sister, may I say something? Ali Agha has dedicated himself to the warfront and to the war effort as a religious endowment (*waqf*). Think long and hard, because he is not the kind of man who will abandon the front as soon as he is married and return to his hometown and domicile himself and his family in a homestead."

---

[31] *Hadīth*: A report of a saying or deed of the Prophet or one of the Imāms or Lady Fātema. The Prophet and the Imāms (as well as Lady Fātema) being immaculate (inerrant as well as sinless in Shi'a belief), their words and deeds are considered to be embodied revelation; thus, reports of their words and deeds comprise a body of scripture that is an indispensable complement to the Quran.

Mother was affronted and said, "It's not as if we said anything about expecting him to quit the warfront! And it is not as if we and Mother were against your and Mohammad's[32] going to the war, Mahmoud Jān."

Upon hearing Uncle Mohammad's name, Grandmother, who was busy offering us some fruit, let out a moan and started to whimper. Mother cleverly changed the conversation and, addressing her brother, said, "It is not as if you have married and settled down, now, is it?"

Uncle Mahmoud smiled. "What? You compare me with Ali Agha? If you multiply me by a hundred, no, by a thousand, I would still not be like Ali Agha!"

Uncle Mahmoud got up and went and brought his photo album and said, "I have a few pictures with him."

As he was turning the pages of his photo album looking for Ali Agha's pictures, he said, "I think he should be no older than twenty-three, but he comes across as a mature man who is in his thirties."

Uncle Mahmoud related stories about Ali and thumbed the pages of his photo album. Up until that day, I always imagined that I would be marrying a tall, brown-haired and brown-eyed man; I never imagined that I would marry a blond-haired, blue-eyed man. Uncle Mahmoud put his finger on one of the photos and said, "This is one of his men. He was injured in one of their scouting operations and had stayed behind enemy

---

[32] Mohammad Dashtī was martyred in Abādān in 1981. His body has not been recovered to date.

lines. No one dared to go and get him. Ali took an ambulance and went behind the Iraqi front line and got him himself. It was a job that no one would have had the courage to perform, even if you asked a hundred ambulance drivers to get it done."

Uncle Mahmoud put his finger on another photo. "And this is Ali Agha," he said.

I felt embarrassed and lowered my head. Uncle Mahmoud said, "He is very concerned about the welfare of his men. He is a demanding commander who demands strict discipline, but he is equally as caring about his forces. When his forces go on scouting missions, he will go with them a part of the way and stand there waiting for them to return. And he will not return until the last man to go has returned to safety. This is because of his consideration and concern for his men. No doubt, he will behave in a similar manner towards his wife and children in his family life."

That day, Uncle Mahmoud kept on telling stories about Ali and his men until noon. It was late by the time we got home. I kept thinking about Uncle Mahmoud's words all of the way back home. I had a good feeling. I felt that I had achieved my greatest wish. It seemed to me that life with a commander whose thoughts were filled with concern for the war effort and who was fighting on the front lines would enable me to find a way to play a role in helping the revolution and thereby to attain to my own goals as well.

That night, Mansūreh Khānūm and Agha Nāser, and Ali Agha and Hājj Sādeq and his wife and daughter, Leylā, and Ali Agha's sister came to our home after dinner. Mansūreh

Khānūm had only one daughter. As soon as she introduced her to me, I was dumb-founded for a few moments, and I just stood there in the middle of the room like a statue. It was Maryam; I couldn't believe it. The same beautiful girl with light brown hair who used to sit in the back of the municipal bus, to whom I was drawn and who I wanted to be friends with. And now I saw that she had come to our home on her own accord and was standing before me, and was going to be my sister-in-law. She was also surprised to see me. At the same time, Ali Agha was surprised to see Uncle Mahmoud, who was one of the men under his command, and kept on asking about what had become of Uncle Mohammad, who had become MIA on the Māh-shahr road at the beginning of the war, and whose body had not yet been returned.

Agha Nāser, Ali Agha's father, was an established man who was kind and whose sense of humor was a prominent feature of his personality. He was of a relatively heavy build, of a medium height, and his hair was graying. His jokes made everyone relax and feel good.

Hājj Sādeq, the first-born of the family, was born in 1959. He was the provincial governor of Qahāvand province; and his wife, Monīreh Khānūm, was an ideological or doctrinal educator. Their two-year-old daughter, Leylā, was already talkative and a real sweetheart. Amīr Agha, the second brother, was born in 1961. He was fair-skinned, with black hair and brown eyes. He was wearing glasses with black frames, and was taller than his brothers. He worked in the Construction Jehād Organization, [which is an organization that was set up after the revolution whose primary mission was to develop the nation's civil infrastructure and to build affordable housing for the poor]. I realized that very night what a kind and caring person he is. Maryam and Ali Agha had taken after their mother in that they were both fair-skinned and blond; whereas Hājj Sādeq and Amīr Agha had taken after their father.

That night, the date for the marriage was set: the eighteenth of Farvardīn (March/ April), 1365 (1987) was to be the date of the marriage vows and a small family get together in our house; and it was decided that the date for the wedding party proper could wait.

Monīreh Khānūm presented me with a bolt of cloth that was suitable for blouses. With the bestowal of that present, I formally became Ali Agha's betrothed. At the end of the night when everyone was preparing to leave, Ali Agha faced the gathering and said, "*Halālam konīd* – forgive me any trespass that I might have committed against you."

He was due to return to the warfront the following morning. I wanted to say "Don't forget to intercede [on my behalf];"[33] but no matter how I tried [to muster up my courage], I was not able to do so.

On the night of that family gathering, I wanted to make a notation in my datebook for the seventh of Farvardīn (March/

---

[33] Don't forget to intercede [on my behalf Come Judgment Day, seeing as you will have attained to the exalted station of martyrdom, God willing, and will thus have propinquity with God and have God's 'ear', so to speak.]

April), but the datebook for the year 1364 had run out of extra days and I had yet to purchase one for the new year.

The winter of 1986 passed and Farvardīn (March/ April) arrived. That year was no different than all of the other new years after the war in that our house did not have a *Haft-Sīn* table spread,[34] nor was it witness to any New Year celebrations or festivities. My mother believed that because there were many families who were in mourning for the loss of their sons who had become martyred in the war, and that we were in the middle of that same war, the propriety of condoling with those families precluded any celebrations. But the spring did not have any such sense of propriety, and it arrived with its usual buds and fresh smell of flowers in bloom, and rains and revitalizing spring breezes.

We visited our grandmothers' homes on the morning of the first day of the New Year, and in the afternoon we were visited by my aunts and uncles, who had come to see Father and Mother. On the second day, we sat at home to receive guests.

---

[34] *Haft-sīn* is an arrangement of seven symbolic items whose names start with the letter *sīn* or 's' in the Persian alphabet. It is traditionally displayed at Nowruz, the Iranian New Year's Day, which is celebrated on the day of the vernal equinox, marking the beginning of spring in the Northern Hemisphere. Other symbolic items that are typically used include a mirror, candles, painted eggs, a bowl of goldfish, coins, potted hyacinth flowers, and traditional confectioneries. A "book of wisdom" is also commonly included, which invariably includes the Quran in Moslem families (or the Avesta in Zoroastrian ones), the *Shāhnāme* of Ferdowsi, or Hafez's *Dīvān*.

An Altar of Roses

Mother's sewing workshop was closed, and we were glad to see more of Mother as a result.

The seventh day of the New Year was the day of our marriage ceremony, but no arrangements had been made yet and nothing had been done yet to further that end. We had not gone to do the shopping for the wedding, nor had we even broached the subject. And not a word had been heard from Ali Agha and his family as yet either.

It was now the fourth of Farvardīn. On the night of the third, Father had heard from one of his friends that one of Ali Agha's lieutenants had been martyred. As always, Mother had woken up early and was busy working in the kitchen. Around nine in the morning she woke me up and told me with sadness, "Fereshteh, wake up! The radio has announced that Mosayyeb Majīdī, one of Ali Agha's lieutenants, has been martyred. His funeral is today. Hurry up and eat breakfast, as we need to attend."

Royā and Nafīseh woke up too. We had breakfast, dressed, and left. The Bāq-e Behesht cemetery was crowded, even though it was the first few days of the New Year celebrations. A large crowd had shown up for the funeral of the newly martyred Mosayyeb Majīdī. Last night's rain had washed the tombstones clean.[35] There were flower bouquets and sweets and Haft Sīn spreads on many of the tombstones.

---

[35] Tombstones are placed horizontally over the grave of the deceased in Islamic lands and not vertically over the head of the deceased, as is the Christian practice.

A Suitor with Blue Eyes

A cool breeze was moving the tall and short trees of the Bāq-e Behesht cemetery. We approached the place that had been set up to accommodate the speeches that were to be made before the burial. It was the most crowded place in the whole cemetery. We saw Mansūreh Khānūm and Maryam in the crowd. I was overwhelmed with relief at seeing them there.

The recitation of the Quran could be heard from the speakers at the impromptu stage that had been set up beside the grave. The city officials and people from the mayor's office and a large number of *pāsdārs* and officials from the armed forces were standing at the head of the crowd. Maryam said, "They have brought [the body of] the martyr; he's over there. His family are up there too."

At this point, the Quranic recitation was stopped and the master of ceremony took his position behind the podium. He had a strong and commanding voice. When he said, "In the name of the *rabb*[36] of the martyrs and the *seddīqīn*[37]," everyone went quiet. A sorrowful quiet had overtaken the Bāq-e Behesht cemetery. The master of ceremony thanked everyone for coming and congratulated the great and noble family of the martyr Mosayyeb Majīdī, the lieutenant commander of the Intelligence Unit of the Lashgar-e Ansār ol-Hosayn Operations, for his martyrdom; and also felicitated the great nation which cultivates and produces

---

[36] The Lord of Providence, Cherisher, and Sustainer of the World – one of the names of Almighty God.
[37] The Sincere. An exalted spiritual station reserved for those who have attained to a close spiritual propinquity to their Lord.

such martyrs; and as he moved his clenched fist towards the crowd, he said,

> For the burial of the martyrs,
> Come, O Universal Savior,
> Come, O Mahdi[38]!

برای دفن شهدا   مهدی، بیا! مهدی، بیا!

A large number of people had come and had gathered up to the gates of the Bāq-e Behesht cemetery and were scattered inside the Golzār-e Shohadā section, which was set aside especially for the martyrs. I was taking a look around when Maryam poked me with her elbow and said, "Look, its Ali Agha!"

Ali Agha was standing on a balcony behind the podium. Seeing him made me hold my breath. I took a few steps back so that I could look at Ali Agha without being seen by Mother or Mansūreh Khānūm or the others. This was the first time that I could look at him at my leisure and without having to worry about the impropriety of gazing. He was still wearing that tan overcoat. His shirt could not be seen as it was concealed behind the overcoat, which was buttoned up. His face looked sad and dejected. And although he was standing erect, he seemed willowy

---

[38] The Mahdi is a title used to refer to the Lord of the Age or the promised and awaited universal savior of humanity, Hojjat eben Hasan al-Askari. The literal meaning of the title is 'the Guided One' or 'the One Who is Guided'.

and emaciated. His beard was haggard and his face was jagged. He started his speech.

"Mosayyeb was a child of the bullets, of the explosion of artillery shells and mortars; Mosayyeb was a child of hunger, thirst, exhaustion; Mosayyeb was the Mālek Ashtar[39] of the age."

I went back a little further and leaned against the back wall and listened closely. He spoke eloquently and commanded attention, even though his voice was filled with sorrow. I thought how difficult it must be for him; how heavy his heart must feel. Was he next to Mosayyeb when he was martyred? What could that have felt like?

Maryam called me and I went and stood next to her. She and Mansūreh Khānūm were weeping. Maryam said through her tears, "Agha Mosayyeb and Ali were close friends. He used to come to our house frequently lately. He had become just like a brother for us, and for Mother he was no different than Amīr or Ali or Sādeq."

The atmosphere of the Bāq-e Behesht cemetery had become heavy. It was as if all of the souls of the dead had risen from their graves and were gathered all around us. Dark grey clouds covered the sky. I felt like finding a quiet, secluded place and crying. I missed Uncle Mohammad. I wished that there would be some news concerning the whereabouts of his body. I wished that his body would be returned, if only for Grandmother's sake. Mother was crying intensely. I didn't know

---

[39] Mālek Ashtar was one of the most worthy and loyal companions of Imam Ali.

if she missed Uncle Mohammad, or was crying for Agha Mosayyeb's loss, or both.

When the procession began to move, I followed behind the coffin with tears in my eyes. The sound of the chant *lā elāha el'allāh*[40] filled the Bāq-e Behesht cemetery. It was a sad and morose scene. It seemed to me that the person who lay in the coffin was a dear son to each and every member of the crowd who had shown up. The people chanted,

> O flower whose petals have been plucked,
> And who has been sacrificed for the Leader;[41]
>
> For the burial of the martyrs,
> Come, O Universal Savior,
> Come, O Mahdi!

این گل پرپر شده،   فدای رهبر شده.
برای دفن شهدا   مهدی، بیا! مهدی، بیا!

My gaze fell on Maryam. She was standing in a corner and holding Mansūreh Khānum by the elbow. She was giving her some water from a flask that she was holding. Mansūreh Khānum was dejected and lifeless, and her face had gone all white. For a brief moment, I became very concerned for her well-being.

---

[40] There is no deity other than God (or Allāh).
[41] The reference is to the Leader of the Islamic Revolution of Iran, who was Imam Khomeini at the time.

A Suitor with Blue Eyes

Maryam said, "Mother suffers from an ailment of the kidneys. Stress is not good for her condition."

Mother and Royā and Nafīseh joined us and tried to comfort Mansūreh Khānūm and to make her feel better. The ceremony had not ended yet; but we left for Imam Khomeini Square, the city's main square, together with Mansūreh Khānūm and Maryam. Mansūreh Khānūm was feeling a little better. Before they departed, it was decided between them and Mother that they would come to our house on Wednesday so that we could all go to the bazaar to do the wedding shopping.

The sun had almost set, and we were seated in the den. The TV was on. Father enjoys watching the news on TV. He said in a loud voice, "Ali Agha [is on TV], everyone."

The Hamedān affiliate of the Radio and Television Network of the Islamic Republic of Iran, the *sedā va sīmā*, was broadcasting a report from the warfront. Ali Agha was seated on a hilltop and was speaking about the Omm ol-Qasr Road and the soldiers who became martyred in that battle. He was saying that in addition to bombarding the front line, the enemy's warplanes would also on occasion dump steel beams and stone boulders and bags of sand on the heads of our soldiers. Everyone was looking at the television eagerly; it was only I who was not able to give expression to my pleasure.

Father was home the following day. The doorbell rang around ten o'clock. Nafīseh, who was six years old at the time, opened the door. She came over and said, "Ali Agha is here, *Khāhar Jūn*, dear sister".

Mother donned her *chador* quickly and ran to the door. No matter how much she insisted, Ali Agha would not come in.[42] I had ironed my *manteaux* and *maqna'e*[43] and *chador* and had placed them at the ready, and so I put them on and left the house with Mother.

Ali Agha and Mansūreh Khānūm were standing at the door to the front yard.[44] I said my *salaams*.[45] Ali Agha was still holding his head in a lowered position. He was wearing his tan overcoat and had pulled his hat down over his forehead, to the point where even his eyebrows could not be seen. He returned my *salaams* in a way that was barely audible. Ali Agha had come to pick us up with a white Renault which he had borrowed from one of his friends. Mansūreh Khānūm sat in the front passenger seat, and Mother and I took our seats in the back. That day, I saw his blue eyes [up close] for the first time in the car's rearview mirror. It had rained the previous night and the streets were clean and the air was clean and fresh.

---

[42] So as not to impose on the hosts.

[43] *Maqna'e:* An Islamic form of head covering for women which covers not only the hair and ears, but also the neck, up to the chin, as is demanded by the sacred law of Islam. Its hem falls down as low as the solar plexus in order to provide an additional covering over the breast area.

[44] All of the front yards in Iran are walled in, in order to provide privacy for the womenfolk, who can thereby go about their business in the yard or enjoy it without having to veil themselves from the gaze of strangers.

[45] The Islamic greeting and prayer for peace: 'May God's peace be unto you.'

Ali Agha parked the car around the midpoint of Sharīatī Street, close to Imam Khomeini Square. We all got out and made our way towards the Mozaffarīeh Bazaar. Ali Agha led the way, with his hands in his pockets. He was bent over, like a hunchback. His head was lowered and he didn't talk. I didn't have anything to talk about either. When we reached the mouth of the Bazaar, he came and stood beside me and said in a tone that I could hear with difficulty, "Excuse me, Zahrā Khānum, it is probably best that when we are in Hamedān, we do not walk together [as a couple], because it's possible that we would be seen together by the family members of a martyr, by a mother, wife, or child of a martyr, and it might become a cause of anguish for them."

I nodded in agreement and said, "That's right."

Mansūreh Khānum said, "Let us first go and purchase the rings."

Other than a couple of jewelry stores, the rest were closed [for the New Year holidays]. Toward the middle of the Mozaffarīeh Bazaar, the Kobrīāī goldsmiths were open for business. We entered their shop and Mansūreh Khānum told the salesman that we were looking for wedding rings. The goldsmith placed his tray of wedding rings before us. Mansūreh Khānum said, "Fereshteh Khānum, make your selection." I looked at the rings on display and my hand went to pick the lightest one. I picked it up and tried it on my finger. It fit. Mother and Mansūreh Khānum looked at the ring on my finger, but Ali Agha's attention was elsewhere. I thought that he was probably thinking of Mosayyeb Majīdī.

Mansūreh Khānūm said, "Fereshteh Jān, this ring is too light. Pick a better one with a heavier gauge."

I looked toward Ali Agha, as I wanted him to weigh in on the subject as well. Behind his heavy light brown beard and mustache I could see a deep grief of mourning. Mansūreh Khānūm insisted again.

He asked the price. The goldsmith weighed the ring and said, "Two thousand and five hundred toumans."

Ali Agha counted out the money and placed it on the counter. The goldsmith wrote out a receipt and placed the ring in a small pink cardboard box which had a flower pattern of tiny red and white flowers on it. He looked at me and Ali Agha and said, "May it [the marriage] bring you blessings. May you be blessed with good fortune and prosperity, God willing."

Mansūreh Khānūm said happily, "Now let's go find the clothiers."

I looked at Ali Agha. His hands were still in his pockets. He seemed happy, but it was also evident that he felt embarrassed. Mansūreh Khānūm said, "We'll buy a nice formal white blouse now, and leave the wedding gown for the wedding in the summer."

I said, "I don't want to buy a blouse under these conditions."

Mansūreh Khānūm said with surprise, "What conditions?"

I said, "Well, it's because Ali Agha's lieutenant has been martyred, and he is in a state of mourning."

Mansūreh Khānūm glanced at Ali Agha and said, "Life and death are two sides of the same coin. Agha Mosayyeb was martyred and joined God in a station that is worthy of his sacrifice and martyrdom. Good for him, as happy indeed is his fate! But those who are alive need to continue with their lives. It is not as if we set the date for the marriage last night. And on the other hand, it is not as if you are going to keep having weddings, so you have to enjoy it when it's time has come."

Mother said quietly, "It's ok. Don't say anything else; let me talk to her."

Mother convinced Mansūreh Khānūm, so that she no longer insisted. Instead, she said, "In that case, let us at least go and buy a mirror and a couple of candelabras."

At the beginning of the Mozaffarīeh Bazaar, opposite the greengrocers' section, there was a large shop that sold chandeliers. We did a complete circuit around the store, looking at the mirror and the candelabras on display. When we got back to where we had started, Mansūreh Khānūm asked, "Did anything catch your eye?"

I went and stood next to the least expensive mirror and candelabra set and asked, "Will this do?"

Mansūreh Khānūm pointed to another mirror and candelabra set and asked, "What about this one?"

It was very beautiful, and seemed to be very expensive too. The set was made of fine bone china, and the multicolority of the embossed flowers made the set all the more beautiful. At the time, the style and make of this set had just entered the market and its novelty was all the rage. The store owner was standing at a respectable distance, and I turned to him and asked him the price. He said, "Three thousand and five hundred toumans, madam."

I said to Ali Agha, "That is too expensive. A mirror and candelabra set is not a necessity which could justify such a large expenditure."

The store owner who was awaiting our decision said, "As a matter of fact, we have its oval model in the warehouse." He then called his apprentice over and said, "Run and get the oval model of this set from the warehouse. On the double!"

We had been placed in a sort of *fait accompli*, and so, no one said anything else. The apprentice was light on his feet. He returned quickly and packed the set properly and with due patience in a large box, which he gave to us. The price of the oval model was a thousand toumans.

On Mansūreh Khānūm's insistence, we bought a small black purse with gold trim which was suitable for formal occasions, as well as white cloth for a *chador* which Mother agreed to sew. We also bought a simple white blouse which had black and red vertical stripes in lieu of a bridal gown, as well as a pair of gold-colored sandals.

Mother bought a bolt of cloth which was suitable for a suit for Ali Agha. It was a beautiful deep navy blue; although Ali Agha never found the opportunity to have it tailored for himself.

It was close to noon. Mansūreh Khānūm had become tired. Ali Agha went and brought the car to the mouth of the bazaar. He took Mansūreh Khānūm to her home first, then took us home. When we got there, he would not come in [for lunch] no matter how much we insisted. And when he took his leave, he said, "Forgive me, Zahrā Khānūm, if you didn't have a good time. I was not myself today." And he said this despite the fact that he had barely spoken more than a few words throughout the whole time.

After he said his farewells and left, I felt like crying. I was hoping that he would stay and have lunch with us. I knew that if he stayed in our company, he would start to feel a little better. I knew that he could sit with Father, whose sense of humor would make him feel better; or that Mother would relate some story, or that Nafiseh would say something funny. I wanted him to come in and take an emotional load off his shoulders.

On the sixth of Farvardīn, the day before the wedding, I came down with what seemed like a stomach flu. Mother was very concerned and anxious. Together with Father, we went to Imam Hospital, which was opposite our street. The doctor on duty in the emergency room examined me and determined that it was a case of food poisoning. They gave me an IV drip in which they injected certain antitoxins, and sent me home after a few hours with a bag of pills and medicinal syrup in my hand.

I don't know if it was the symptoms of food poisoning or the fear and anxiety of the marriage ceremony, but in any event, I didn't sleep a wink until morning. When I got up and looked in the mirror, I was taken aback. My face had become yellow, as if I had contracted jaundice. There were two half-moons puffed up under my eyes. It seemed that all the blood had drained away from my face.

The house was eerily quiet. Mother was out and Father was getting dressed to go out. Our house did not in the least resemble a house in which there was soon to be a marriage ceremony. I asked Father about Mother's whereabouts. He said dejectedly, "Mr. Rostamī's son, and his brother's son, were martyred. Your mother has gone there to pay her respects."

Mr. Rostamī's house was across the street from ours. Two brothers had married two sisters and were living in the same house together. The way Father related it, the sons of both brothers became MIA in Operation W'al-Fajr.[46] Hearing this news made me feel even worse.

I thought about the afternoon and the marriage ceremony, and about Mr. Rostamī's family who had given two martyrs [to the cause of Islam]. The thought of their loss was difficult for me, being one of their neighbors. I constantly kept thinking of their mothers, and my heart would go out to them and I would start to cry.

It was now eleven in the morning and there was no sign of any preparations for a wedding or its attendant festivities in our house. Everyone had been affected by the loss which had been inflicted on the Rostamī family. Mother had one foot in their home and another in our own. I was busy cooking in the kitchen when Nafīseh yelled out, "Fereshteh Jūn, Uncle Mahmoud needs you outside."

I turned the stove off and hurried out. Uncle Mahmoud was standing in the front yard, together with Mother. They were

---

[46] On Fāw Island, which is Iraqi territory.

busy talking. As soon as he saw me, Uncle Mahmoud said bitterly, "What's going on?? Fereshteh, why have you not made any preparations? Why have you not laid out the marriage spread?!"

I looked at him with surprise and shrugged. Uncle Mahmoud repeated again, "What do you mean? What's going on??"

I said, "I don't know. No one told me to do anything."

Uncle Mahmoud looked at his watch and raised his voice at Mother and me: "It's eleven o'clock!"

Mother said, "Mahmoud Jān, our neighbors, the Rostamīs, have given up two martyrs."

Uncle Mahmoud hurried to the door of the front yard and said quietly but angrily, "Well, what is it that you want to do? Are you planning on having an orchestra or some sort of a music-fest, God forbid?"

He then turned to me and said, "Fereshteh, go and tidy up the living room. I'll be there in a minute."

Uncle Mahmoud said this and left. Mother became all anxious and started to take out her own wedding spread, and the prayer mat of her wedding which was made of a *termeh*[47] fabric. She laid out the prayer mat toward the *qiblah* or direction of prayer (facing the Ka'ba in Mecca). She gave the Quran and its lectern to me and said, "You have good taste; do the arrangement yourself."

---

[47] *Termeh* is a type of Iranian handwoven cloth, produced primarily in Yazd province.

The mirror and candelabra set was in our house. I took them out of their box, wiped them down, and cleaned the mirror surface so that it sparkled, and put them in the middle of the wedding spread. I placed the Quran on its lectern in front of the mirror, so that the Quran's image would be reflected in the mirror.

Royā came into the living room holding a vase of fresh flowers. She said that Ali Agha had brought them. I asked if he wanted to come in, and Royā said, "No, he went with Mother to the Rostamīs' house."

I placed the vase of fresh flowers next to the mirror and candelabra set. Now the reflection of pink and white primroses could also be seen in the mirror. I thought that I should maybe go over with Mother and Ali Agha to pay my respects to the Rostamīs.

A little later, Uncle Mahmoud came back, bringing a whole bunch of stuff with him. He placed some items that he still had from his own wedding spread next to the one I was arranging. A basket of hazelnuts and pewter colored walnuts, a few pieces of *sangak* flatbread which had been decorated with silver acrylic paint, and two oyster shells which is where the wedding rings would be placed temporarily; as well as some *nabāt* or crystalline sugar, and some *noql*, [which is a candy made of almond slivers covered with musk-willow scented confectioners' sugar]. He had also brought some flowers.

Uncle Mahmoud got everyone to get a move on with his arrival. Father left the house and returned with a few boxes of sweet pastry. Then he would go and come back with some boxes of apples and oranges. He would go and buy *gaz* nougat and chocolates. And each time he returned, Mother had a fresh order ready for him to fulfill.

Grandmother showed up in time for lunch. As soon as she saw me, she said, "Vajīheh, have you not taken Fereshteh to the hairdressers?"

Mother looked at me and shrugged. Grandmother complained under her breath. "Get up! No one has seen a bride look like this before! Hurry up and at least see to her face."

Mother was a woman of many talents. In addition to being an expert seamstress, she was a skilled hairdresser and makeup artist. At Grandmother's behest, she added waves to my hair. As she was doing so, she told Grandmother how she and Ali Agha had gone to the Rostamī's house to pay their respects and to ask them for their permission [to hold the marriage ceremony, notwithstanding the martyrdom of their sons]. Ali Agha had said, "We are not planning a special ceremony; but we will only do so if we have your consent and approval." When my hair was done, I went and put on the blouse that we had bought. But as soon as I entered the room, Grandmother said disapprovingly, "What on earth is *that*? Haven't you bought a proper bridal gown?"

I said, "This will do just fine. It will do as a bridal dress, and at the same time, out of respect for Ali Agha, it has black stripes as well." Grandmother shook her head and grumbled some more. Mother bit her tongue and signaled me not to say anything more about it.

The guests arrived after lunch, before we had a chance to get back up and to see to all the arrangements that still had to be attended to. The aunts and uncles on both the maternal and paternal sides of the family were there, together with their wives and husbands, as were a few others from among our close relatives who had been invited. Ali Agha and his immediate family arrived at three thirty, together with a few close relatives. Ali Agha was wearing that same tan overcoat and brown shirt, with charcoal grey trousers. He had brought a large cake, which he placed in the center of the wedding spread.

I was seated beside the wedding spread in a white *chādor* which had a pattern of little blue flowers on it. The women had gathered all around the room. Ali Agha came into the room momentarily. He wanted to sit next to me; but when he saw that there were women all around, he took his leave and joined the men who were gathered in the den.

Uncle Mahmoud was taking some pictures. Maryam was busy rubbing two large heads of solid conically shaped sugar together over my head.[48] Suddenly a ruckus was raised, and the sound of laughter and people sending *salawāts*. Mother went to the den and returned. Mansūreh Khānum and Maryam followed her lead and returned also. Maryam said, "Ali Agha's friends have arrived. Ali Agha had not invited any of his friends, so I don't know how they cottoned on to this intelligence."

Mansūreh Khānum said with glee, "Amīr says that one of his friends found out and told everyone else. They followed

---

[48] A ritual meant to bring about felicity for the bride and groom.

our car. They were hiding in the next street over. As soon as we came in, they hurried over and followed us in, saying *yā Allāh, yā Allāh*.[49] Thank God that Ali is now surrounded by his friends." Uncle Bāqer could be heard singing a tune:

> If you are a true believer (*mo'men*) and your word is true and sincere (*sādeq*)
> You will agree with us
> That we should send *salawāts*[50] [in order to hasten]
> The blinding of the eye of the hypocrite (*monāfeq*).[51]
> In the heavens, the angels
> Mingled His love with the spirit [of man];
> He has written on His Throne
> *Salawāt* be unto Mohammad (unto whom be peace).

---

[49] Men say *yā Allah* (literally, O Lord!) when entering a house to which they are strangers and hence *nāmahram* (see footnote 8, above), so that the womenfolk can know that a *nāmahram* man is coming in, so that they can cover themselves. Once they have done so, the women say, *befarmāīn*, meaning that the women are now covered so that permission is granted for the man to enter the sanctuary of the home.

[50] The invocation of blessings on the Prophet Mohammad and on the purified and immaculate members of his house.

[51] Hypocrisy (*nefāq*) is considered a sin that is worse than unbelief (*kofr*), because at least the unbeliever is sincere in his or her unbelief, whereas the hypocrite is one who puts up a pretense of belief while harboring unbelief in his hearts

Doubtless Ali was the Wali[52]
[For] he was raised [for this purpose] by the *nabi*;[53]
He was the [spiritual] king of all,
So send *salawāts* unto [the spirit of] Mohammad.

گر مومنی و صادق
با ما شوی موافق
کوری هر منافق
صلوات بر محمد (ص)
در آسمان فرشته
مهرش به جان سرشته
بر عرش خوش نوشته
صلوات بر محمد (ص)
بی شک علی ولی بود
پرورده ی نبی بود
شاه همه علی بود
صلوات بر محمد (ص)

The atmosphere changed with the entrance of Ali Agha's friends. The sound of the men sending *salawāts* in unison motivated the womenfolk to join in and send *salawāts* too. A little later,

---

[52] *Walīy* (regent, sovereign, lord and master; patron, guardian, protector, custodian). The plural form of *walīy* is *owliā*: those of God's creatures who have spiritual propinquity to Him, inclusive of prophets and Imāms and, to a lesser degree, the *olamā* and *foqahā* (the scholars of Islam); in a distant sense: "saints". The *walīy* is usually an abbreviation of *walīy al-amr*, who is the Just Ruler and Guardian-Sovereign of the affairs of the *mo'menīn* or true believers.

[53] *Nabī*: prophet.

A Suitor with Blue Eyes

Mother, who was standing in front of the door of the living room, said, "Agha [reference to the clergyman] has pronounced the marriage vow sermon."

Something sank in my heart. I thought it was like the month of Ramadān and it was before dawn and there was only a little time left before the *azān* or call to prayer would start. I started praying hurriedly. I asked God to grant us good fortune and make us prosper spiritually and materially, and to make it a part of our lot that we would be able to go on pilgrimage to Mecca and to Karbalā.[54] I then picked up the Quran from its lectern and started to read it.

Uncle Ahmad had become my *wakīl* [or the person in whom I placed my trust for the purposes of disposing my affairs with respect to the marriage contract and bond]; and had pronounced the equivalent of the "I do" part on my behalf in the midst of the all-male gathering. Uncle Ahmad came into the den holding the large notary register as well as the marriage contract in his hands. He asked me to sign my name in several places. Mother said, "Ayatollah Najafi[55] pronounced the marriage vow sermon."

The men could again be heard sending *salawāts*. Uncle Bāqer was singing:

> Open the desire of your tongue, while you still have life
> and motion,

---

[54] Where Imam Hosayn, the Lord of the Martyrs, is buried.
[55] A great Shī'a magister and doctor of sacred jurisprudence who passed away in 1997 at the age of ninety. He was a son of the City of Hamedān.

An Altar of Roses

Every moment, in order to send *salawāts* upon the beautiful visage of Mohammad.

بر گشا کامِ زبان تا که تو داری حرکات
دم به دم بر گل رخسار محمد (ص) صلوات

The house was filled with the sound of *salawāts*. Mother said from the doorway, "Ladies, the bride-groom is coming over." The women whose *chādors* had fallen back on their shoulders arranged their attire properly, after which Ali Agha entered the room together with Father and Uncle Mahmoud. Ali Agha sat next to me and greeted me with due modesty and decorum. Uncle Mahmoud placed a large register on my lap and showed me the places where I needed to sign. Maryam picked up one of the oyster shells which held one of the wedding rings and held it in front of Ali Agha. Ali Agha in turn picked it up clumsily and, forgetting what he should do and because he was seated to my right, took my right hand and placed the ring on my finger. I quietly said, "Not on this hand, on my *left* hand!"

I raised my left hand and brought it toward him. Ali Agha had turned as red as a beet. He took the ring off my right-hand finger and placed it on the correct finger this time.

My father had bought a carnelian gemstone which had been set in a silver ring for Ali. He put it on Ali Agha's ring finger.

Last New Year's, when our whole family had gone to Mecca in order to make the *omrah* or minor pilgrimage there,

A Suitor with Blue Eyes

Father had purchased a classy Rado watch for his future groom. This he now gave to Ali Agha as a wedding present.

My gaze fell upon the mirror for a moment, and I saw that Ali Agha was looking at me. I felt embarrassed and quickly turned my gaze away and lowered my head. This was the first time that Ali Agha was able to see me properly and up close.

The following day, Mother went to her sewing workshop and my sisters and I were occupied cleaning the house. The symptoms of the food poisoning had not fully left my body yet. When Mother returned home for lunch she said, "Ali Agha came over this morning when you were all asleep and invited us to his *hey'at* or religious community group.

That night, the whole family went to the *hey'at*. There was a white illuminated notice board outside their apartment block which announced: *The Hey'at of the Way of the Martyrs*. Amīr and Ali Agha were the founders of the *hey'at*, and it was the first night that the *hey'at* or group assembly was being held in their home. And it was the first time that we were going to their home. It was on the fourth floor of the Honarestān Apartments. It was 130 square meters in size (about 1400 feet), and had three bedrooms. It was a men's *hey'at*; the women's section was made up solely by my mother and I and my sisters, together with Mansūreh Khānum and Maryam and Monīreh Khānum. I found out that night that Mansūreh Khānum's parents (who were referred to as Hājj Bābā and Khānum Jān), and Khānum Jān's only sister, Khāleh Fātemeh, and her brother, Dāī Mohammad, who Mansūreh Khānum resembled closely, lived in Tehran. I also found out that Maryam was recently married to the son of one of Khānūm Jān's neighbors, who worked in the Foreign Office (or State Department), and their wedding was set for the summer, after which Maryam would be moving to Tehran.

Ali Agha came to the room in which we were seated and welcomed us. It was evident that he was very happy to see that we had made it over. We did not set eyes on him again until after the end of the ceremonies, after which he gave us a ride home in one of his friends' car. When we were saying our goodbyes, he waited until Father made his way into the house and then said, "Hājj Khānūm, we're going to be going to Qom[56] tomorrow together with Agha Mahmoud and his wife. Do I have your permission to take Zahrā Khānūm with us also?" Mother hesitated for a moment and said, "Did you mention it to her father?"

Ali Agha thought about what he wanted to say for a brief moment then said, "The truth is that I was too shy to bring it up."

Mother smiled and then said, "OK, let me discuss it with him tonight. Come over tomorrow morning, and if he is OK with it, Fereshteh will go with you."

Ali Agha didn't say anything more and said his farewells and left. Mother got Father's consent for me to go. She packed a small travel bag for me that night, in which she placed a couple

---

[56] The city in which the shrine of Her Eminence Lady Ma'sūmeh, Imam Rezā's sister, is buried. As a pilgrimage destination within the borders of the Islamic Republic of Iran, the importance of this shrine is second only to the shrine of Imam Rezā himself, who is buried in the sacred city of Mashhad.

of changes of clothes, my *chādor-e namāz* or the *chādor* that is set aside specifically for the purposes of performing the ritual devotions and prayers, a towel, and my identity booklet or *shenāsnāmeh*. She woke me up for the pre-dawn prayers and gave me some words of guidance.

I was eating breakfast when Ali Agha rang the doorbell. Father opened the door. Uncle Mahmoud and his wife had come too. Seeing her brother and his wife made Mother happy and she entrusted me to Uncle Mahmoud, giving specific instructions to Uncle Mahmoud's wife.

Ali Agha had borrowed an old Peykān from a friend; it was a true clunker. He drove it himself. Uncle Mahmoud sat shotgun, and his wife and I sat in the back. Mother splashed a bowl of water after us as we were heading out to the car, and Father bade us farewell by reciting prayers and *salawāts* for us, and by having us pass under the pocket Quran which he always had with him. Ali Agha depressed the gas pedal and the car took off after an initial complaint.

Zan Dāī (Uncle Mahmoud's wife) and I started chatting together, and Ali Agha and Uncle Mahmoud did the same. When we were about halfway to Qom, Uncle Mahmoud started telling jokes and reminiscing funny stories. He got us laughing so much that before we knew it, it was noon and we had already arrived at Sāveh. We went to a *chelow-kabābī*, a restaurant that specializes in kabābs, served with steamed rice. Ali Agha ordered a *soltānī chelow-kabāb* for me and for himself, [which is a skewer of lamb filets and a skewer of a combination of ground lamb and veal]. Because I was seated opposite Ali Agha, I was too embarrassed to eat anything. I nibbled a little on my rice and kabāb, and then stopped eating.

I don't know why Zan Dāī was playing with her food too, but she stopped eating before her plate was half finished. Uncle Mahmoud, who was looking for suitable subject matter for his jokes, said with good humor, "Don't worry, Ali Agha; with the kind of appetite that our wives have, we will be rich enough to make the pilgrimage to Mecca before you can say '*Hājī, Hājī, Makkeh*'!" He then took what remained of his wife's *kabāb* and made a meal of it. And as he was eating it with gusto, he said, "And both of us will have gained a whole lot of weight, too, 'cause these two have an appetite like a bird's. Speaking for myself, I know that within a couple of months I'll become like this." He puffed out his cheeks and made out like he was obese, and then continued, "By the same time next year, we'll each own our own homes, let alone a new car."

Uncle Mahmoud continued on like that, and we kept on laughing. By the time we got to Qom, it was evening. The men went to look for a hotel. When they found one, they came back and asked for our identity booklets. Mine and Zan Dāī's were just plain birth certificates and so could not really be used as photos ID's, and were not acceptable to the hotel administrator.[57] No matter how much Ali Agha tried to reason with the manager of the hotel, it was to no avail. Thus, we had no choice but to go

---

[57] It is against the law in Iran for a hotel proprietor to provide accommodations to a couple unless he is satisfied that they are legally married. Fornication is against the law, of course. (Marriages are registered in one's birth certificate/ identity booklet.)

to the *amāken* authorities [who are tasked with enforcing the public decency laws]. It took two or three hours before we were able to find the *amāken* office and to get their written authorization, and to return to the hotel.

Ali Agha and Uncle Mahmoud took our luggage up to our rooms while we waited in the lobby. When they came back down, we headed out toward the shrine, with Uncle Mahmoud and his wife taking the lead and talking, while Ali Agha and I followed behind them in silence. I remembered what he had said earlier and so I put a few paces distance between us. When he realized I had fallen behind, he stopped so that I could catch up, but I stopped short. He started again, thinking that I would catch up, but when I continued to keep my distance, the cup of his patience ran over and he asked, "Are you tired?"

I answered, "No. You said yourself that we should not be seen walking together, in the house of the martyrs. Remember?"

Ali Agha smiled and grabbed me by the wrist and pulled me over to him and said, "That was for when we are in Hamedān. No one knows us here in Qom."

By the time we got back to the hotel, it was midnight. Our rooms were on the second floor. Uncle Mahmoud took a key out of his pocket and opened the door to a room and offered passage to his wife to enter into the room. I was wondering where I was to spend the night. Ali Agha opened the door to the room next door and said, "*Befarmāīd*; after you."

I felt conflicted. I both felt embarrassed, as well as having a feeling of insecurity come over me. I was stuck at a crossroads. I looked at Zan Dāī. I was pleading with them to take me with them into their room, but they said goodnight and disappeared into their room. And so I had no choice but to enter the room. I felt insecure. The atmosphere of the room weighed me down. There were a couple of armchairs next to the window, and I sat down in one of them.

Ali Agha paced back and forth in the room and busied himself doing nothing with the various appurtenances that were in the room. There were two single beds in the room, separated by a small nightstand. Additionally, there was a small refrigerator, a TV, the two armchairs, and a small work table. Ali Agha asked, "Are you not tired? Do you not want to sleep?" Not knowing what to say, I said, "No."

It seems he was aware of my state of mind. He rolled up his sleeves and went into the bathroom. A while passed and he did not come out. I got up and stood by the window, which afforded a view of the golden dome and the minarets of the shrine of Her Eminence Lady Ma'sūmeh. It was a beautiful view that was easy on the eyes, such that I didn't want to look away from it. Even though it was late, there were plenty of cars which passed by with their bright lights. The flashing neon lights of the shops around the shrine which sold *sowhān*[58] and *tasbīhs* (the Moslem's rosary), and [all of the] mementos [and paraphernalia that

---

[58] *Sowhān* is a traditional Iranian saffron and pistachio flavored wheat sprout flat brittle confection made most famously in Qom, among other places. Its ingredients consist of ground wheat sprouts and wheat germ, flour, pistachios, egg yolks, rose water, sugar, clarified butter or vegetable oil, saffron, cardamom, with slivers of almonds or pistachios added as a topping.

pilgrims like to purchase and take back with them to their hometowns] were still on. There were many pedestrians walking back and forth on the streets and sidewalks around the shrine.

    Ali Agha came out of the bathroom. His face was wet and he was rolling down his shirtsleeves. When he saw me, he said with surprise, "Have you not gone to bed yet?"

    I said, "I'm not sleepy."

    He smiled and said, "I can see that you are both tired as well as sleepy. I want to offer my ritual devotions (*namāz*; Arabic: *salāʿ*). And there are a few things that I need to see to. If you are uncomfortable [with me in the room], I can go downstairs." I said, "No; *rāhat bāshīd*: please do not be concerned on my account."

    He said, "Then you should not be concerned either. Go to bed. You want me to turn the light off?"

    Before I had a chance to respond, he switched the light off and stood facing Mecca and started to make his *namāz*. I took advantage of the opportunity and took off my *chādor*. I pulled the blanket over my head, and because I was so tired, I fell asleep quickly.

    I awoke with the sound of the *azān* or call to prayer, which was being recited from somewhere close by. I unconsciously looked at Ali Agha's bed and saw that it was empty. The street lights had lit the room. I sat on the bed. I heard the sound of running water from the faucet, and saw that the bathroom light was on. I stood up and put on my *chādor*. Having made his ablutions, Ali Agha came out of the bathroom and greeted me with a *salām*. He was surprised to see me up and said,

"O, *salām*. Are you up already? It seemed you were very tired. As soon as you put your head on the pillow, you were out like a light."

I said, "Yes, I was tired."

He said, "Agha Mahmoud and I want to go to the shrine for the morning *namāz*. Want to come with us?"

I said, "I haven't made my ablutions yet."

He opened the door.

"I'll go and roust Agha Mahmoud while you make your ablutions."

After we returned from the shrine and had breakfast, we headed for Tehran. About forty minutes into the journey, Uncle Mahmoud said, "Damnation! We forgot to buy some *sowhān*!"

Ali Agha let his foot off the gas pedal and slowed down and asked, "What should we do? Go back?"

A little further ahead there was a U-turn lane. Ali Agha took it and we headed back to Qom. Fortunately, we found a rest stop a little way shy of Qom, and turned in, bought the *sowhān* and headed back to Tehran.

We had journeyed for about an hour when the car started to make some unhealthy noises. Ali Agha pulled the car over to the unpaved shoulder of the road, got out and lifted the car's hood. Uncle Mahmoud got out to see if he could be of any help. Zan Dāī and I got out of the car too. Zan Dāī asked, "What's the problem, Mahmoud Agha?"

Uncle Mahmoud said, "She's on strike."

We took advantage of the opportunity and stretched our legs some by walking around a little. There was a cool breeze blowing. A little farther, there was a rise and some hills and a green meadow with a few trees. There were some birds pecking at the crumbs left behind by past travelers who had used the area as a rest stop, but the sound of the trucks and cars passing by at speed precluded our being able to hear the chirping of the birds.

Ali Agha and Uncle Mahmoud rolled their sleeves up and got busy dismantling parts of the car's engine compartment. It took an hour before the car's starter turned the engine and we were able to get back on the road, after sending prayers of peace (*salawāt*) [to the Prophet of Islam and to the purified and immaculate members of his House]. Uncle Mahmoud had found a new subject for his jocularity and had started making fun of the car's condition. Within less than a kilometer, the car let out that same unhealthy screech and came to a stop.

Uncle Mahmoud groaned. Now it was Ali Agha's turn to make light of the situation with the heavy accent that he put on. "I said you dis maa-sheen very sensaateeve, but you upset him. Now he refuse to von't move!"

The two of them got out and carefully pushed the car over to the shoulder again. We remained seated in the car and kept on sending *salawāts* as fast as we could and prayed hard that nothing bad would happen. This time, the car had run out of gas. Ali Agha gave an empty five-gallon container to Uncle Mahmoud and said, "See vaat you deed? You make fun of dis maa-sheen, so now he on *es*-straayk! Vaat is dis means? Dis means vee maast get him some gas."

It took a long time for Uncle Mahmoud to go and come back and fill the tank with enough gas to get us to Tehran. We had started just past first light [on what should have been a two-hour trip] and got to Tehran at four in the afternoon – hungry and thirsty and tired. We had our late lunch at the outskirts of town, in one of the streets off Āzādī Square, then took a look at a few hotels, but were unable to find one who would rent us two rooms, with Zan Dāī and I not having valid photo ID's. After chewing on the problem and kicking it around some, we decided to head to Karaj[59], because Ali Agha believed that the inn keepers there would not be as strict as they were in Tehran, and that we would ultimately be able to find a place to rest and spend the night.

Zan Dāī had fallen asleep and I was entering these events in my datebook under the date of the tenth of Farvardīn 1987. Uncle Mahmoud said in a low voice so as not to wake Zan Dāī, "Vaat you write about in your books?"

Ali Agha chuckled, "Zahrā Khānūm, if you are writing about our journey, don't mention any of the bad parts. Just write that we had a grand old time."

Uncle Mahmoud escalated: "You write anyting bad for me, you in big trouble by me. You un-der-estand vaat does dis means?" He then recounted all of our adventures in such a funny way that our laughter woke Zan Dāī up.

---

[59] A city about an hour's drive west of Tehran.

By the time we got to Karaj, it was dark. Ali Agha and Uncle Mahmoud found an inn which was happy to accommodate us without the need for picture IDs, and rented us two rooms.

After we solved the problem of where we were going to stay for the night, we decided to take a stroll in the streets of Karaj. Uncle Mahmoud and Zan Dāī did everything in their power to get Ali Agha and I to walk together as a couple. Uncle Mahmoud would shove Ali Agha toward me, and Zan Dāī would push me towards Ali Agha. But all of their efforts notwithstanding, we both felt embarrassed and walked at a safe distance from each other with our heads lowered down. We had dinner in a restaurant outside of the hotel and hung out and took in Karaj's sights until late.

We returned to Hamedān the following morning. Ali Agha dropped me off at our house and "returned me" to my mother all safe and sound, said goodbye and took his leave. Before he left, he gave me his address so that I could write him.

Love Letters

Uncle Mehdi brought the wedding pictures over a week after Ali Agha left for the warfront. I looked through them quickly, and when I was satisfied with the quality of the prints, I looked through them again, this time carefully and with due deliberation. The pictures made their rounds several times in the hands of Mother and Father and my sisters, and when their appetite for seeing them again finally waned, I took them and went to our bedroom. At times, I would look at a single picture for half an hour. Looking at the pictures increased my longing for Ali Agha to the point that at midnight I picked up a pen and started to compose a letter addressed to him.

The countdown started from the following morning. I would mark the days of my datebook like a prisoner marking the passage of time on the walls of her cell. Ali Agha had left on the twelfth of Farvardīn of 1365 (1987); and it was the sixth of Ordībehesht (April/ May). In the evening, the doorbell chimed. An inner voice told me that Ali Agha was behind the door. I put on my *chādor* and ran to the door. It was Amīr Agha. He greeted me hurriedly and asked about everyone's well-being one by one, but quickly. He asked after Father and Mother, as well as after Dāī and Grandmother. And eventually he took an envelope out of his pocket and said, "Sister Fereshteh, Ali sent you this letter."

I became overcome with so much joy that I forgot how to thank him and was at a loss as to how I was to bid him farewell. I took the letter and read it several times over between the space of closing the door and making my way to my room.

It was a very short and simple letter and did not contain anything other than the usual *salāms* and questions asking about my health and general well-being. But it was a great emotional reassurance for me. It was as if Ali Agha was beside me and had taken the brand of his love for me and branded my heart with it. In the letter, he had written:

In the name of God,
the Most-Beneficent, the Most-Merciful

In the name of Allāh,
the Sentinel of the Honor
of the Spilt Blood of the Martyrs [to His Cause]

Warm *salāms* and greetings from the front defending truth and justice (*al-ḥaqq*) against injustice and iniquity and nullity (*al-*

bātel), whose soil is stained with the red blood of the martyrs; which blood acts as a reminder of the blood of Imam Hosayn, whose blood was shed on the plain of Karbalā; and whose memory instills the love of [encountering] the countenance of God (*leqā'ollāh*) [in the hearts of the faithful].

Warm *salāms* from many distant parasangs[60] from the hilltops and the plains and the scorching heat of the Karbalās of the Iranian plateau.

And warm *salāms* from the real Mālek Ashtars and Habīb eben Mazāhers of the world, who are the real and in the flesh [latter day] companions of Abā Abdollāh[61] al-Hosayn.

If you were to ask about me, I am well, praise God. And if it be acceptable to God, I am busy in His service, and hope that a day will come for the victory of Islam over the unbelief that is rampant throughout the world, and the uprooting of iniquity and injustice by the blessed hands of the Valī-e Asr,[62] where I will be

---

[60] The parasang is a historical Iranian unit of itinerant distance, the length of which varied according to terrain and speed of travel. The European equivalent is the league.

[61] Abā Abdollāh is a title of Imam Hosayn which characterizes him as the Sire (Abā) of the [true] Devotees of God. And this is because by sacrificing himself in the cause of Islam, he kept true Islam alive, thus siring all true believers who came after him and who follow his line.

[62] *Valī-e asr*: this is one of the titles of the Twelfth Imam, the Imam al-Mahdī, who is believed will return to the physical plane at God's behest at the end of time (as we know it) in order to establish a long reign of peace and equity and justice on Earth prior to the Resurrection. It is a title of the Lord of the Age and of the universal savior of humanity.

able to see you, Lady Zahrā, together with your honorable, *hezbollāhī* and revolutionary family, at close quarters once more.

I beseech you to remember me in your prayers and to ask Almighty God at the times of your ritual devotions for His forgiveness of my sins; and also to ask him to accept from both of us [the work that we are doing] in this sacred struggle (*jehād*) which I have undertaken and in which you are a partner. I will not take up any more of your time... Mahmoud Agha (Uncle Mahmoud) is well. Give my regards to your honorable parents as well as to my sisters. That is all for now. I entrust you to God.

A servant of Islam,

Ali Chītsāzīān

When it came time to sleep, I placed the letter under my pillow and took it with me in my purse on the morrow wherever I went. I treated it like the letter was Ali Agha himself!

I endeavored to keep Ali Agha's letter with me always. Whenever I opened my purse and saw the envelope, it gave me a good feeling.

On the 23rd of Ordībehesht, a Tuesday, Ali Agha came back to Hamedān. He made our house his first port of call. He came back on the morning and evening of the following day too, and waited behind the door for a half hour or so because we were all holed up in Grandmother's house, not knowing anything about his pending visit.

Each week on Mondays and Thursdays, we would go to the Bāq-e Behesht Cemetery in order to participate in the funeral processions and wakes of the martyrs [of the Iran-Iraq War]. The day that Ali Agha came was a Thursday. That day, we marched in the funeral procession of the martyrs [of the war] together with Mother and Father and everyone else. In the Golzār-e Shohadā, [the martyr's section], I suddenly saw Ali Agha. First I thought I was mistaken. But then I pointed him out to Father. Father went forward and took him into his arms as if he was his own son, and kissed his face and forehead. He held onto Ali Agha's forearm and was looking him up and down with great pleasure. Ali Agha had turned as red as a beet with embarrassment. He had lowered his head and was thanking Father. A few of his friends were beside him as well. Father had become so excited at seeing Ali Agha that he insisted that he come to our house for dinner that night, and would not take no for an answer.

Ali Agha came to our house after the evening call to prayer, the *azān-e maghreb*. He was wearing a navy-blue shirt with the same army fatigue trousers with the eight pockets. His hair had grown longer and was covering his forehead and had changed his appearance. Upon seeing Ali Agha, Father once again embraced him and kissed his cheeks and forehead several times. He took him by the arm and sat him next to himself and started a warm conversation with him. He asked him about what progress was being made on the warfront, and how soon the war would come to an end. After a little while, Mother called Father away on some pretext. When he came out of the living room, Mother somehow kept him occupied and indicated to me that I should go and see Ali Agha. I took the wedding pictures with me so that I could show them to him.

Ali Agha loved the pictures. He looked at the pictures of just the two of us seated in front of the wedding spread and said, "These are the best ones." He took advantage of the opportunity and said, "Lady Zahrā, *Zahrā Khānūm*, tomorrow is Friday and no one will be home. Come to our house at three o'clock."

I agreed that I would. But on the morrow, when I mentioned this to Mother, and contrary to my expectation, she disagreed and said, "If there will not be anyone else present, it is not right. If Ali Agha calls for you himself, there would be no problem. But it is not proper for a young lady to pick up and go to someone else's home on a Friday afternoon all by herself."

There was nothing that could be done about it. I should have known that she would not give her consent. She was very sensitive about our welfare. We were not allowed even to visit the homes of friends and acquaintances. I acquiesced [to her better judgement] without another word. We had learned not to speak over Mother's decisions once they had become final. And we knew that she wanted what was best for us.

The closer it got to three o'clock, the more the butterflies in my stomach fluttered their wings and the more anxious I became. We did not have a telephone so I couldn't tell him what had happened. I was afraid that he would be upset with me and get angry. At the same time, I felt sorry for him, because I knew that he was looking forward to seeing me. I could not think of any way to get a word to him. I just kept on praying that Ali Agha would somehow be inspired to come after me himself. Eventually three o'clock came around, and after that, it took several hundred hours before the hands of the clock reached four o'clock, and half past four, and five o'clock.

I was beside myself. I kept thinking, "What is Ali Agha going to think now? He must be upset and even angry with me." It was the first time that we had made a rendezvous together where I had not kept my word. Father and my sisters were watching TV; but it was as if I was in a different world. I could not hear or see anything in the external world. I was staring at the TV, which was broadcasting the Friday afternoon matinee movie, but my heart and mind were with Ali Agha. I was on edge and could not abide anyone or anything. I kept thinking of the kind of reaction I could expect tomorrow from Ali Agha. Will he stop speaking to me? Or will he go back to the warfront without bidding me farewell? Will he be angry and reproach me, or will he come and complain to me about my behavior? I had an intense sense of anxiety and worry.

I passed that afternoon with great difficulty. It took so long to pass that I thought nightfall would never come. And so, I made an excuse that I had a headache, and went to my room and went to sleep without taking dinner.

When I was coming back from school around noon of the following day, I heard the sound of a motorcycle behind me. I had my senses about me because I felt that someone was following me. I quickened my pace without looking around to see who it might be. When I was a few steps short of our house, I heard a familiar voice from behind me.

"*Salām*. Where are you rushing off with such a quick stride?"

It was Ali Agha's voice. I turned around and looked at him. When I saw that there was a smile on his face, I breathed a sigh of relief.

He asked, "Are you ok?"

There was not an ounce of reproach in his face or in his voice.

I answered, "I'm fine. Thank you."

He asked, "So then why didn't you come yesterday?"

I felt ashamed and answered with anguish, "I'm so sorry. It was my own fault. Mother didn't give her consent. She said it was not proper for me to go on my own on a Friday afternoon. The streets are deserted."

Ali Agha didn't say anything but nodded, as if he was in agreement.

He said, "I was worried about you. I thought that, God forbid, something untoward might have happened to you. But you are well, praise God; right?"

I smiled and took out the key to the house from my purse. I said, "In any event, I'm really sorry. Mother said, 'If Ali Agha were to come by himself and the two of you were to go together, there would not be a problem'".

Ali Agha nodded again in agreement and said, "Hājj Khānūm is right. And you did the right thing to listen to her. So then I will come after you in person this afternoon."

I breathed another sigh of relief and turned the key in the door and said, "Do come in."

But Ali Agha had some things he needed to take care of, so he said goodbye and left. I ran through the yard and my spirits were flying as high as a kite by the time I got to the kitchen. Mother was not home. When she came home a few hours later from the workshop and I explained what had happened and what had been said, she gave her consent, and I began preparing the clothes I was going to wear.

It was a quarter to three when Ali Agha showed up. He had borrowed a friend's car. This was the second time that we were going to their house. No one was home. His family was visiting Hājj Sādeq. This time around, I was able to pay more attention to the home and its furnishings because there was no one else there. There was a small vestibule as we entered the house. To the left was the half bath for the guests, and to the right was a large coat closet which also doubled up as the storage space where the bedding for the guests was kept in a pile. To the right was a long and narrow kitchen on whose walls creeping vines could be seen. There was a bright window at the back of the kitchen which got a lot of light, in front of which a large variety of house plants had been potted. Pictures of nature or children could be seen on all of the doors of the white cabinets; they were so beautiful that one was tempted to step into the kitchen just to look at the pictures there. At the back of the kitchen next to the window there was a small steel door which opened up to a small balcony, which afforded a good space for keeping onions and potatoes and jars of pickles and the like. Mansūreh Khānūm's good taste in the way she had arranged everything in her kitchen appealed to me.

The house had a den as well as a formal living room, and the two were separated by a light grey curtain which had a pretty pattern of large yellow flowers on it.

Every room that I entered had a large window that illuminated the apartment with plenty of natural light. There were some more of the same vines that were in the kitchen in small pots on the radiator in the den whose vines and heart-shaped leaves climbed the walls and hung down from the ceiling. And there were beautiful flowers which enhanced the beauty of the home.

At the back of the house, that is, at the end which faced the entryway, there was a smallish wooden door which opened up to a small vestibule, which led to the bathroom and two facing bedrooms. Ali Agha opened the door to the bedroom on the right. It seems this was the bedroom that he shared with Amīr Agha.

There were pictures of many martyrs and of Imam Khomeini tacked on all of the walls with thumb tacks. There were headbands of martyrdom and army dog tags hanging from some of the pictures. There was a bookcase in the room also.

Ali Agha sat down with his back to a wall and invited me to join him. I sat down and my nostrils were filled with the scent of tee-roses which was the scent which he was wearing. He got up and went toward the bookcase and picked out a photo album from among the books and sat back down next to me and said, "Here, let's take a look through this album."

He leafed through the pages of the photo album slowly. He had circled some of the heads of the people with a red marker.

He would place his finger on these albums and say, "This is my friend, the *Shahīd* (martyr), Amīr-Hosayn Fazlollāhī. He was martyred on Majnūn Island. And this one is *Shahīd* Mohammad-Ali Jerbān."

The scents of his body and perfume and breath had intermingled. Even though his voice was almost broken with the sorrow of the loss of his friends, I had a good feeling. I wished that the world would come to a stop in that very moment so that he and I could stay at each other's side in that same state for years. I felt that the room with all of the pictures of the martyrs had a different feel to anywhere else. Ali Agha would turn the pages and his finger would pause on a few pictures on each page. When he was on the verge of tears, he would get up and leave the room on the pretext of going to bring tea or some fruit.

And on more than one occasion he got me to get up from where I was sitting using the excuse of his wanting me to get something or other from the bookcase. I got the feeling that because he was too shy to look at me directly, he was using these maneuvers as an excuse to get a better look at me.

I asked, "Ali Agha, I have heard that the boys in the Lashgar-e Ansār[63] have a lot of love and respect for you. They say that you take prisoners who have been sentenced to death and those who have been convicted of high crimes, take them to the war front and treat them in such a way and work on them in a

---

[63] Recall that Ali was the CO (Commanding Officer) of the Intelligence Unit of the Lashgar-e Ansār ol-Hosayn battalion or regiment.

way that changes them such that they become different – that they turn into people who have been completely transformed."

Ali Agha smiled and asked, "Who did you hear that from?"

I answered with pride, "Well, you know, one hears things, here and there."

And then I asked him very formally like a reporter: "Are these kinds of people not dangerous? Have they not caused any problems for you to date?"

Ali Agha said with confidence, "No, not at all. I always tell my men…" He smiled and continued, "And I will tell you too, Lady Zahrā. You have become a valuable member of our forces. One's code of moral conduct and how one behaves and comports oneself is the most important thing in society. If we work on how people behave toward each other, we will produce a society that is ideal and headed in the right direction. If people's morals and comportment within an Islamic society are correct, that society will become a Virtuous City.[64] We must enter into the hearts and minds of the people if the country is to get back on the track of living in accordance with divine ordinances and norms. Imam Khomeini said, 'The front that universities must fight on is producing [righteous] people.' If we are to follow the line of the Imam, we must act on his instructions."

---

[64] This is a phrase borrowed from the title of a book on political philosophy by the celebrated Moslem philosopher Fārābī. The Christian analogue would be Saint Augustine's *City of God*.

At this point, the bell of the apartment sounded. Ali Agha got up to leave. He opened the closet door and tied his holster around his waist, holstered his Colt pistol and left the room. I had no idea up to that point that Ali Agha carried a firearm.

He returned after a little while, upset and dejected. I rose up a little bit and asked with concern, "What is it?"

He shook his head slowly from side to side and said, "I just got word that one of the guys in the pictures I just showed you was martyred a few days ago. It's Hosayn Sharīfī, who I said had been injured, and whose picture was taken when he was in the hospital. They've brought his body back to Hamedān; I have to go."

I got up and picked up the side plates of fruit and the tea cups and put them on the tray and took them into the kitchen. While Ali Agha was getting ready, I put the fruit back in the fridge and washed the teacups and plates.

His friends were waiting downstairs in front of the apartment building. Ali Agha dropped me off with that same borrowed car and left.

As soon as Mother saw me, she asked with surprise, "Are you going or did you just get here?"

I said, "I'm back."

She looked at me with surprise and asked, "What happened? Did you quarrel, God forbid? But you only just left!"

I was thinking of Ali Agha's sidearm. I told Mother about what I had seen. She shook her head and said, "It is a bad situation. On one hand, there is the Bathist regime in Iraq who has declared war on us and invaded our country. And on the other hand, there is the fifth column of the enemy within, the *monāfeqīn*[65], who pose a different kind of danger to our boys. Praise God, our youth are smart and have their senses about them; they have to take precautions."

The following morning, Mother took Nafiseh with her to the sewing workshop. I had taken a break in my studies and was getting ready to start studying again when Ali Agha rang and came in. We started chatting, and this time it was my turn to take the lead. I brought my photo albums and we started looking at them together. Ali Agha didn't have too much time and was in a hurry to leave.

The next day was a Monday. I waited for him a lot, but he didn't show up. I wanted to see him every day now that he was in Hamedān. I missed him. It seemed that I had become accustomed to seeing him and having him around. Mother and I went to the Bāq-e Behesht Cemetery. I thought that the funeral of Hosayn Sharīfī might be in procession and that we might be able to see Ali Agha there.

The cemetery was very crowded. I kept my eyes peeled for him but didn't see him. I looked for him throughout all the time we were in the cemetery and even on the sidewalks when we were on the way back home, hungry for a glimpse of him.

Tuesday was also a holiday and so there were no classes on Tuesday either. I had just started studying when the doorbell rang. It was Ali Agha. I asked him to come in, but no matter how

---

[65] See footnote 20, above.

much I insisted, he did not come in. He was going back to the front and had come to say goodbye.

I brought a bowl of water and splashed it on the ground behind him as he was leaving, and I stood in the doorway and watched him leave. After he had gone some distance, he turned and looked around. When he was assured that there was no one in earshot, he said in a loud voice so that I could hear, "Take care of yourself." Then he uttered the formulaic expression of one who is going away on a long journey: "*Halālam kon* – forgive me any trespass that I might have committed against you."

And I responded in a low voice that was audible only to myself, "God forbid. *Shafā'at yādet nareh* – don't forget to intercede [on my behalf Come Judgment Day, seeing as you will have attained to the exalted station of martyrdom, God willing, and will thus have God's ear, so to speak.]".

He waved at me. I placed the fringe of the white *chādor* I was wearing on my arm and waved back at him. I waited as long as it took for him to go the length of our street and turn into the main avenue.

His departure marked another phase of my marking the passage of time in my datebook. I marked the passing of each day with a heavy sigh and a mark next to its date, and would write, "Two days have passed… ten days… twelve days…"

It was the seventh of Khordād, and thirteen days had passed since Ali Agha had left. It was a quarter to eight and I was getting dressed for school. The doorbell rang. I had become habituated to listening out for the doorbell, and so I got to the door like lightning. Ali Agha was behind the door: he was covered in dust and looked exhausted. When I saw him, it was as if I had been given the whole world. I asked him in; and Mother had also come out to the door. She was glad to see him, like he was her own son. She took him by his forearm and pulled him into the front yard.

Mother asked, "When did you arrive?"

"Right this minute. One of my men was martyred. I need to get back tomorrow."

Mother said, "In that case, do come over for dinner tonight."

That day was the day of my birthday. Mother always remembered everyone's birthday. After Ali Agha left, she said, "I want to hold a birthday party for you."

I said, "No, Mother. Didn't you hear Ali Agha's friend was just martyred?"

Mother had wanted to invite others to the party in addition to Ali Agha and his family, but she saw that I was right and changed her mind. That evening, she congratulated me on my birthday and gave me the present that she had bought for me and said, "The war will be over soon, God willing. That's ok; these days will pass. If God wills, this same time next year, we'll have a birthday party for you and your son together in your own house."

That night we had Ali Agha and his family over for dinner. It was the night of that same afternoon in which he had sprained his ankle practicing his martial arts, about which he had not uttered a word of complaint. I noticed it toward the end of the evening. I had insisted on taking him to the hospital to have it looked at, but he demurred, saying, "It's nothing; it'll heal in time."

Finally, I relented and said, "You have so much forbearance! How can you stand so much pain? I couldn't stand it for a minute."

He smiled and said, "You have to practice. I would like my wife to have forbearance and perseverance."

I remember, that night Mansūreh Khānūm's kidneys were giving her trouble and Hājj Sādeq took her to the hospital. I took Ali Agha to my room. I asked, "What's the matter? Are you not feeling well?" He said, "I sprained my ankle in the gym this afternoon."

I rolled up the cuff of his trouser leg with difficulty. He was bashful and kept pulling his leg back. I pulled his sock down and took it off. His leg was very pale. His ankle was swollen and bruised. I became alarmed and said, "Get up; we need to take you to the hospital."

He chuckled and said, "*Na bābā*. Nah, it's nothing; it'll get better."
I was looking to call out to Mother, but he said, "No, no; don't do that."

He put his sock back on quickly. No matter how much I tried, I could not prevail on him to let me take him to the hospital. One of Ali Agha's friends came after him at the end of the night. They had gone back to the *Sepāh* barracks, where his fellow soldiers had reset his sprained ankle after massaging it in hot salt water.

Ali Agha came over to our house early Thursday morning. He would not come in, no matter how I tried. He was heading for the front again.

For the first time tears welled up in my eyes in front of him and I started to cry. He took me by the hand and said, "Have you forgotten our resolution so soon? Did I not say last night that I wanted my wife to have forbearance and longanimity? I might not return this time. I don't want you to show weakness. I want you to be patient and have long-suffering, like Her Eminence Lady Zeynab."[66] But all these words notwithstanding, I could not stop the flow of my tears, which would not quit. I knew that he did not express his feelings freely. He had not once become emotional in the time that I had known him, nor had be complained about missing me. But I was his exact opposite: fragile, sensitive, and emotional. I said my goodbyes through my sobs and my tears.

I closed the door and leaned against it. I couldn't bring my sobbing under control. I thought he might knock on the door at any moment and come in to comfort me; but a few minutes passed and there was no sound on the other side of the door. After five minutes had passed, I opened the door slowly and looked out into the street, but there was no longer anyone there. I couldn't believe he had the heart to leave me in this state. When I entered the house, I started wailing again loudly.

---

[66] The august sister of Imam Hosayn, who survived the massacre of the Plain of Karbalā and lived to tell the tale and spread the word, which she did with courage and eloquence.

He had said I needed to have patience and forbearance. I should have been able to forbear it and suffer through it. After all, it was my own choice; my own decision. It was no one other than myself who had decided to be a partner in the difficulties of the war effort. It was I who had wanted to be the wife of a *pāsdār*, a Revolutionary Guard. I thought of the *pāsdārs* as people who had great patience and forbearance, and who comported themselves with immaculate decorum. I told myself, "Ok, it's a deal. I'll be patient and suffer my fate, come what will. But watch over him, dear Lord! Dear God: injuries and wounds I can handle, but pray God, not martyrdom or being taken prisoner. So watch over him, dear Lord!"

A Second Honeymoon

The exams of the month of Khordād of 1365/ 1987 were over. Father went to his shop early in the morning. And as for Mother, in addition to her running the sewing workshop, she also participated in other activities in support of the war effort which the womenfolk of Hamedān ran on their own accord. She would sometimes take Nafīseh with her, and would not even return for lunch. On these occasions, the household chores would be divided up between Royā and myself.

It was Tuesday, the 10th of June, 1986. The doorbell sounded. I put on my *chādor* and traversed the ten or fifteen yards from the house to the door of the front yard with several large strides. As soon as I opened the door, I saw Ali Agha standing there. His arm was in a sling suspended from his neck.

After greeting him quickly, I asked, "What happened?"

153

He answered as if it was no big deal, "Oh, it's nothing. It's just a few small pieces of shrapnel."

I invited him in. He was tired, and was not himself. He had given his hair a buzz cut, his beard was long and hirsute, and his lips were colorless and chapped. His boots were covered with so much dust that one could not tell what color they were underneath.

"You should take better care of yourself; one would have thought you've returned from a warfront or something," I quipped.

He smiled and said, "It was a major operation; on Majnūn Island."

I pleaded, "Come in!"

He said, "I can't; I'm very tired. I just wanted to see you first. Is Vajīheh Khānūm home?"

Mother was not home. I asked with surprise, "No, she's at the workshop. Why do you ask?"

He said, "The men are worn out and need a break. The *Sepāh* has invited some families to go on an all-expenses paid vacation to Mashhad."

He ran his hand over his long beard and said, "I'd like to take you with me. Do you think Vajīheh Khānūm will give her approval?"

I didn't say anything. He said, "I'm going to go and have a lie down and rest. I'll come back in the afternoon and see if she will give her approval."

Father and Mother didn't have any objections and consented. We started our journey at the break of dawn of Thursday, the 12th of June, 1986, in front of the *Sepāh* headquarters. Our group was split into two buses: one bus was for those who were married and their families, and the other bus was for those who were single.[67] Ali Agha sat me in the second or third row. He put his duffel bag on the empty seat beside me and went to the bus of the single men.

The buses took off and a few hours passed, after which we stopped to take a rest. Ali Agha came back into our bus, but he didn't stop at my seat and went to the back of the bus. At first, I thought that he was going back there just to say hello or to show his face and would come back soon, but he didn't come back, no matter how long I waited. I turned around and looked back, and I saw that most of the men were sitting with their wives and were either busy talking or having a piece of fruit or some other snack. And Ali Agha and a few others who were seated at the back of the bus were talking up a storm and laughing. I caught his eye and waved him over. It took a little while before he came over. I took his duffel bag off the seat and put it behind my feet and said, "Sit down, I'm bored stiff!"

He sat, but he was restless, and I knew that he wanted to go back. I said, "Does the bus qualify for Hamedān rules too?!"

He looked surprised. I said, "Lest the families of the martyrs start to gossip in the streets."

---

[67] Celibacy is looked down upon by Moslems, as it goes against the exemplary model set by the Prophet, as well as going against human nature, of course, which requires certain urges and needs to be fulfilled in a healthy and socially responsible way.

He smiled and nodded his head. He said, "Yes, the bus qualifies. I feel embarrassed around my men. I'm afraid they'll think I'm ignoring them."

I protested, "It's not as if you know what they're thinking; what if they don't even think like that?"

He said, "True; they might think that Ali Agha has flow the coup and married and left them alone to themselves."

I said, "Everyone else is sitting next to their wives; and it's not as if anyone is saying anything about them."

He said with impatience, "Everyone has his own peculiar traits; this is how I am."

I didn't say anything more. I understood his character now. But that character trait notwithstanding, he sat next to me for a half hour or so and then went back. A little later, the sound of someone singing could be heard from the back of the bus. It was one of Ali Agha's guys. He had a good voice. He sang elegies, but his local Hamedānī folkloric songs were nicer and made everyone laugh.

My fellow travelers would laugh at peculiar accents and idiomatic expressions in the folkloric songs as they ate some fruit which they had brought for the journey, which they offered to me as well. It was a little past noon. The bus made a stop at a restaurant in a rest area. The women who had little children stood in line outside the public restrooms. One or two of the children had become restless. I went to see if I could offer my help to one of the ladies; I wanted to try to get the children who had become restless to the front of the line for the restroom. Just

A Second Honeymoon

as I was thinking of doing this, a man arrived and bypassed the line of women and went into the restroom.

The women's voices rose in protest. I don't know who got the news of what had just happened to the menfolk, but I now saw Ali Agha running towards us, together with a few of his men. His wrath could even be seen from a distance. When he got to where we were, he told us to go back to where the buses were parked with an imperative tone, after which he entered the restroom. He kicked the door in, and a little later we saw him dragging the man out by the scruff of his neck with the hand that wasn't in a sling. His voice could be heard saying, "Don't think us *pāsdārs* are unmannered!"

The man kept looking around, stunned and lost for words. His hands were holding his trousers together. Ali Agha's voice was loud: "We have taken up arms and are fighting on the warfront in order to protect your *nāmūs* [the order, honor, self-respect, and dignity of one's self and one's wards and house]; and then you lower your head and pretend not to see anything and go straight past the line into the women's restroom right before our eyes?!"

I didn't catch what the man said or did in response, but when Ali Agha came back to the bus he was distraught, and ordered the drivers of both buses to take off.

We were all so upset that none of us spoke; even Mr. Rafī'ī's group, who had been loud with singing songs and elegies, were sitting quietly on their seats. The bus started and we were back on the highway before too long.

Ali Agha had made room reservations at the Qoo Hotel in Chālūs with the help of the local Friday congregational prayer leader there. There were two large halls with beautiful ornate mirrorwork on the walls and cornices; the womenfolk settled in one, and the menfolk in the other. We were given blankets and pillows which were new and clean.

No matter how much I looked, I could not find Ali Agha. He was busy making the necessary arrangements for dinner and other necessities. I wandered around the hotel with another lady. The Caspian Sea could be seen behind the hotel. We went and sat on the beach. The weather was fine, and the sound of the waves, and the gentle way that they lapped the shore and ebbed back, the dusk, and the infinite expanse of the sea, imparted a strong sense of tranquility. The pungent smells carried by the waves, and the occasional squawking of seagulls, had lifted my mood; sounds which inspired the imagination and were gentle on the ears. We were lost in our own thoughts when Ali Agha showed up. With Ali Agha's arrival, my lady companion bid us farewell and took her leave. Ali Agha asked, "Are you having a good time?"

I responded, "What am I supposed to do? You're always busy running around seeing to things, and I don't have anyone to talk to. So I looked for somewhere that was secluded."

Ali Agha stared into the sea and said, "Life is like the sea. If the waters of the sea stay in one place, they will stagnate like a swamp. And like the sea, one must always remain in motion; but movement has its difficulties. The grandeur and beauty of the sea is due to its movement; for if we still these waters, they will turn into a fetid swamp. I want to be like this sea; I like to be in motion. I want to go through hardships in order to reach the ocean. I will do whatever it takes to get to the ocean. You're the same way, aren't you?"

Ali Agha's words had made me go deep into my thoughts. I was wondering about the nature of the ocean which he wanted to reach, and where it could be. Without any particular purpose, I said, "Uh huh!"

The following morning, Ali Agha put everyone to work bringing the bivouac mats and breakfast materials to the place behind the hotel where we had stood looking at the sea and talking about the ocean. After breakfast, the menfolk had a swim in the sea with their clothes on. But Ali Agha did not wade in because of his arm. He stood to the side and gazed into the infinite expanse of the sea.

Ali Agha and I were standing at some distance from each other on the shore. Mr. Hosayn Rafi'i and a few other people went to see Mr. Mehrabān, whose leg was in a cast up to his knee and who walked with a cane. They took him by the arms and legs and swung him back and forth like a hammock. For his part, Mr. Mehrabān was yelling and screaming for relief, but as no one came to his aid, they continued swinging him without mercy and flung him into the sea. The poor soul could not get himself out of the water, no matter how he tried. A few people took mercy on him and helped him out of the water and sat him down is a corner where he could get dry. And then it was the turn of the head of the rabble-rousers, Mr. Hosayn Rafi'i. A few people swarmed towards him and grabbed his arms and legs and did to him exactly what he and the gang had done to poor Mr. Mehrabān; with the difference that there was nothing wrong with Mr. Rafi'ī and he was able to get himself out of the water without any problems. Meanwhile, his ID cards and wallet had come out of his pocket and were floating on the water. Mr. Rafi'ī waded in the water trying to collect all of his documents and wallet. Some of the guys wanted to go and help him, but Ali Agha said, "Don't help him."

I said, "Ali, that's not right!"

Ali Agha smiled and said, "No, he deserves it. Let him get a taste of his own medicine. You reap what you sow."

Mr. Rafi'ī's documents and wallet were in the clutches of the waves and his cash was floating on the surface of the water. Mr. Rafi'ī yelled, "Come and help me! What do I care, you rascals; it was your travelling money!" But no one stepped forward to help him. Rather, they laughed and started making fun of him in unison by chanting the same folksong which Mr. Rafi'ī had sung on the bus. Now they all sang it back to him in unison, snickering at his misfortune.

Eventually Mr. Rafi'ī was able to gather his things and made his way out of the water and towards Ali Agha along with a few others whom he had mustered in order to exact his revenge. Ali Agha was dressed in very dapper apparel. They jumped him and dragged him into the water and dunked his head into the sea right in the shallows. I got concerned and ran forward and yelled, "Leave him be! Ali Agha has injured his arm. It's going to get infected!"

But his subordinates were unmoved and continued to dunk his head under the water and bring him back up for air several more times, my pleas landing on deaf ears. Eventually, they let Ali Agha go, and he started to make his way towards me with a big smile on his face and water dripping from his clothes and shoulder harness. I said with great concern in my voice, "Why don't you say something to them, Ali?! You have to keep your wound dry."

Ali Agha smiled and said, "Let them have their fun. They've come here to get some rest and relaxation. It's all in good fun; it's not a problem." Then he went and changed into some new clothes and got rid of his bandage and shoulder strap.

Meanwhile, Ali Agha and I, in our capacity as the newlyweds, had become the new item on the agenda of the boys' fun. They had latched onto the fact that Ali Agha kept his distance from me, and they insisted that they wanted to take a picture of the two of us together as a couple. So, upon their insistence, we posed together for a picture as a couple. But the guy taking the picture couldn't keep the camera steady and both our faces came out as a blur, as if we were in a fog or something.

We eventually made our way to Mashhad. Private rooms had been reserved for married couples in the hotel there, but Ali Agha was rarely in the room and I was usually on my own. One day I decided to get him to stay in the room come what may. I used the air conditioner as an excuse and told one of Ali Agha's men who was passing by in the lobby to tell him that the air conditioner in our room is not working, and can he come and fix it?

The man said with surprise, "The air conditioning doesn't work? Allow me to see what the problem is." Having gotten my permission to enter the room, he started looking into the situation and before long he said, "But there is nothing wrong with this air conditioner, Mrs. Chītsāzīān!"

I was embarrassed and uttered, "Well, uh, it's too loud."

The man who was very humble and always averted his gaze said without looking up, "All of the air conditioners are as loud as this, my sister. The air conditioner in our room is no different than this one."

And with that little episode, I forgot about getting Ali Agha to come to the room. It was not long after that when I became aware that Ali Agha had been in contact with the warfront and that he had been told that the Iraqis had attacked Majnūn Island – the same place where he had carried out some operations – and that the commander of the Battalion of His Eminence Ali Akbar, Hājj Rezā Shokrīpūr, had been martyred. Thus, rumors of our return to Hamedān started to go around and started to gather pace. It was even said that the menfolk might be flown to the front by plane, and that the women would take the bus back to Hamedān. During these exchanges of information, I also realized that another one of the boys who also worked in intelligence by the name of Alī Tābesh had also been martyred a few weeks ago on the same Island. On hearing all this news, the men's spirits sank and the atmosphere changed and our premature return to Hamedān became a certainty. And so I said to Ali Agha, "Let's go to the bazaar today."

Ali Agha asked with surprise, "The bazaar? Whatever for?"

I said, "We have to buy some souvenirs for our folks."

Ali Agha put his hand in his pocket and took out six thousand Toumans which he gave me and said, "Take this and go to the bazaar and buy whatever you want. Go with one of the other women; I don't like going shopping."

In those days, six thousand Toumans was a considerable sum of money. I didn't object. I asked, "Do you not want something yourself?"

He said, "No, nothing. Use it for yourself."

I said, "Your shirts are all worn out. I want to buy you new ones. What colors do you want?"

But he would not give in to my desire to buy him shirts. It was evident that he had no time for such things. And so, because he didn't want to argue, he just said, "Khaki; the color of my military fatigues."

That day, one of the ladies and I went to the Imam Reza Bazaar. I bought a pretty pink prayer *chādor* for myself, and two fancy blouses for Mother and Mansūreh Khānūm. Ali Agha's sister Maryam had recently married and moved to Tehran; I bought some items of clothing for her as well as for his brothers. And for Father and Agha Nāser, I bought two identical and beautiful prayer rugs. For Ali Agha, I bought a khaki shirt and a pair of army pants, the kind with a lot of pockets; and I also bought some saffron, dried barberries, and crystalline sugar (*nabāt*). And despite all this shopping, there was still a lot of money left.

When I was back at the hotel, I showed him everything that I had bought. He smiled and said, "What patience you have for these things, my love! How can you stand to do so much shopping for everyone?! And with such good taste!"

The men were distraught because of the news of what had happened on Majnūn Island. And what was particularly disturbing to them was the fact that the enemy had attacked the western flank, which is where the forces from Hamedān were positioned. Thus, everyone packed their things and boarded the bus.

We were sitting in a restaurant in a rest stop on the way from Mashhad to Hamedān when suddenly one of Ali Agha's men yelled out, "Ali Agha!"

I got up from behind the table and ran outside. Some of the men were running in front of me. I saw Ali Agha in an area that was green with verdure and looked like a park. He was flying in the air, delivering kung-fu kicks to a young man in a red tee shirt, and then turning around immediately and doing the same to a tall broad-shouldered man who was with the other man. His arm was no longer in a sling and he was making martial maneuvers with both his hands, just as if he was in a Bruce Lee movie. The two guys were defending themselves, but they were no match for Ali Agha. Ali Agha's men surrounded him and calmed him down and things cooled off. I knew not to approach him in these circumstances. Some other men from Ali Agha's battalion also arrived, and they all made their way inside the restaurant. Someone brought a glass of water, and another ordered some tea to be served. From what was being said, I gleaned that one of the two men had made a pass at the wife of one of our fellow travelers and Ali Agha just happened to be behind her and heard the insult. Ali Agha was very strict when it came to these kinds of matters; so much so that even after half an hour had passed, his face and even the skin of his head, which he had shorn with a buzz cut, were still crimson with rage. He was seething with anger at the fact that someone would have the ill manners and audacity to make an insulting comment at a married woman who was properly veiled with a *chādor* and who had a child in her arms. What was worse, rather than apologizing when being called out to account for their behavior, they had become indignant and had turned violent.

I was sitting in a corner of the restaurant. After some time had passed, those two men came into the restaurant and went over to where Ali Agha was sitting. I was very concerned. I thought they had come in to start another fight. But they had become ashamed of what they had done and had come to ask his forgiveness. They pleaded shamefully, "Forgive us! We are deeply ashamed! We didn't know you were a soldier, otherwise we would not have disrespected you in such a shameful manner."

It was seven at night on Sunday June 22nd, 1986 when we arrived in Hamedān. Ali Agha drove me home and came in for a little while; but because Father was not present, he said he would call again tomorrow morning. But he didn't show up the next morning, and came in the evening together with Uncle Mahmoud instead. They sat for an hour or so and talked up a storm with Father. They said that the bodies of sixteen martyrs had been brought back to Hamedān, one of which was Shahīd Shokrīpūr.

The next day, on Tuesday the 24th, Ali Agha and Uncle Mahmoud left for the front at noon. Before leaving, they came to our house to say their farewells. I asked, "When will you be back?"

He replied, "I don't know. Pray that I will be back in time for the wedding."

It was summer. On one hand, Mother was busy with her activities which supported the war effort and the boys on the front lines; and on the other hand, she was busy preparing the articles which were to be included as part of Ali Agha's dowry. Twenty-four days had passed since Ali Agha had left for the front. Amīr and Hājj Sādeq came to our house on Thursday night. They had brought a letter from Ali Agha for me. I took the letter and ran to my room after bidding them farewell. I opened it and read it:

In the Name of God

In the name of the faithful and intimate
companions of the Lord of the Age

"Salām Alaykom.

"I hope that you are well and that you are thankful for the endless bounties which God has bestowed upon us. We should be grateful and prostrate ourselves before the Almighty for giving us such a dearly beloved Leader, the *Pīr* or wise old sage of Jamārān,[68] whose sturdy steps brought light to our otherwise unenlightened eyes, with which light we were able to see the right way to live out our lives, and with which light we are able to distinguish truth from falsehood and right from wrong, and to fight until the last drop of our blood against the forces of iniquity and injustice and oppression.

"Please give my warm and heartfelt *salāms*[69] to your father and mother and to your sisters: I pray God that you and your noble family are always successful in your struggles in the Way of God; and I ask that you pray God for this humble soul so that I will be able to work all the better in God's Way. Perhaps He will see fit to accept such a request, coming from you.

"Concerning the date of the wedding, kindly convey to your honorable family that they should be prepared for the ceremony to be held, God willing, on the Eid al-Qorbān, which falls on the 16th of August, 1986 this year. I will be there a few

---

[68] The reference is to Imam Khomeinī, the leader of the Islamic Revolution of Iran at the time. He lived in a part of town called Jamārān.

[69] *Salām alaykom* or *salām* in short is the traditional way in which Moslems greet each other, after the tradition of the Prophet. It is a salutation that is a prayer and invocation of blessings: 'may [God's] peace be unto you', like the traditional Catholic salutation of *dominus vobiscum* (which is Latin for "the Lord be with you"). The traditional Catholic response of *et cum spiritu tuo*, (meaning "and with your spirit [also]") has its Islamic equivalent in the standard Islamic response: *wa alaykom as-salām*: 'and unto you also be [God's] peace'.

days before that date, unless something prevents me from leaving.

"I have nothing else to say other than to entrust you to God's hands and good graces."

I breathed a sigh of relief after having read the letter. I was relieved because Mother had already invited guests to the wedding. Five days before the wedding, Ali Agha had returned to Hamedān and he was supposed to come over for dinner to our house together with his family so that we could start planning for the wedding. As usual, Mother had prepared a delicious meal.

The aroma of rice and saffron and Mother's *Khoresh Gheimeh* had filled the whole house. In the early evening, I washed down the patio in the front yard and drew back the house's curtains and opened the windows. Everything was clean and in order. Mother had finished the purchases for Ali Agha's dowry and had wrapped them up in large and small boxes, some of which she had placed in the small storage room at the top of the stairwell at roof level, and the rest of which she had stored in a small storage room that was in the corner of the front yard. Royā and Nafiseh were counting down the days until the wedding. The comings and goings to and from our house were increasing daily. Grandmother, my cousins, and aunts would come over every day in order to be of some help to Mother.

It was night. We had turned on the lights of the front yard. Every once in a while I would spray down the patio with water in order to cool the place down; and the last time I did this, I washed the walls down too. I looked at the front yard and at the small green trees and at the flowerbeds which were full of flowers. I had sprayed them with water and they sparkled with life and energy under the electric lights of the yard. I thought about how much grander our wedding ceremony would be if we covered the front yard with a canopy and strung up the trees and the spaces between them with lights. I imagined myself in a wedding gown and a beautiful white lace mantilla bridal veil. I imagined Ali Agha was standing next to me and the guests were showering us with sugar candy, flowers and gold coins. I thought it would be good if we had a special place for the bride and groom.

The doorbell chimed and Ali Agha and his family entered into the front yard. From the moment they stepped in, something within me told me that there was some bad news to be had. Contrary to their usual selves, Mansūreh Khānūm and Agha Nāser and Ali Agha were not happy and full of verve. But not having realized this, Mother had started to talk with enthusiasm about all of the things which she had already been able to accomplish in preparation for the wedding. She talked about the fact that she had already invited the guests and ordered the confectionary, for example; and how we were planning to lay carpets down on the patio in the front yard. Mansūreh Khānūm bit her lips and was fussing with the edge of her black satin *chādor* which had a pattern of large embossed flowers on it, also in black.

Agha Nāser signaled to Mansūreh Khānūm that she should speak up about the news that they had to impart. Mansūreh Khānūm said hesitantly, "The truth is that one of our family members has passed away, so we will not be celebrating [anytime soon]."

All of a sudden everything fell apart. Mother's face lost its color and went white. Nevertheless, she meekly asked, "You mean to say you want to postpone the wedding?"

It seemed like Mansūreh Khānūm felt sorry for Mother. She glanced at Agha Nāser and Ali Agha and said, "No, our situation should not affect you. By rights you should carry on with what you have started. You have gone through a lot of trouble, invited guests and made all these preparations. You should have a celebration among yourselves, and we will come quietly and take our bride away."

Father and Mother were taken aback and looked at each other and asked each other's opinion with the silent code of familiar facial gestures. Mother said, "We have invited a whole lot of guests!"

I was so glad to see Ali Agha that my elation was not dampened by what had happened. Ali Agha insisted that we should not cancel the wedding. And so eventually we agreed not to do so.

From the morning of the next day, Mother picked up the pace of the work she had to do to complete the preparations. Despite the fact that Father was not in a good financial situation at the time, she managed to prepare a good and full dowry for Ali Agha and myself. She tried to do everything to make the wedding celebration a memorable one.

Mother went to the bazaar and instead of a wedding gown, bought me a very beautiful cream-colored blouse, which cost twelve thousand five hundred Toumans, which was not an inconsiderable sum at the time. During those days, there were heated discussions as to how we were to hold a small but respectable wedding celebration.

Mother was determined to hold the wedding come what may. She would say, "It would be doing an injustice to the bride and groom. They don't realize it now, but they would regret not having had a wedding celebration each time they went to someone else's wedding. We have a duty to make the occasion of their marriage tie into a memorable occasion."

Ultimately, Mother pulled it off perfectly, even though our wedding ceremony was a simple affair where we did not put up a canopy or string up any lights or cover the patio with rugs, and it consisted of a simple gathering where people got together and enjoyed each other's company while partaking of some fruit and confectionary, with a special place reserved with a single seat for the bride, with no groom.

No matter how much we insisted, Ali Agha would not agree to come. He would say, "The gathering is a women's-only affair. I feel too shy to come and sit among a sea of women. And I know women's habits: as soon as they see the groom, they start clapping and making all sorts of noises."

Ali Agha came to the house the following morning. He said that his friend's wife was accepted to Mashhad University, and that they had put all of their belongings into one of the rooms of their house and emptied the rest of it and given its key to Ali Agha. They said that we could use the house without having to pay rent as long as they are in Mashhad.

Ali Agha said, "Come with me and let's go take a look at the house. If you find it to be acceptable, we can start moving our belongings in."

The house opened up onto two different alleys. The door that opened up into its front yard was in an alley that was opposite our own. The residents of the second floor used that door. The door which we were to use opened on to Qāziān Alley, which was still pretty close. It was a two-story residential building built on stilts which provided a parking area on the ground floor, and was located in the middle of the Qāziān Alley, number 17. Ali Agha turned the key and opened the door. There was a wide staircase with short risers. The house was large and bright with plenty of natural light which made it pleasing to behold. On one end, its windows opened onto the front yard, and on the other end, they opened onto Qāziān Alley. The layout of the house was very important for me; and the fact that it was so close to Mother's house was wonderful. Ali Agha asked, "Well, what do you think? Do you like it?"

I said, "Very much."

We then proceeded to look over the den, the living room, kitchen and bedrooms. One of the bedrooms was locked, which was obviously the room in which the owners had stored their belongings.

Ali Agha was pleased with the fact that I had taken to the house. He said, "Zahrā Khānūm, if it is ok with Vajīheh Khānūm, let us go get our dowry gifts and set everything up here."

A Second Honeymoon

I said, "Why would it not be ok with her. They are ready when you are."

Ali Agha showed up later that same day with a few of his friends and took the household appliances and other gifts which were all part of the dowry. My mother had included a 2x3 meter carpet, and it was only after we had spread the carpet out that we realized how large the living room was.

That evening Ali Agha went to the Sepāh Cooperative store and bought two 3x4 meter carpets,[70] one of which we spread in the living room, and the other one in the den. But despite the large size of the carpet in the living room, the periphery of the room was still bare. Ali Agha then purchased some glue-down carpeting which we cut up and used to fill the voids left around the periphery of the living room.

It was the evening of the 28th of Mordād, and Ali Agha and his family were supposed to show up at my Mother's house and take me to our new home. Mother had invited her brother's wives and other close family members to her house for the occasion. After we ate dinner, we washed the dishes and tidied up, and waited for the groom and his family to show up. Mother had started crying from early evening on. She had burned some wild rue (*espand*) in a portable censer and would circle my head with the smoke [as a way of warding off evil]. No matter how I tried, I could not stop my tears from running down my face either.

---

[70] Just under 130 square feet each.

I was wearing that beautiful cream-colored blouse which Mother had bought for me, together with the *chādor* which I had worn on the day we made our marriage vows. It was already past ten o'clock. And then eleven o'clock came and went and they still hadn't shown up. I don't know why I felt anxious. I said to Mother, "Are you sure they said they would call tonight, Mother? Maybe they were thinking it's tomorrow night and there's been a misunderstanding."

Mother had begun to doubt herself too. We kept on waiting, not really knowing what to do. The family was busy talking, but for me, the minutes dragged. Another hour came and went. I told mother, "I feel sleepy, Mother. Maybe some problem has come up for them."

Mother had become agitated. She hugged and kissed me and said, "They'll show up any minute now." And then she started to weep in my arms.

And that is exactly what happened too. The doorbell chimed and Ali Agha and Amīr and Hājj Sādeq and Monīreh Khānūm and Maryam entered the house. Ali Agha was wearing a light blue shirt with charcoal grey trousers. He looked different. He came forward and greeted me and asked how I was. Mother was holding a Quran in her hand. She opened it and recited a few verses for us. Ali Agha asked Father and Mother for their permission. Father and Uncle Mahmoud took me by the hand and took me from the living room into the entryway and then out to the front yard to the sound of Mother's supplications and weeping.

Mother kept repeating her ritual supplications under her breath and would move around aimlessly back and forth, as if she was looking for something. Nafiseh was observing my departure with sadness and concern. Mother came over and stood next to me and kissed me several times. She whispered in my ear, "*Halālam kon, mādar jān* – forgive me before God any trespass that I might have committed against you, my dear child."

She then said aloud through her tears, "Pray God that you will be blessed with good fortune. Pray God that you [= both of your lives] will come to an honorable conclusion. Pray God that all good things that are licit and lawful in accordance with God's laws come your way, my beloved."

When we got to the car in the alley, Father took Ali Agha's hand and placed my hands in his and said, "Ali Agha, I entrust my Fereshteh to your hands. Guard her like you would guard your own life." Ali Agha said, "Entrust her to God, Ḥājj Agha."

And Father said, "Of course. Of course I entrust both of you to God's good graces."

I had lowered my head and could not see anyone. I heard Ali Agha's voice as he said, "Ḥājj Agha, I hope to be a worthy groom to you. And I hope that I will be a good husband for Zahrā Khānūm."

Father said, "Of course you will be. Upon my word with God, if my daughter lives a single day with someone such as yourself, it is a hundred times better than her spending a whole lifetime with an ignoble and dishonorable man."

He then put an arm around Ali Agha's neck and kissed him.

Both my aunts helped me get into Ali Agha's friend's car, and then they got in themselves and sat on either side of me. The car belonged to Ahmad Sāberī, one of Ali Agha's friends; and he was driving it, with Ali Agha riding in the front passenger seat next to him.

We passed by a few streets and arrived at Imāmzādeh[71] Abdollāh, [which is a famous 'square' (or circus, actually) in Hamedān where the shrine is located]. Mr. Sāberī circumambulated the Imāmzādeh Abdollāh circus seven times with his car. He was in a good mood and was having fun at Ali Agha's expense. During all of the time that we were circumambulating the Imāmzādeh Abdollāh shrine, my eyes were fixed on the shrine's dome and I was praying for our good fortune and that our lives would come to an honorable conclusion.

After making this kind of pilgrimage to the Imāmzādeh, we made our way to Imam Khomeini Square and then from there to Bū Alī Street. We only had Hājj Sādeq's car in tow. Hājj Sādeq and his wife and daughter were seated in Hājj Sādeq's brown Peykān,[72] together with Maryam and Amīr Agha. There was no honking of horns nor any letting out of strange sounds from that car. When we drove a few more blocks, Mr. Sāberī asked, "Shall we go to Sang-Shīr?" Ali Agha didn't say anything, so we went there and after a few more blocks we got back to Qāzīān Alley.

---

[71] Imāmzādeh: the shrine and pilgrimage destination of a saint who is a son or daughter of one of the Twelve Imams.
[72] The Iranian version of the Hillman Hunter.

Ali Agha got out and opened the back door and took my hand. Agha Nāser and Hājj Bābā and Khānūm Jān and Mansūreh Khānūm and Mother and my sisters were waiting for us in front of the door to the house. The smell of wild rue smoke had filled the alley. Agha Nāser took me by the hand and we went inside the house. When we were in the stairwell, Agha Nāser started to recite this elegy:

> Today that this celebration is manifestly good (*hasan*),
> It is such by the grace of God and of Hojjat[73], the son of Hasan.
> The new bride is like the Jasmine flower,
> And the groom, like the Anemone.
> The goblet of the bride and groom spilleth over,
> From the love of Mohammad and Ali and Zahrā.

> امروز که این جشن به توجه حَسَن است
> ز الطاف خدا و حجت ابن الحسن است
> مانند گل یاس بود تازه عروس
> داماد گل شقایق و یاسمن است
> از عشق محمد و علی و زهرا
> لبریز بود ساغر داماد و عروس

The others kept sending *salawāt* as they followed us. When we entered our own home, the guests stayed for a few minutes, and then they came forward and congratulated us and wished us

---

[73] An honorific title of the Lord of the Age or the Twelfth Imam.

prosperity and happiness in our new life, bid us farewell, and left. When the house was vacated of its guests, Hājj Bābā put my and Ali Agha's hands together and prayed for us. Almost everyone had left other than the uncles' wives. Ali Agha went and made his ablutions. I also made my ablutions and stood behind him ready for offering our ritual supplications, deferring to him to lead the prayers.

After the prayers, we sat and he talked to me for a while. He repeated everything which he had told me and asked of me at the time we made our marriage vows. He said, "Your father and mother are my father and mother as well. And you should think of my parents as being yours as well. If both of us treat both our families with respect and honor them, no problems will arise. You are a woman of faith who holds [correct] beliefs and who veils herself [in accordance with the ordinances of the sacred law of Islam]. There is nothing more that I require of you; because a Moslem woman is familiar with her duties and responsibilities; and furthermore, you have been raised in an honorable family of faith."

Ali Agha had guests on the following day; there were a few of his subordinates, as well as some relatives from both families. The mothers were in the neighbor's home on the second floor, and the womenfolk were in our home. We ordered out for dinner, and after dinner was finished, one of Ali Agha's friends started to perform *maddāhī* or to sing panegyrics for the *Ahl al-Bayt* or for the Fourteen Purified Members of the House of the Prophet. When the sound of their sending *salawāts* could be heard, the women would send *salawāts* as well. A little after dinner, the menfolk said their goodbyes and left.

That was the simple way in which our unceremonious wedding ended and our life together started. Mansūreh Khānūm and Agha Nāser and Amīr Agha stayed over at our house. Mansūreh Khānūm was highly fond of her children. Even though she was not feeling well, she took responsibility for the cooking. I was responsible for maintaining hygiene and cleanliness in the house, which included vacuuming and washing the dishes, as well as cleaning and washing the fruits and vegetables. And Amīr Agha did the shopping for the household. He was a kind and gentle young man, and had a strong emotional bond with all of us. It sometimes happened that Mansūreh Khānūm would send him out four or five times to shop for different items before noon; but I never once heard a word of complaint out of him.

Mansūreh Khānūm and Agha Nāser and Amīr Agha went back to their own home after four days. That day, I was left to myself. It was the first time that I cooked. I made some pan-fried kebabs with rice. It was around noon. The aroma of the kebabs had filled the house. The door chimed, and I went to the door and asked, "Who is it?" It was Ali Agha. He said, "It's me. We have guests."

I ran and put on my *chādor* and opened the door. Ali Agha came in along with a friend who said "*Yāllāh*" a couple of times [in order to indicate that a *nāmahram* man is entering the premises]. After welcoming them, I went into the kitchen, and Ali Agha followed me in. I was a little upset, and I said, "If you wanted to invite a guest, I wish you would have let me know sooner."

He smiled and said, "Its only one guest; surely there must be some bread and cheese that we can all eat?"

I said, "Yes, there is. But I would be ashamed to serve such a lowly meal to any guest."

He said very calmly, "Don't worry yourself about these kinds of things at all. We won't complain, even if you don't feed us any lunch. We're just going to talk about our own business. If you give us a morsel of bread and cheese and some sweetened tea, we would be much obliged and in your debt."

Ali Agha's response was disarming. He said, smiling, "So what have you cooked whose aroma has filled the whole house up, my love?" I said, "Pan-fried kebabs with steamed rice."

He took in a deep breath and said, "Mmmmm. Truly, a good wife is a blessing. Anyone who doesn't have one is missing out."

I smiled and gave him the tablespread [to spread out on the floor in preparation of serving the meal]. There was enough food to go around. The two of them ate in the den and I ate in the kitchen. Our tablespread was full of God's bounties: aromatic herbs such as mint and parsley and tarragon and savory; yoghurt, and slices of Persian melon; and there were soft drinks as well. I remembered one of the adages that Mother used to say: "God provides for the upkeep of guests".[74]

---

[74] Literally, the saying is something like this: "Guests bring the provisions for their daily sustenance with themselves".

My Beloved Flower

It had been a week since we had started our life as a couple. One morning after we had offered our pre-dawn ritual devotions to the Lord, Ali Agha said, "Zahrā Khānūm, I have to leave today. Do you know where my duffle bag is?"

I asked with surprise, "Leave? Where to?"

He smiled and said, "Where to? Well, to the front, of course; where else? Where else do I have to go to?"

I looked at him with disquiet and said, "Can't you go a little later?" He said, "No; the enemy has acted dishonorably…"

I packed his duffle bag. I placed his towel, bathroom accessories, underclothing, a few shirts and trousers, and some pieces of fruit and other snacks in it. He said, "This is where the difference between a married man and a bachelor can be seen. I have lived to see the day in which I am personally the beneficiary of humanitarian aid!"

Tears were welling in both our eyes. Ali Agha was not one to give expression to his feelings very often. He bent over and started to tie his boot laces. He was wearing the watch that he had been given as a wedding present and it was loose on his wrist. I thought I must remember to have it adjusted the next time he comes back from the front. When he looked up at me, I saw that his eyes and face had turned red down to his throat. He spoke through barely-contained tears: "My beloved flower, take care of yourself and *halālam kon* – forgive me any trespass that I might have committed against you."

I felt like crying out loud. I wanted to tell him to take me with him. He was looking into my eyes. His blue eyes were stormy like the sea. I said, "You take care of yourself too. *Shafā'at yādet nareh* – don't forget to intercede [on my behalf Come Judgment Day]".

And then without saying another word, he suddenly ran down the stairs and as he was walking away hurriedly with his back to me, he waved and said, "I'm going now, my beloved flower. *Khodā hāfez* – God be with you."

The Eleventh Rose Garden

It had been about four days since Ali Agha had left. I had gone back to my mother's house from the very first day. It was evening. The doorbell chimed. That day felt different somehow, from the moment I had woken up. One minute I was fine, and the next I would be overwhelmed with a great sense of anxiety. I was restless and could not stay on task. I felt strange; and I didn't know what was going on. As soon as I heard the chime of the front door, I ran barefoot to the door, all the while praying to God under my breath: "God, let no harm come to Ali Agha. God, let Ali Agha be whole and healthy. God, let the person who is behind the door not be the bearer of bad news..."

As soon as I opened the door, I was stunned. I couldn't even open my mouth to offer my *salaams*. It was Ali Agha: happy and smiling, and without any injuries on any parts of his body.

I stepped aside so that he could come in. I took his duffle bag from him and he smiled and said, "The humanitarian provisions are depleted."

I said, "There's plenty more where they came from!"

He asked, "Who's here?"

"Everyone."

When we were sitting down together and Mother had served tea, I said, "I wish you hadn't said you need to go back tomorrow. I already have the butterflies."

Father and Ali Agha smiled. After dinner, Mother took me aside and said, "If you want to spend the night here together, it's alright with me; you are welcome to do so. But it would be better now that your husband has come back for just one night for you to spend the night in your own home. Ask him if he has any laundry that I can do for him."

Ali Agha left the following morning. My overnight bag was by the front door. I had not had the opportunity to unpack it when we came over the night before. I picked up the bag and left the house. The street was empty and there was not a soul to be seen; and Ali Agha had disappeared like a bird taking fight. My house of hope was on the other side of the street. I ran over to our own street with tears in my eyes and pressed my finger on the doorbell. On Friday September 12th, 1986, several battalions were supposed to be deployed to the front from Hamedān province. Mother and I went into the street, where we saw that a large crowd had gathered to see the troops off and to wish them well. The smell of the smoke of wild rue had filled the street where the buses which were taking the troops drove through.

The Eleventh Rose Garden

The womenfolk sprayed the bus windows where the soldiers had put their heads out with rosewater from china and steel rosewater atomizers. And the soldiers waved to the crowd from behind the buses' windows.

Around noon we went to the *Masjed-e Jāmeʿ* or Congregational Mosque, and returned home after making our Friday ritual devotions in congregation. I was tired and had a headache, and so I went to bed early. When I woke up for the pre-dawn ritual devotions, my head still ached so I went back to sleep. The sun was shining brightly inside the room. Mother had gone to her sewing workshop, and Father had gone to his barbershop early in the morning, as was his habit. When I heard the doorbell chime, I got up out of bed, put on my *chādor*, and got myself to the door so fast that my body was shaking all over. I couldn't think who it could be that was behind the door, and what kind of message he would have. When I opened the door and saw Mansūreh Khānum standing there, my legs went out from under me and I froze.

Mansūreh Khānum was well dressed as usual. She realized how concerned I had become at the sight of her and said, "Don't worry, dear Fereshteh; there's no problem. It's just that we are leaving for Tehran to pay a visit to Maryam, and we thought we'd come and take you along with us. As fate would have it, you were not able to attend her wedding, so…"

I breathed a sigh of relief and said, "Thank you. But I wish you had said something earlier! I am not prepared to travel now."

At this juncture, Hājj Sādeq who was standing at a little distance away, came forward and after exchanging the standard greetings, said, "The truth is, Fereshteh Khānum, that Ali has been injured."

Hearing Ali Agha's name and the news of his injury made the world start to spin over my head. I grabbed hold of the front door to steady myself against a fall. Mansūreh Khānum held my arm and said, "I swear to God it's nothing major. It's just that we wanted to go to Tehran but thought that if we didn't come and tell you the news in person, then you would be upset with us when you heard the news the next day; that's all."

I was not feeling well. It was as if I was not standing on solid ground. My heart was pounding hard against my chest.

Mansūreh Khānum said, "Fereshteh Jān, I swear it's nothing. I wouldn't lie to you."

Royā and Nafiseh were still asleep. I couldn't bear to wake them. I picked up my carry-all which was in the corner of the room and quietly left the house. I got in Hājj Sādeq's car and said, "Let's go so that I can give Mother the news."

Mother's workplace was on our way. It was a workshop on the second story of a residential building on Bābā Tāher Street. It had several large rooms: a room where the cloth was cut, a room where the pieces were seamed, and a room where they were sown together. Mother was in charge of the whole operation. She would go back and forth between the rooms and patiently monitor the work. The whirring sounds of the Singer and Marshall sewing machines was mingled with the sound of the cutting machines. *Chādorī* women were busy sewing away behind the sewing machines. Mother was standing over a lady in the sewing room telling her something. Hearing the *clop clop* sounds of the manual machines took me back in time to when I was a child and to Mother's sewing. She made such beautiful clothes for us with these same black manual machines which had an image of a lion on them: pleated skirts and fancy blouses of printed cotton and chintz. I stepped forward and said, "*Salām*, Mother. *Khasteh nabāshīd*. I pray that you are not weary."

Mother was surprised to see me and became concerned. I said, "It's nothing to worry about. Ali Agha was injured, and they have taken him to Tehran for treatment. And I want to go to see him with Mansūreh Khānūm and Hājj Sādeq."

Mother's face lost its color, but she tried not to show any signs of her concern. She held my hand and said, "God willing, it will not be anything serious. Do you want me to come with you?"

I said, "No; there's no room in the car. There is Monīreh Khānūm; and Ali Agha's friend wants to come along too."

Mother recited the *āyat ol-korsī* or Verse of the Throne under her breath. She said, "Let's go downstairs so that I can offer my *salāms*."

She went up to the car and greeted Mansūreh Khānūm and Hājj Sādeq and Monīreh Khānūm and asked how they were doing. She then embraced me and kissed me and bade me farewell. I then got back in Hājj Sādeq's brown Peykān, sitting in the back with Mansūreh Khānūm and Monīreh Khānūm. Mother was looking at me with concern in her eyes and whispering supplications under here breath. I was turned around and was looking behind me. When we reached Imāmzādeh Abdollāh, I could no longer see my mother. Hājj Sādeq said, we're going to the Sepāh [Headquarters]; Mr. Farzān is waiting for us at its gate."

Mansūreh Khānūm said, "This Hosayn Agha Farzān is in our Ali's debt. When he joins us, I'll ask him to tell you the story himself. They say he was martyred. Ali is very fond of him. When the news of his martyrdom reached him, he went to the *Me'rāj-e Shohadā* martyr's cemetery to pay his final respects. In the cold-storage room in the mortuary, he noticed that the plastic sheeting that they had wrapped his body in had fogged over. He immediately mounted Hosayn Agha's body on his shoulders and took him to the hospital. And that is how Hosayn Agha came back to life."

Hosayn Agha joined us a little later and sat in the front passenger seat. As soon as he was told I was Ali Agha's wife, he started to sing Ali Agha's praises, and then related a whole bunch of stories of their exploits. He said, "Even though Ali Agha is a commander, he is the first person in any operation to strike out from the front line and make his way to the enemy's fortifications."

He also said, "It was Ali Agha who was the first person in the war to tell us not to use our walkie-talkies, because they could be monitored. He told us to use wired communication devices."

He spoke at length about his bravery and courage. He said, "But all that notwithstanding, Ali Agha is the most compassionate, caring, and humble person in the whole battalion."

Hosayn Agha told us so many stories about Ali Agha's exploits in the war that we were in Tehran before we knew it. Sāsān Hospital was a large and modern hospital. Its ceramic wall and floor surfaces sparkled with cleanliness; one could see one's own reflections in them, they were so clean. We got in an elevator which looked more like the elevators of fancy hotels than hospital elevators. We ascended a few floors, after which the doors opened and we stepped onto sparkling white ceramic tiles which were so clean that they made our shoes squeak when we tread on them. I was restive. All sorts of thoughts coursed through my mind. I had no idea what kind of state I would find Ali Agha in. We finally entered a two-bed room. There was a lady standing by his bed.

Hājj Sādeq and Hosayn Agha went forward and greeted and kissed the person resting on the bed. Mansūreh Khānūm then went forward and after saying hello, asked, "How are you, dear? Are you ok?"

I thought to myself, "Can that really be Ali?? He was a young man with a slight beard and mustache, a shaved head, emaciated, with a lifeless face. He didn't look like Ali Agha at all. Monīreh Khānūm stepped up too. I was the only one who was still standing at the foot of the bed, looking in stunned silence at someone who everyone referred to as "Ali Agha".

I was always someone who was easily taken over by my emotions, but at that point, I tried to control myself and remain calm. He was hooked up to an IV drip, and a catheter hose could be seen beside the bed on the floor. At that time, I was an eighteen-year-old girl, full of the spirit and verve of life. I was full of love for and devotion to a man who was my husband and in whose person all of my hopes and dreams in life resided. But after two weeks of making a life together in common, he was sprawled on a hospital bed like this, and I didn't know what I could do for him. I bit my lip so that I would not cry in front of the others. Just then Ali Agha's eye caught mine. He smiled and nodded his head, indicating that I should come closer. I was so upset and life weighed so heavily on me just then that I thought my legs could not bear to hold up my upper body. The room was swirling around me. I held onto the bedframe. Monīreh Khānūm was standing next to me and realized my state and took hold of my arm.

"What is it, Fereshteh? Are you not well? If you are not well, let's go get some fresh air."

I let her lead me, and I made my way dizzily out of the room. As soon as we were in the hallway, I could no longer hold back my tears and they came flooding out. The middle-aged lady who had been standing by Ali Agha's bed had followed us out. Monīreh Khānūm said, "This is Aunt Fātemeh, Mansūreh Khānūm's sister. She's Ali Agha's only aunt."

Aunt Fātemeh talked me down with such patience and calmness that I started to feel better after a while and we both made our way back inside the room. She sent everyone away and took my hand and brought me next to Ali Agha. She said, "Ali Jūn, did you see your wife, Fereshteh Khānūm?"

As soon as he saw me, he said, "What's the matter, Fereshteh Khānūm? Were you crying?"

I was surprised at how 'Zahrā Khānūm' became 'Fereshteh Khānūm' all of a sudden. I lowered my head and busied myself wiping away my tears with the tissues that Aunt Fātemeh had given me. Ali Agha asked again, "Well, what's the matter then, Zahrā Khānūm?"

Now I was crying and laughing at the same time. I said, "It's nothing. Are you ok?"

A special tranquility had come over him. He said, "I am well too, praise God."

He had one hand on his stomach and the other one on my head. I wanted to take hold of his hand, but then I remembered the condition that he had set. I opened some fruit juice for him instead. I wanted to hold the glass up to his mouth, but he took it with the hand that was on his stomach. The others had wandered to the window and were talking to each other. He had a few sips then gave the glass to me and said, "I don't feel like having any more; you have it."

Hājj Sādeq and Hosayn Agha and Monīreh Khānūm went to visit other veterans of the war who had been wounded and were hospitalized there. Mansūreh Khānūm and Aunt Fātemeh were busy talking at the window at some distance from us.

Ali Agha look at me with his kind blue eyes. "Fereshteh Jān, it was so good of you to come. It never occurred to me that you would."

I took courage and placed my hand next to his on the bed. He slowly brought his own hand next to mine and took hold of it and squeezed it. He smiled and we communicated a lot just then, just by looking into each other's eyes. I said, "The war has put a distance between us."

I then said, "What happens tomorrow is of no consequence. What is important is that you are feeling ok right now and that we are with each other."

There was a spiral-bound notebook on the amber-colored steel table next to us. He had drawn a landscape with a mountain, together with the sepulcher and dome of Imam Hosayn's shrine. I picked it up and looked at it. There was a flag at the top of the mountain. It appealed to me. I said, "You've drawn it so beautifully!"

There were names all around the dome. I started reading the names: Qāsem Hādī, Mossayeb Majīdī, Mohammad-Bāqer Mo'menī, Amīr Fazlollāhī, Mohammad Qorbānīān Movahhed, and Hasan Sarhaddī."

I asked, "Did you draw it?"

He nodded his head.

I said, "You draw so well!"

My encouragement seemed to have worked; he asked, "You want me to draw you something?"

Pleased with this, I took out the diary that I always kept with me from my purse and gave it to him. Ali Agha said, "Give me one of those flowers."

There was a bouquet of red and pink and white gladiolas in a vase on the table at the foot of his bed. I took out a stem. It was wet, and so I snapped off the stem and gave him the flower.

He bent his knees and brought his feet up and placed the flower between his two feet over the sheet and started to draw using a blue pen. He drew beautifully. He drew the gladiola with several fast strokes of the pen, and next to it he drew a candle and a butterfly. The butterfly had been shot with an arrow. It had fallen to the ground and a few drops of blood were oozing out from its wing. Under the drawing he wrote:

> The devotees [of God] all departed on the Path of Love;
> Make haste lest you be left behind.

He recited the couplet with a loud voice. I snickered and said in jest, "You've come to Tehran and become a full-bred *Tehrounī*, and so you've gone all lovey-dovey on me."

He chuckled and quickly crossed out the word "Love" and replaced it with "Death". Seeing the word Death upset me and I frowned. I said, "Do you have any other tricks up your sleeves? Other than upsetting me, that is."

He wanted to make me feel better. He gave me my diary and said, "Presented to my dearly beloved wife, Fereshteh Khānūm, the love of my life. Keep this as a memento from me, dearest."

I took the diary and said, "What if we stayed in Tehran, Ali? It suits you; you have become like a regular *Tehrounī*. 'Presented to my dearly beloved wife… Fereshteh Khānūm… the love of my life... dearest'. Of course, if you said, 'my love' instead of the country bumpkin 'dearest', it would have been closer to the mark."

He laughed a lot, and his laughter got me laughing too. He said, "When you entered the room, you looked like an angel (*fereshteh*); truly, the name Fereshteh becomes you."
I felt embarrassed. He tore out the drawing he had drawn for me and held it up to me. I put it in my purse. He put his hand back on his stomach. There was no watch on his wrist. I asked, "What happened to your watch?"

He said very nonchalantly, "One of the guys took a liking to it and asked to examine it, so I told him to keep it."

I got upset again. I said, "Ali, that was a wedding present! It had been purchased in Mecca. My poor father had picked it out with such attention and care. It was a genuine Rado!"

He shook his head and said, "Don't worry about the fate of material things so much. Think more about the life of the world that is to come, and win over the hearts of others with your acts of kindness and righteous deeds, as these are ultimately what you will take with you to your grave."

I didn't say anything, but I felt sorry for the loss of the watch. At nightfall, I wanted to stay in his room as the single nighttime companion that hospitals allow, but Hājj Sādeq said, "I'll stay".

Ali Agha wanted me to stay too, but there was nothing to be done, so we went to Hājj Bābā and Khānūm Jān's house, which was located in the neighborhood known as *Chāhār-rāh-e Kokā-kolā*.

I was very concerned about Ali Agha's well-being the first night I spent in Tehran. His operation went well and was successful, but his injury was a serious one. The doctors had said that he needed complete rest and plenty of it. I was anxious. I was concerned that he might get up and walk around and fall or have something else happen to him. I knew that Ali Agha was not as concerned about his own health and well-being as he should be. That night I prayed until the early morning hours, asking God to bring him back to health. Those days coincided with Tāsūā and Āshūrā.[75] I remember going and standing on the sidewalk and looking at the processions of the men flailing their chests (*sīneh-zanī*) [as a symbolic gesture of commiseration with the suffering of Imam Hosayn and his retinue, as well as a ritual form of redemptive suffering]. I remember covering my face with my *chādor* and wailing as loud as I needed to. When my emotional and spiritual load was thus lightened in this way, I would uncover my face and ask the people around me to beseech God for my husband's recovery.

We stayed in Tehran for about a week in Khānūm Jān's house. Uncle Mohammad had recently come back from abroad on his own and without his wife and kids. He said that he had come to stay indefinitely. Maryam lived in the same alley, on the second floor of her mother-in-law's house. We spent most of the mornings together, and went to the hospital during visiting hours

---

[75] Āshūrā: the tenth day of Moharram; the day on which Imam Hosayn was martyred. Tāsūā is the day before Āshūrā and is another important day of mourning and commemoration in the Shi'a spiritual calendar.

in the afternoons. When I went to visit Ali Agha, I wouldn't budge from his bedside; and I only wished that I could spend the nights with him too.

After a week Hājj Sādeq insisted that we return to Hamedān, which we did, even though I wanted to stay and Ali Agha was ok with my staying as well. Several times he whispered to me, "Stay, Fereshteh." But none of us dared to contradict Hājj Sādeq.

The day we returned to Hamedān was the 28th of Shahrīvar (August/ September). I was deep into my own thoughts the whole way: I didn't talk to anyone, nor did I have anything to eat. I felt a part of my body was left behind in Tehran. I was sick with worry, loneliness, and the sense of being away from him. I don't know what had gotten over me all of a sudden, but I couldn't stand being away from Ali Agha. It was a strange feeling. I hated myself and cursed myself. I felt as if someone had placed their hands on my throat and was squeezing it. For the life of me, I couldn't get myself to calm down and relax. I had the butterflies. I kept thinking, "Why did I leave Ali Agha alone? Why?? If only I had shown some courage and not stood on ceremony, I would be with Ali Agha now." I felt a little better by the time we arrived at Hamedān. I would curse myself a thousand times a day. Why did I come back? Why did I not stay by my husband's side? Was Ali Agha not my husband, after all is said and done? Who was closer to him than me? Why did I not insist on staying? These thoughts were slowly driving me to distraction and making me physically ill. I had lost weight. My anxiety had turned into heart palpitations. My prayer rug was open on the floor in the direction of the Ka'ba in Mecca 24 hours a day, and I was constantly in a state where I was either offering my ritual devotions, or I was praying to God for help, or I was invoking His Blessings on Ali Agha by way of *zekr* (the invocation of God and His blessings by the ritual or formulaic repetition of phrases).

On the 9th of the following month, *Mehr*, the news reached us that Ali Agha's friends had brought him home. I was in my mother's house. I packed my bag and ran over to our own house. Ali Agha's friends had brought him over. We laid out a bed for him and put him to sleep. He had two crutches under his arms. Seeing those two crutches made the world spin around my head. I thought, what if Ali Agha will never be able to walk again? After I came home, Ali Agha's friends said their goodbyes and left. The first thing I did after I closed the front door was to fold back the corner of his blanket, and then I breathed a sigh of relief. I don't know why I was concerned about his legs; but by the grace of God, both his legs were whole if not healthy.

That same day, Mansūreh Khānūm and Agha Nāser and Amīr Agha and Hājj Sādeq and Monīreh Khānūm and Leylā all came to see Ali Agha and stayed with us. From the following day onward, visitors and guests streamed into our house to visit Ali Agha and see how his health was improving; from the Commander in Chief of the *Sepāh* or Revolutionary Guards Corps to corporate executives and regular office workers, to the Friday Congregational Prayer Leader [of Hamedān], to the Commander in Chief of the Army.

Monīreh Khānūm was an ideological educator (*morabbī-e parvareshī*), and because it was early in the month of *Mehr* [(which is the start of the school year)], she would go to school every day. And Āghā Nāser would go to his car wash every day, which was at the beginning of the road to Malāyer, past the Bāgh-e Behesht cemetery. That left me and Mansūreh Khānūm and Leylā, Monīreh Khānūm's daughter. As well as Ali Āghā, of course, who was bed-ridden, and Amīr Āghā, who was on a leave of absence from the *Jehād*.[76] Every morning Amīr Āghā would take a long shopping list that we women had prepared and go to the market to fulfill all of its items.

I was Ali Āghā's private nurse; as was my wont. I would take him fruit juice and *fālūdeh* and fruit cooked and preserved in syrup (*compote*) at a fix hour in the morning between breakfast and lunch, and would sit next to him at lunchtime and make him have his lunch, which included rice with chicken or braised lamb shank. If he didn't have an appetite or did not eat his meal, I would take the food away and bring it back ten times until I would finally take an empty tray in triumph back into the kitchen.

The days of Ali Āghā's convalescence were arduous but sweet. Amīr Āghā was usually home so that he could attend to any guests who showed up. As for me, I was running around with a dozen chores to do from the moment I awoke for the pre-dawn ritual devotions to the time I went to bed at night. The times when I took Ali Āghā his food, or when I sat next to him to give

---

[76] It is not clear which *Jehād* is referred to here; it is most probably either the Education *Jehād* (or Drive), or the Farming and Agriculture *Jehād* (or Ministry of Agriculture).

him his medications, was when I was able to rest a little. At night, I made my bedspread below his feet, in such a way that I would be awakened as soon as he moved about. I loved nursing him; it fulfilled me and made me feel whole.

Ali Agha's health gradually started to improve. Now he was able to meander about in the house with the aid of his two crutches, even though he usually relied on my hands and shoulders. Those days went by like greased lightning. They were good days; they were days in which Ali Agha and I were at each other's side and talked to each other to such an extent that it made up for the allotment of many years.

On the 17th of October, 1986, one of the crutches was set aside in a corner of the room. Ali Agha donned his *Sepāh* uniform and made his way toward the stairs. No matter how much Mansūreh Khānūm and I pleaded with him not to go down the stairs, our pleas fell on deaf ears. And Amīr was not home to help him down the stairs either, worse luck. He made his own way down the stairs and was gone for a few hours, after which he returned. He asked for his duffle bag, and no matter how much Mansūreh Khānūm and I pleaded with him again not to leave and to give himself more time to recover, he would not listen.

That same day, he made his way to the warfront with the aid of a cane. And with his departure, everyone else said their goodbyes one by one and left also. That big house which had been witness to the comings and goings of so many guests and visitors, suddenly fell silent and felt lonely. No one could stand being in the house for a minute without Ali Agha's presence. I packed up his bedding and stored it away with tears in my eyes. I kissed his crutches and placed them inside the wardrobe. I packed my bag, locked the door behind me and made my way to my Mother's house.

On the Twelfth of Dey, [(January), about three months later,] Ali Agha returned, full of joy and happiness. I hadn't ever seen him so happy and excited before. He would have taken flight had it not been for his feet keeping him down. He said, "We're going to go and see the Imam [Imam Khomeini] with the boys."

We looked at him with so much envy and desire. Mother pleaded, "Ali Agha, can you make it so that we can come along too?"

This was everyone's desire, even though we knew that it was an impossible request. He left [for Tehran] on a Tuesday, and he returned on the Thursday of the same week, with high spirits. Everyone who was home greeted him by kissing his face. With Ali Agha's arrival and all of the wonderful stories that he had to tell, the atmosphere of our home was completely transformed. He kept on relating the tale, and we kept on interrupting him with our questions.

After dinner Mother gave me the duffle bag which I always had at the ready, and bid us farewell as we made our way to our own house. The alley was dark. It had snowed a lot and the street had iced over and was like a sheet of glass. I treaded carefully over the ice and made my way forward slowly. I was shivering from the cold. I slipped and almost fell a couple of times, and each time I was about to fall I grabbed hold of Ali Agha's arm. Even then I was aware of the arrangement that we were not to be seen to be too close together in public, and so as soon as I had steadied my step, I released his arm.

When we got home, Ali Agha was still all excited from his visit to Imam Khomeini, and so he said, "I don't know why I'm still hungry, Fereshteh. Will you make us something to eat?"

It had been more than two and a half months since I had locked the door to the house and left for my mothers'. I went into the kitchen, and he followed me in. I opened the cabinet doors quickly to see if I could find something to fix up. And then I went to see if there was anything in the refrigerator. I straightened up and stood next to the sink. Ali Agha was leaning against a cabinet with his hands between his back and the counter and was looking at me. He said with a special excitement in his voice, "Fereshteh, when we had our private visit with Imam Khomeini, one of the boys stepped forward and kissed the Imam's hand. When doing so, he had tried to take the imam's ring off his finger for its *tabarrok*.[77] He had managed to bring it out halfway, but not more. When it came to my turn, I first slid the ring back into its place, and then I kissed[78] the imam's hand. The imam cracked a smile and nodded his head in approval." He then talked about a few square meters of white cloth which he had taken with him and

---

[77] *Tabarrok:* the property of a relic or some mundane object which has been blessed or charged in some other way with sacral properties.

[78] The practice of kissing someone else's hand is considered to be harmless and even laudatory if it is for the purposes of showing respect for one's parents or for righteous *sādāt* (descendants of the Prophet), but is to be avoided in the case of people in positions of authority, inclusive of religious scholars.

which the imam had ran his hand over in order to charge it with *tabarrok* blessings.

The following night we were invited to Hajj Sādeq's house. Amīr and the others were there too. We cut up the cloth into about 150 small pieces which we divided between us. Ali Agha has a *tasbīh* or Islamic rosary whose beads were made from baked clay from the Plain of Karbalā. I don't know where he had gotten it from. It always had a pleasant scent. We cut its string and put a bead in each of the pieces of cloth. We folded the pieces of cloth into little parcels and placed them all in a plastic bag. Ali Agha wanted to distribute them to the members of his battalion as a souvenir from his visit to the imam. But before anything else, he gave Mansūreh Khānum's and my share to each of us: a piece of the cloth which had been charged with *tabarrok* blessings by the imam, and two beads from the *tasbīh* from Karbalā.

That night was Ali Agha's last night in Hamedān. He was due to leave for the front the following morning. I had packed his duffle bag, but I was still putting little things in it as I thought of them. Wherever I went, he would come after me. Eventually he said, "You move around so much, Fereshteh. Settle down for a minute; I want to speak to you."

I looked at him with surprise. He took my hand and we sat in the middle of the room, facing each other. He said, "If I ask you a question, will you [promise to] tell me the truth?"

My heart was pacing fast. I couldn't think what it was that he could possibly want to ask me about. I said, "Sure, go ahead. What's on your mind?"

He smiled and said, "I'm sure you have realized by now that I'm not one to wear my emotions on my sleeve."

I smiled and said, "That's for sure!"

Then it was his turn to smile. He said, "But this time I want to talk to you about what I am feeling in my heart of hearts."

I had no idea what he was trying to get at. I looked with surprise into his blue eyes. He said, "I'm going to leave tomorrow, but it will be hard for me to do so without you. I don't know why I have become like this!"

My heart was beating so fast that it was as if I could feel it pushing up against my throat. I was holding my breath and I had to force myself to breath. Was this really Ali who was saying these kinds of things? He always had difficulty expressing his feelings before. So what had happened now? He said, "Will you come with me to Dezfūl?"

Those days were the peak of Dezfūl's being the target of bombardment and rocket fire. But I became excited at the possibility. I took his hand in mine and said, "You scared me! I thought you wanted to say something scary! Well of course I'll come with you. Why not?"

A smile that was mingled with concern came to his face. He asked, "What about your father and mother? Will they not object?"

I breathed a sigh of relief and said, "I'm sorry, but am I mistaken in thinking that I am *your* wife? My fate is in your hands; and those poor souls will not object to your decision."

He said with that same tone of concern in his voice, "It's just that it is very dangerous there."

I became so happy at hearing this that I got up and started to pack my belongings without giving a second thought to the dangers of the area where I was heading toward. I said, "Is it not dangerous for you?"

He said, "We're different. Think about it seriously, Fereshteh."

I had opened the door of the wardrobe. I wanted to take a few sets of clothes. I asked, "What's the weather like over there?"

He said, "Its heaven! Like its spring."

I turned around and winked and said, "You clever devil; so you wanted to go to Heaven on your own, huh?"

He smiled and didn't say anything else. He got up too and we packed a few necessities overnight. Some pots and pans and plates and knives and forks and spoons and other kitchen utensils; as well as a suitcase full of clothes, Ali Agha's photo albums, and a few blankets.

And we packed up the rest of our belongings in moving boxes so that we could take them to Mother's house. We were at it almost until morning. Ali Agha had suddenly decided that we should vacate the house and return it to its owner. He said, "When we are away, there might be someone who might want to live here."

As we worked together, Ali Agha told me that a house had been given to him and his friend, Hādī Fazlī, in one of the developments around Dezfūl; and that Hādī and his wife and small child had moved into it a few days ago. We had stacked the moving boxes in the entryway. Dawn was only a couple of hours away. We made some room among the boxes and napped for a couple of hours.

When we woke up in the morning, we went and put all of our belongings in the small storage room at the top of the stairwell in my mother's house, as well as in the small storage room that was in the corner of her front yard. Ali Agha informed Mother and Father about our decision to go to Dezfūl. They received the news with no objections. Mother only emphasized that we should be careful and take good care of ourselves, and to call them when we arrived, and to stay in touch.

Ali Agha loaded all of the equipment and belongings that we were taking with us in the back of the khaki-colored four-wheel-drive SUV. Mansūreh Khānum was not in Hamedān. She had gone to Tehran a few days before the fifth of Dey, which was the day Monā, Maryam's first daughter, was born.

After saying our goodbyes to those who were in Hamedān, we got in the SUV and headed for Dezfūl. After we passed Ma'mūlān, Ali Agha put in a cassette in the car's stereo system which was a recording of revolutionary songs and elegies about the great men and women who were martyred in the cause of Islam and the Islamic Revolution. There was one song in particular which I liked very much. As soon as one side of the tape ran out, Ali Agha would flip it and play the other side:

> It is night and the visage of the homeland is dark,
> And it is a sin to sit idle in the face of darkness.
> Give me my rifle so that I can be on my way,

For anyone who is a devotee [of God and His laws] has been mustered.
Brothers in faith are restless; brothers in faith are burning [for justice].
The breast of brothers in faith are fields of tulips.[79]
The night is a dangerous stormy sea full of swell,
Which I am facing with my thoughts of purity.
Bring me a dagger and a shroud,
For blood spills out from passionate hearts.
My brother is but young; he is drowning in blood.
My brother's forelock is a [raging] volcano.
You who are familiar with the ache of the devotees,
You who are a fellow soldier and a fellow bondsman,
Look at the blood of our loved ones on the walls,
And blow the Trumpet of the Morning of Light.
My brother is but young; my brother is restless.
My brother's forelock is a [raging] volcano.

شب است و چهره ی میهن سیاهه
نشستن در سیاهی ها گناهه
تفنگم را بده تا ره بجویم
که هر که عاشقه پایش به راهه
برادر بیقراره، برادر شعله واره، برادر دشت سینه اش لاله زاره

---

[79] The tulip is used as an allegory of devotion because of its red color and the black color of its base which is thought of as the mark of a brand on the heart of the devotee which seals his or her devotion to God and to the ordinances of His dispensational order.

شب و دریای خوف انگیز و طوفان
من و اندیشه های پاک پویان
برایم خلعت و خنجر بیاور
که خون می بارد از دلهای سوزان
برادر نوجوونه، برادر غرق خونه، برادر کاکلش آتشفشونه...

Ali Agha sang along under his breath too: "My brother is but young; my brother is restless; my brother's forelock is…"

Ali Agha was right. That year, Dezfūl's weather was like Heaven on Earth. It was unbelievable. When we left Hamedān that morning, there was so much snow piled up on either side of the roads that at times the walls of snow were taller than the brick and mortar walls of the houses. Icicles hung from the gutters and eaves of the roofs, and it was so cold that one could not come out into the street without putting on a hat and gloves and a heavy overcoat. And then we suddenly went from a town that was iced over into Heaven itself. The weather was moderate and spring-like. The orange and lemon and bitter orange trees were full with foliage and were vibrant. Their green leaves delighted the eyes. The aroma of flowers filled the city streets. The smell of Eucalyptus was inebriating. The weather was so good that once we passed Khorram-Ābād we started to peel off our layers of clothing one by one. Unlike the people of Hamedān who were doubled over and hunch-backed from the cold, in Dezfūl, people were going about their business in tee shirts and short sleeved shirts, all bright eyed and bushy tailed.

I had imagined Dezfūl to be empty of residents, but this was not the case. The city was vibrant with the energy of life. Children could be seen playing in the streets, with the womenfolk standing at the front doors chatting. The streets were green with the leaves of trees and springtide verdure.

We passed several streets. Occasionally we would pass a house that had been destroyed by a bomb or missile, or would see bent steel columns and girders sticking out of a pile of rubble. Broken windows and spalled asphalt and pavement, streets marred by pock marks and holes, and decapitated palm trees told the bitter tale of the war.

We entered the Pānsad Dastgāh development and passed a few streets and alleys. The streets of this development were less crowded than the streets of the city proper. They had not yet been paved or even had any trees planted. We entered a side street. Ali Agha was still singing along with the song: "My brother is but young; my brother is restless; my brother's forelock is… And here is the Eleventh Rose Garden."

Then he came to a stop in front of the house and said, "My brother is restless; my brother's forelock is… And welcome to your new abode."

Would that we had not gone

When we entered the house, Agha Hādī and Fātemeh were busy arranging their belongings. Their things were stacked in the entryway and they had not yet settled in. The house seemed very chaotic and untidy. There was dust and dirt everywhere. I immediately thought that it needs a full and thorough cleaning. The following morning the men left and events took place which arose as a result of a mistake which I still regret and which came about as a result of my not thinking clearly, which in turn was due to my inexperience and naiveté. Two or three days after we arrived at Dezfūl, someone knocked on the door around ten o'clock in the morning. I thought it must be the factotum whom Ali Agha had mentioned would be calling. I put on my *chādor* and went to the door and asked who it was. The voice was unfamiliar. It said, "It's me, Ali Agha's assistant, Saīd Sedāqatī." He then said, "I've come to check to see if you need anything."

I said, "Ali Agha and Agha Hādī went to the front Saturday morning. They said they won't be coming back anytime soon."

Saīd Agha said with surprise, "I'm on my way to Ahvāz. My wife is in Ahvāz, together with Hājj Hosayn Hamedānī's wife, Mr. Bashīrī, and a few other households. Come and let us go there together."

I said, "But Ali Agha would be unaware of where we were. They could come back any time and worry about what had happened to us."

Saīd Agha said, "When I deliver you to Ahvāz, I'll go back to where Ali Agha is and tell him myself. But please hurry up. No good will come of your staying here."

As our fate would have it, the status changed to red right then and the sound of the air defense guns could be heard booming. Saīd Agha repeated with great concern, "Hurry up! Let's go!! I'll wait for you in the car."

I was undecided as to what to do. I related everything to Fātemeh, who said, "I think it's better that we go, Fereshteh. Honestly, when the status turns to red at nights, I get very scared. Let's go to Ahvāz; and when Hādī and Ali Agha want to return to Dezfūl, we will return with them."

That made my mind up and I started to pack up our belongings and pack our clothes. But I still did not have a good feeling. It was as if someone kept saying, "Don't go!"

Even today, when I remember those days and those events, I wish that we had not gone to Ahvāz with Agha Sa'īd; that we had not even been home to open the door for him. Then things would have turned out differently. But unfortunately, I had opened the door; even though I knew even then that I should have resisted the temptation, but I don't know why I didn't do so. I don't know why we even went with Sa'īd Agha when my heart wasn't in it. We got in Sa'īd Agha's Land Rover, and he began making his way to Ahvāz at speed. Throughout the journey, I was full of anxiety and I recounted each of my concerns under my breath to Fātemeh as we travelled south. Sa'īd Agha had become aware of my anxiety and said, "Why are you so worried? Don't worry yourself. I said that I will certainly be seeing Ali Agha today, and I will be sure to tell him of the move."

We finally arrived in Ahvāz. We went over the bridge on the Kārūn River. We passed by a few busy streets and a large hospital and stopped in front of an attractive detached house. Sa'īd Agha honked his horn a couple of times and then said, "If all the womenfolk are together in one place, our minds can rest better, assured that we have done everything we can for your safety."

Momentarily a woman who had on a white *chādor* with a flower pattern opened the door. I could see through her *chādor* that she was pregnant, and we later learned that she was Sa'īd Agha's wife. She greeted us and welcomed us and led us into the front yard. Unlike our house in Dezfūl, the house was very large and elegant and pleasing to behold, and its front yard was full of trees and raised soil beds which were full of plantings and flowers. There was a hammock in the middle of the yard as well. We bonded with Sa'īd Agha's wife very quickly, whose name also happened to be Fātemeh. I told her that I was concerned that

Sa'īd Agha would forget to tell Ali Agha and Agha Hādī about our move. She said, "Sa'īd forget? Impossible! Be assured that he will let your husbands know." Hearing this put my mind at rest a little. The house had many large rooms, and each family lived in one of the rooms. The kitchen and restroom were shared, of course. After a little time had passed, Hājj Agha Hamedānī's wife came and greeted us and welcomed us to the house. Her three children were next to her: Wahab, Ali, and Zahrā. Because Sa'īd Agha did not return that night, we spent the night in their room; although I could not sleep because I was so worried and anxious. I awoke for the pre-dawn ritual devotions with a great sense of anxiety. We were gathered around the tablespread for breakfast when the sound of the doorbell got me halfway on my feet. One of the ladies went and answered the door and came back into the room and said, "Fereshteh Khānum, Mr. Chitsāzīān wants to have a word with you."

I looked at Fātemeh and bit my lip and shook my head in self-reproach and quickly put on my *chādor* and ran to the door. Fātemeh could not stand the tension and followed after me. Ali Agha was standing behind the door looking well dressed and dapper. It was evident that he had been able to take a shower. Agha Hādī was beside him and looked anxious and annoyed. As soon as he saw Fātemeh, he bellowed, "Where have you been??"

Ali Agha didn't say anything. He was standing there looking at me without a word. I greeted him quietly and took his hand and said, "Come in. Have you had breakfast?"

He still didn't say anything. I couldn't breathe. I now realized why I had been so overcome by a sense of anxiety and foreboding. I said with trepidation and concern, "Didn't Agha Sa'īd tell you? He assured us that he would tell you."

Ali Agha glanced at Agha Hādī and said with surprise, "Who? Which Sa'īd??"

"Sa'īd Sedāqatī."

"No, we haven't seen Sa'īd since yesterday."

Instead of Ali Agha being irritated with us, I became upset but controlled myself so that I would not start to cry. Fātemeh Khānūm, Sa'īd Sedāqatī's wife, came to the door and invited the men to come inside. Agha Hādī and Fātemeh and Zeynab went into one room, and Ali Agha and I went into another. The house had plenty of empty rooms to spare. I was angry at myself for not having listened to what was in my heart. I knew that my heart never lied; I knew this from many first-hand experiences. I don't recall if I cried or not, but I do remember being very upset. I said, "I swear, darling, it wasn't our fault. Sa'īd Agha assured us that he would be seeing you and that he would tell you. I swear to God that if I knew that you would not be told, I would rather have my legs broken than leave without letting you know." I then started to implore him: "Ali, I beg of you not to be upset with me. I'm sorry. I apologize."

Ali Agha smiled and said, "You mean to say that I am upset now?"

Seeing his calm demeanor and smile gave me a new lease on life. I got up and happily went and got him some breakfast. The *lavāsh* flatbread of Ahvāz is slightly thicker than its

Hamedānī analog, and they are delicious when they are fresh and warm. I flew like a light butterfly back and forth, bringing him bread and tea and jam. But despite the fact that he didn't say anything and was eating his breakfast without a word, I knew that he was upset with me. I had gotten to know his ways over the last few months. When he was upset about something, he would go quiet and not speak. After he finished eating his breakfast, he got up and said, "We have to leave; we have a lot of work to do. You should stay here for now."

I did not say anything for fear of upsetting him. I was happy the episode had come to an end. I went into the hallway and said in a loud voice, "The ladies should not come out [unveiled]; the menfolk are leaving."

When Ali Agha and Agha Hādī left, I ran toward Fātemeh's room. She was in a bad mood. She asked, "What happened? Was Ali Agha cross with you too?"

"No." And then I asked with surprise, "Why? Did Agha Hādī say something to you?" Fātemeh was restless. She sighed deeply and said, "Hādī was very angry. He had a right to be too. It's just our bad luck… Of all the days that they could have chosen to come back home, they had to choose last night!"

I was stunned. I said, "Really? They went home last night??" Now it was Fātemeh's turn to be surprised. She said, "You mean to say that Ali Agha didn't tell you??" I shrugged involuntarily, after which Fātemeh started to recount what had happened.

"Our luck being what it is, they went home last night. As soon as they saw that the lights were not on and that there was no trace of us, the poor dears didn't dare to set foot into the hall. Hādī said, 'I would urge Ali Agha on, and Ali Agha would urge me on.' They thought that something must have happened to us. And the fuse had blown, for some reason. Well, they eventually reset the fuse with some difficulty and enter the house. On one hand, they were happy to see that nothing had happened to us in the house; and on the other hand, they sat in wait and began to worry as to where we were. They worried so much that they couldn't sleep. Eventually Ali Agha said, 'Fereshteh has family in these parts; maybe they have gone to see her folks.' They started to feel a little better with this thought, but because they could not sleep, they got up and started working on household chores. They took all of the bedding material and shook the dust out of them and laid them out. Hādī said that they arranged all of the blankets in a neat row around the living room."

At this point Fātemeh winked and said, "The best part is that they cleaned all the windows! Didn't you see how spic and span they were? They had become so dirty with sweat that they went and showered in the early hours of the morning."

Fātemeh recounted the tale with feeling and a special sense of excitement; and as she was relating the tale, and later too, I thought about why it was that Ali Agha hadn't told me any of these things and why he was able to conceal the fact that he had become so concerned. That event deepened my understanding of Ali Agha. It was then that I realized that he was not like the others. At least he was very different from me and the people around me. That incident changed the way I looked at him. Throughout the ten or so days that we spent in the house in Ahvāz, Ali Agha and Agha Hādī came to see us on a few occasions. But after that, they stopped coming over.

When we were in Ahvāz, we went to the bazaar with Fātemeh Khānūm, Sa'īd Sedāqatī's wife. We even bought some things for our house in Dezfūl. On most mornings, I would take Hājj Agha Hamedānī's kids into the front yard and give them rides in the hammock. But that day it was only by God's grace that the kids were asleep and I went into the yard and sat on the hammock alone. I suddenly heard the sound of an airplane. It was flying at such a low altitude that I knew at once that it was an Iraqi warplane. It was a scary-looking black Mig. I don't know what kind of power God had given me at that moment, but even though I was very scared, as soon as I saw two missiles separate from the airplane and start coming towards me, I got up from the hammock and started to run at such an incredibly fast speed toward the wall that later on I couldn't even believe what I had done. I placed my hands on my ears and opened my mouth and started to recite my *ashhad*.[80] I could see the missiles coming right at me. I was waiting for everything to explode and for my body to be torn to shreds or into a thousand pieces.

The sound of bombs falling behind me shook the ground and time stood still and everything went dark. A pall of dust and smoke filled my eyes, and the smell of sulfur filled my nostrils and throat. I breathed with difficulty. It seemed that the bombs

---

[80] This is the testimony of faith which all Moslems recite if they feel that their life is in danger and that they are about to enter into the *barzakh*, which is the domain one's soul enters between death and the Resurrection.

exploded a few hundred meters from where I was. Then I realized that the target of the raid was the Golestān Hospital which was located behind our house. There was a terrible stench in the air and the heat was suffocating. I don't know how I was able to escape that terrible plight. When all the dust had settled and I was able to look around, I saw that there was a great amount of large and small shrapnel and projectiles spewed all over the front yard in front of my feet; but thank God none had hit me.

That same night I dreamed that Ali Agha was wounded in the waist. I woke up from the nightmare and could not go back to sleep until the morning. I was overcome by a sense of dread that night. I told everyone about my dream in the morning. I couldn't eat any breakfast, no matter how hard I tried. I was restless and couldn't settle down. I went from the kitchen to our room, and from there to the front yard and back. A little later, Agha Hādī and Agha Sa'īd came, without Ali Agha. Right then I knew that my dream was true, and that this was the reason for my sense of dread. But no matter what I did, they didn't tell me the truth of what had happened.

What they said was that there had been a communique over the wireless from Headquarters where they had asked for Ali's presence in a meeting, and that Ali Agha had gone to Hamedān. Then they said in unison, "And we want to go to Hamedān also; you should come with us too."

I knew something had happened and that all this dissimulation had been planned. But despite this I said, "No, I won't come. That one time that I left with Agha Sa'īd without telling Ali Agha was enough." Agha Sa'īd said with irritation in his voice: "This time it's different. We were with Ali Agha just now. He sent us to you himself. He was in a hurry and had to leave with a few others ahead of us."

I said, "Agha Sa'īd, that's exactly what you said last time. You said that you would be seeing Ali Agha for sure that day. Do you remember? There is no way that I am going to step foot outside of this house without Ali Agha."

When they were confronted with this position, they started begging and pleading with me. And then when they realized that I was not going to pay any heed to their entreaties, they started to plead with Uncle Mahmoud. An hour later, Uncle Mahmoud came over with Mohammad Khādem, a friend of Ali Agha's, and repeated the same words: "We want to go to Hamedān; you should come with us too."

I said, "Swear on your own life, Uncle: has something happened to Ali Agha?"

He said, "I haven't lie to you. I said he had an urgent meeting and he had to go to Hamedān."

Additionally, the ladies of the house came over and insisted that I go to Hamedān with Uncle Mahmoud. They even help me pack my bag. And so, when I saw that the situation had changed like this, I thought it best for me to get to Hamedān, and the sooner the better. We got into Mohammad Khādem's Land Rover. Uncle Mahmoud came along too. He sat in the front with Mohammad Khādem, who was driving, and I sat in the back.

When we got in the car, I asked Uncle Mahmoud to stop by Dezfūl on the way up so that I could pick up some of my clothes. It was only when we arrived there that I realized that I hadn't brought the keys to the house with me. Uncle Mahmoud had to climb the wall. He opened the door to the front yard, but I didn't have the key to the house either. Uncle Mahmoud climbed onto the roof of the house and somehow made his way down the light well in the back of the house, found the suitcase that contained my clothes and brought it out with great difficulty.

We were on the Pol-Dokhtar Road when suddenly Mohammad Khādem said, "Look over there: an Iraqi Mig!"

It was true. An Iraqi Mig was tailing our movement on the road at a very low altitude. Mohammad Khādem said, "Sit tight!" He then put his foot on the pedal and speeded through the winding path of the Pol-Dokhtar Road as fast as he could. The Iraqi Mig had seen us and started to lower his altitude even further down, so that he was flying exactly over us.

I was so scared that I was holding onto Uncle Mahmoud with both hands from the back of his seat. The car swerved so much at every turn that we thought the car would turn over at any moment and fall into the valley, or alternately, that we would hit the side of the mountain. The Mig was so low that we could see its pilot. The puttering sound of the jet's machinegun fire made me even more scared. The bullets would hit the pavement, the mountains, and the small rocks on the shoulder of the road, and would ricochet back towards us. Mohammad Khādem drove like a racecar driver, and thanks to our good fortune, there were no other cars on the road. If there were, we would surely have run into them before the Mig could have done us any damage.

What I prayed for in those frightful moments was that if Ali Agha had been martyred, that God should martyr me too so that I could join him. This thought gave me peace. I let go of Uncle Mahmoud's seat, rested my head back on my seat's headrest, and started to recite my *shahādatayn*, oblivious to the fact that martyrdom requires one to be blessed with good fortune. And that is undoubtedly why the Mig overtook us before too long and changed course and disappeared behind a mountain. Uncle Mahmoud said its target was the power plant.

We arrived at Hamedān that evening. A black pall of smoke had blackened the sky. Unlike Ahvāz whose spring-like weather had already arrived, and where the trees were green with foliage and where we had even planted some seeds for garden greens in our little garden, Hamedān was cold; it was as if we had come to Siberia. The trees were bare and bent over under the weight of snow.

Khādem brought the car to a stop and asked someone what had been hit. The man answered, "They hit the oil storage facility and the Darvīsh-Ābād gas station four days ago. There was a small bus full of passengers at the gas station which went up in flames, martyring all the passengers."

I was astonished. That meant that the oil storage containers had been burning for three or four days! From the 30th of Dey until now.

The man said, "There have been around four or five hundred injuries, and about fifty or sixty martyrs."

Because the weather had been so nice in Ahvāz, we had forgotten to wear warm clothes. Uncle Mahmoud said, "By the way, do you know what happened, Fereshteh?"

Suddenly my heart froze like the icicles in the street. My teeth started chattering harder against each other. I felt as if my blood had frozen in my veins. When Uncle Mahmoud saw that I was not responding, he said, "Ali Agha..."

But I didn't let him finish his sentence and interjected, "Was martyred??!"

Mohammad Khādem turned and faced me and said, "No, Hājj Khānūm. No, I swear to God that Ali Agha has not been injured."

I was so agitated and upset that if you had stuck a knife in me, I would not have bled out. I yelled at them, "Enough! Stop lying to me!! I told you that I had had a dream last night, didn't I? I knew that something has happened to Ali Agha. Why are you playing mind games with me?! Why didn't you tell me the truth in Dezfūl? Why did you mess with my mind all the way from Ahvāz to here? Just stop the car right here; I want to get out!"

Uncle Mahmoud tried to calm me down. "Listen, Fereshteh Jān. We didn't tell you on purpose because we didn't want you to be upset all the way from Ahvāz to Hamedān, and start to imagine the worst case. I swear to God that Ali Agha is ok. He sustained an injury and is in a hospital in Shīrāz."

I said, "I want to get out of the car." Khādem turned in to the street my mother's house was on. Uncle Mahmoud was very upset. He said, "Fereshteh Jān. Please forgive us. I swear to God, we did this for your own sake!"

As soon as Khādem stopped in front of Mother's house, I pulled the door handle and opened it. Mother was waiting behind the door; it was as if she knew we were coming. As I was getting out I said, "You were very wrong to play with my emotions like that for such a long time." Then I slammed the door on them. Mother ran to me. I embraced and kissed her. She smelled wonderful, as always; and her embrace calmed me down.

I complained to her about how Uncle Mahmoud had treated me: "They think I'm a kid or something; like I don't have the constitution to take bad news. They didn't tell me that Ali Agha has been injured. They said he has some meeting he needed to go to. But I knew; I had a dream about it last night."

Mother stroked and kissed my head. She said with kindness in her voice, "It's ok, dear. Amīr Agha told us that it is not serious. Ali Agha is very strong, praise God. He'll recover soon."

The nature of the injury was that he had been shot by a bullet which had ricocheted into his side and lodged itself in his chest in a way that the doctors couldn't extract it. The following week, Ali Agha went to visit his friends at the Veteran's Hospital in Tehran with the bullet still lodged in his chest. From there he made his way to Hamedān, after which we picked up a few belongings and went back to Dezfūl.

Pink and Purple Curtains

When we went back to Dezfūl together after an absence of about a month, I promised myself never to leave his side. It was the Bahman (January/ February) of 1987. The day we arrived back in Dezfūl, Ali Agha bought a few kilos of chicken and said, "Fereshteh, make a tasty dish for the occasion of a meal before an operation. We have to get back to the front after lunch."

I got busy skinning and cleaning the chicken and marinating it in turmeric powder and plenty of chopped onions, after which I put the pieces in the pressure cooker on the stove and set it to cook on a high flame. Agha Hādī and his family were in their own room. Not thirty minutes had passed when I heard a frightful explosion from upstairs. It shook the whole house. At first I thought we had been hit by a bomb. Ali Agha and Agha

Hādī ran up the stairs barefoot, and Fātemeh and I ran after them.

The pressure cooker was no longer on the stove. Its lid had fallen off to one side, and the pot itself was on the other side of the kitchen. The pieces of chicken and the greasy yellow liquid from the pot were all over the walls and ceiling and floor of the kitchen. I lowered my head with an overwhelming sense of shame. Ali Agha had a big smile on his face as he gathered the pieces of chicken and placed them into his mouth with a childish grin. He picked up the pressure cooker pot and said as if he had found some hidden treasure, "Thank God there's still a little chicken in it!"

We ended up eating what little chicken was left, and ate it with great gusto.

Life in Dezfūl was very different for someone such as myself who was born and raised in an area that had cold winters. It was the very beginning of those days. Fātemeh and Zeynab and I were in the downstairs rooms, which is where we slept, and our husbands were not present. I had just woken up and was putting the bedding away. Just as I picked up my mattress, Fātemeh let out a short shout which woke Zeynab up. There was a frightful black insect under my mattress. It had two long calipers and eight ugly legs and a tail which bent forward like a bow back over its body. Fātemeh grabbed my forearm and said, "It's a scorpion!"

I had heard the name 'scorpion'; and I even knew that the venom of its sting is deadly like some snake venoms are. Fātemeh took a couple of steps back out of fear and precaution.

I said, "Don't worry. This region is full of scorpions; they live in warmer climates. If you don't bother them, they won't hurt you."

Fātemeh said, "We should kill it."

Calmly, I said, "If you kill this one, what are you going to do with that other one over there?" And then I pointed to the baseboards and to the corners of the room. When we examined the room, we found three or four more scorpions. Fātemeh was more concerned for Zeynab's sake. I said, "Don't worry. They'll go away themselves. Scorpions come out of their lairs at night looking for food, but go back to hiding under cricks and in nooks and crannies during the day."

I bent over and picked up the mattress and placed it in a corner of the room. Fātemeh was from Maryānaj, a large suburb of Hamedān city, and had been raised in the prairies and on the foothills of the great Mount Alvand. And so, after a little while had passed, she gathered back her senses. I got a broom and started to sweep the scorpions out of the bedroom. The dreadful scorpions ran away from the broom so fast that we couldn't figure out when or where they disappeared to. We didn't see them again throughout the day, but they showed up again at nightfall. I couldn't sleep for the first few nights because I was constantly afraid that there might be a scorpion under my blanket or on my pillow. As soon as I heard the slightest noise that resembled the possible movement of an insect, I would get up and switch the light on. But I soon got used to the idea and it became normal.

Every morning when I woke up and carefully gathered up my bedding, I would find a few scorpions who had made themselves a nice resting place under my mattress or pillow.

An Altar of Roses

Gradually the sight of scorpions became normal for me. Every morning I would pick up a broom and sweep them away; and I did this without a pother, although I never did get over my fear and loathing of them when I saw them.

One day Ali Agha and Agha Hādī came in and happily announced that we were to have guests over for dinner. Fātemeh and I thought that a couple or three guests would not be a problem. Shaped pasta such as Fusilli and Conchiglie, the seashell shaped ones, had just come on the market, and so we bought some of the twisty-shaped Fusilli and made a large pot of it with a generous portion of Bolognese sauce which we poured over the Fusilli. The dish had a nice color to it. It was a Friday, and the guests arrived at around eight in the evening along with their wives and kids. When Fātemeh and I looked to see how many there were from behind the window, we saw that there was a line extending from the front door, past which there were people already inside the house, through the front yard, passed the door to the yard. And the line kept moving forward, but it seemed that the line was never going to end. Ali Agha said a *yāllāh* and came in. As soon as he said his *salāms* I protested; "Ali Jān, you said 'a few' guests. You didn't say that you had invited the whole city of Dezfūl!"

Ali Agha smiled and said, "Don't be upset with me."

I said, "What do you mean, 'don't get upset'? We only have one pot of pasta. Come and take a look and see if it's going to be enough to go around!"

Ali Agha replied calmly, "No one is going to leave to find their diner elsewhere. Don't worry yourself; 'God provides the sustenance of guests'."

Meanwhile the guests had made their way in where the women had gathered around in the den and the men were sitting down in the living room, and Fātemeh and I were preoccupied with the question as to what we were going to have to do about feeding all these guests. No matter how we tried, we could not see how we were going to be able to feed so many people with one pot of pasta.

And so, we excused ourselves and went into the kitchen and grated all the potatoes which we had and broke the ten or twelve eggs that we had on hand and made potato and egg flans in three large pans. When it came time for serving dinner, we divided the pasta into several serving dishes. It looked very appetizing, especially at the bottom of the pot, which had become pan-fried and crisp in the *tahdīg* or 'bottom of the pot' Iranian style. The pasta was served to the men and the potato and egg flan was served to the women, together with tomatoes and pickled gherkins and other pickled vegetables and aromatic herbs.

After we had gathered up the dinner spread, the din of the men's voices could be heard in the den and it was evident that they were busy having a grand old time. And Ali Agha was the gang leader of the jokesters. I was sitting by the door and was positioned in such a way that I could see him through the gap in the door. He was acting like a conductor in a game where he went around the room and made everyone make all sorts of acrobatic movements, putting their bodies in all sorts of unusual and precarious positions, which made everyone laugh at their expense. The laughter and good fun were infectious and it got the women laughing along with the men folk. Everyone had a wonderful time that evening. When the guests left at the end of the evening, Ali Agha said, "See how everything worked out? Everyone had a great time and no one went home hungry."

I said, "That's easy for you to say. It was Fātemeh and I who were in a panic as to how to pull it all together."

Ali Agha said, "May God reward you. I'm sorry for having gotten you all concerned. The fact is that there is nothing to entertain the troops in the area, and so I figured the more the merrier. But I should have informed you."

The following day the thought occurred to us that if we were to live in this house and to have people over, we needed to make curtains for the house. And so Fātemeh and I set off for the bazaar and asked around to find a fabric store. The city was only half occupied because it was so close to the warfront. Most of the stores were closed, with the exception of those which sold the bare necessities of everyday living. And so, when we found a fabric store that was open, we bought ten or twelve meters of cloth: a pretty pink and white checkered pattern for the kitchen, and a flower-patterned fabric with a purple background for the living room. Our hearts were set on improving that house, and so we got to work on the sewing machine as soon as we got back. Zeynab had become tired, so Fātemeh put her to bed and started cooking. I sewed the living room curtains first. The living room windows faced the front yard and could be seen from the street and until then we had covered them with our prayer *chādors*. And so, when the curtains were ready and Fātemeh and I hung them up, they changed the look and feel of the whole house. A house's curtains and carpets are what give it the finishing touch and make it beautiful. We didn't have any carpets, but those curtains truly turned the house into a home. The curtains were purple with small yellow and orange flowers.

After the living room, it was the kitchen's turn. The kitchen's curtains brightened it up and changed its feel for the better. There was a large metal table to one side of the kitchen on top of which we had placed all manner of pots and pans and plates and cutlery, and beneath which we stored bags of potatoes and onions and cans of pinto beans and chick peas and lentils. I sat behind the sewing machine and worked it to make a large table cover with an apron large enough to cover the table's legs. And I sewed an elastic band around the perimeter, working some pleats in, to keep it from sliding out of place. I prepared the table with Fātemeh's help and placed the table cloth over it and neatly arranged all of the various kitchen utensils under it. The best part was that all of that stuff was now covered and was stored away out of sight. I also sewed a pretty apron for the kitchen sink which did not have a cabinet to rest on. And I used that same checkered cloth to make a tablecloth and some kitchen towels. The cloth added a lot of color to the house and all that color lightened our spirits and made us all excited to see the change. We would go out of the room and come back and look at our handiwork. We would stand in the living room and say, "It's so much better! It's so beautiful! ..." And then we would go to the kitchen and say, "Ah, that's so much better... now it looks like a proper kitchen!" I made some pot holders and hot pads and such with the rest of the fabric, and hung them on the kitchen wall.

After our home improvement project for the upstairs was finished, we went downstairs. We agreed that each of us would work on our own respective rooms. I found an empty cardboard box in the street and placed it in the corner of the room in lieu of a table. I placed Ali Agha's photo albums inside it to weigh it down and stabilize it, and covered it with a piece of the living room fabric. I had brought a table cover from Hamedān with me which I had embroidered with white silk thread. The center of the table cover had several white swans which stood out as if embossed as I had filled them with cotton. The swans had red beaks and were spreading their wings. Crocheting had become all the rage and most teenage girls and women had taken it up as a pastime. I placed the table cover on the cardboard "table". I dusted and swept the room. And on the following day I went out with Fātemeh and Zeynab to the bazaar and we bought a tableware set. And we busied ourselves in this way on various home improvement projects for the next few days.

One night when the lights were all on and we were busy cooking in the kitchen, Ali Agha and Agha Hādī had seen the new curtains from the street. The curtains were even more beautiful when they were backlit like that. They had become really excited to see the beautiful colors of the curtains of the living room and kitchen, and Agha Hādī had said to Ali Agha, "Look! Our home has curtains now. And what beautiful curtains they are!"

Pink and Purple Curtains

When Ali Agha and Agha Hādī entered the house, they were really surprised to see the beautiful way in which the house had been transformed. They got really excited and would go from one room to the next to take in the changes. That evening the two of them were tired and covered in dust as usual, and went to sleep right after dinner. Fātemeh and I took advantage of the opportunity and went to the front yard and cleaned and polished their boots to a high shine, and then washed their army uniforms. The two of them were very surprised when they saw their uniforms hanging on the washing line and saw their boots had been cleaned and shined.

Around that time, Fātemeh and I had both started to miss seeing our families. There was a gentleman by the name of Mr. Bakhtiārī who was a colleague of Ali Agha's and who used to pay us a visit every other day to see to our shopping needs. He rang the doorbell that morning and, as if we had been given a godsend, Fātemeh and I quickly said that we wanted to go to the communications office so that we could call home long-distance.

The communications office was located in the center of town and was always crowded. We had to wait for an hour for our turn in a large hall that had several telephone booths. There were a few rows of wooden benches which were mostly occupied by soldiers waiting to call home. Zeynab was fussing and had exhausted Fātemeh's patience when our turn finally came. I called our neighbor Sakīneh Khānūm and got her to rouse my mother and bring her to the phone with great difficulty, after which we talked at length and caught up. After we finished talking on the phone, we left and joined Mr. Bakhtiārī, who was waiting for us a little further up the street. As soon as we got to the car we heard the sound of the high-caliber machine-gun fire of the anti-aircraft batteries. The streets were not crowded. Fātemeh was holding Zeynab in her arms. Suddenly we heard the loud noise of several jets, after which the sound of successive explosions rocked everything.

I didn't know what to do. Fātemeh said, "Let's cross the street." But as soon as I started to cross the street my eyes were filled with dust and smoke. It had turned dark everywhere. I couldn't see a thing. But I could hear people screaming and groaning. In the middle of that dust and smoke, I was hit with a heat-wall and saw a large red-hot piece of shrapnel coming toward me. I don't know what kind of supernatural powers God had given me just then, but I was somehow able to duck and fall to the ground to avoid it. I heard the sound of the shrapnel as it crashed hard against the wall of the store that was behind me and made a hole in the wall. All of this took place in the span of a few brief moments. I had lost sight of Fātemeh. I called out to her, "Fātemeh, Fātemeh…"

I heard the sound of another large explosion from further afield. It was a frightful moment. I could hear the sound of shrapnel buzzing past my ears like so many locusts attacking a field. Ali Agha had told me to lie flat on the ground in such an event, and so I lay down on the hard pavement of the street and put my hands over my ears and opened my mouth. Throughout all this time, I kept thinking of Fātemeh and Zeynab. After a while, things started to quiet down a little. I looked up and saw Mr. Bakhtiārī's car through the dust and haze. I got up and ran doubled over and threw myself in the back seat of the car. Fātemeh and Zeynab joined us at just about the same time. I picked Zeynab up with tears in my eyes and kissed her. Fātemeh closed the car door and asked with fear and dread in her voice, "Fereshteh, are you ok?"

I was fine. I held Zeynab's head to my breast and could hear her heart beating fast like that of a small bird's. We had a very bad freight that day, but we decided not to tell our husbands about it so as not to worry them. When the men were present, we didn't miss anybody or pine for home; but as soon as they would leave, our pining for home and other company would start. Once when they were heading back out to the front I said, "Ali Jān, I miss Hamedān a lot."

He asked, "Hamedān or Hamedānians??" I smiled and said, "You know what I mean."

Ali Agha came back the following night and said excitedly, "Fereshteh, put your *chādor* on. You have company! Its family."

Surprised, I asked, "Family? Which one?"

He smiled and said, "Weren't you missing the 'Hamedānians'?"

I put on my *chādor* and went to the front yard. Ali Agha winked and said, "Here you go: I present to you, your cousin!"

He had brought Vahīd, Uncle Bāqer's son, whom he had found on the front. Vahīd had gone forward and greeted him and introduced himself, making it known that he was family. And Ali Agha had taken him by the arm and insisted that he must come to dinner that night to our house, saying that I was missing my family and that it would cheer me up.

And it really did cheer me up. Vahīd and I started chatting, taking turns exchanging stories.

"Vahīd, do you remember the kinds of mischief we got up to when we were kids?"

Vahīd smiled and said, "Do you remember how naughty I was as a kid?"

When Ali Agha saw how busy we were exchanging reminiscences, he spread the table spread himself and brought out the dinner; and then picked up all of the plates and such and took them to the kitchen. When I heard the sound of the plates and pots and pans being washed, I felt sorry for him as I figured he must be tired, and so I got up to go and wash the dishes myself. But he wouldn't let me. He said, "What do you mean? Weren't you just now pining for the company of family? Go back and talk to your cousin; it'll make you feel better."

But I didn't go back and helped him with the dishes instead. When I went back to the living room, I saw that Vahīd had fallen asleep without any bedding in the corner of the room. I felt so bad. I felt sorry for him. I wanted to wake him up and make a bed for him, but Ali Agha wouldn't let me. He said, "Let him be. Let him sleep. These soldiers have slept on rocks and stones so much on the front that they are used to it. So for Vahīd it is as if he is sleeping on a bed of goose down in the Hilton Hotel!"

Pink and Purple Curtains

I still couldn't bear to see him sleep like that. I said, "Ali Jān. He's a guest in our house. Think, if his mother was here, would she let him sleep without any bedding?"

I placed a blanket over him and gave Ali Agha a pillow to place under his head.

For us Hamedānīs, Dezfūl weather started to get too warm from the middle of March onward, to the point where we started using the swamp cooler[81] from then on. The men had found a beat-up old swamp cooler and welded a stand for its housing to the metal window frame of the bedroom. Its sheet metal duct wound its way through the house like an endless serpent. When things were all quiet at night is when we realized what a horribly loud and unbearable racket it made! It would take us several hours to get used to the noise and be able to fall asleep.

One morning when I had woken up to make my predawn prayers, I was taken aback as soon as I opened the front door to the yard. Ali Agha was sleeping on the patio, without a mattress or any covering. He had placed his boots under his head and was sleeping in a fetal position. I was surprised, as he had come back early. My heart went out to him. I bent over and shook his shoulder.

"Ali? Ali Jān? Wake up, why are you sleeping here?"

Ali Agha woke and sat up. It was still only half-light. When he saw me, he smiled and said *salām* and asked how I was.

---

[81] A "swamp" cooler or evaporative cooler is a simple air conditioner that cools air through the evaporation of water-soaked fibers or cellulose that air is drawn before being distributed throughout the house.

"Why are you sleeping here?" I asked.

He picked up his boots to set them to the side and a scorpion ran away toward the wall. He said, "I knocked on the door last night, but you were fast asleep."

I asked, "Didn't you have your key on you?"

He said, "I thought that Fātemeh Khānūm might be sleeping in the living room; it wouldn't have been proper for me to just barge in unannounced."

I sat next to him and took his hand in my own and said, "I'm sorry. It must have been the noise of the swamp cooler. I didn't hear you. Were you able to get some sleep?"

He said, "As a matter of fact, I slept fine, because I knew you were on the other side of the door. And I had some sweet dreams too."

Although Ali Agha had just gone back to the front that night and was not about to return very soon, we still didn't turn the swamp cooler on from that night on, just in case.

March came and went and it was New Year's Eve;[82] our first New Year's Eve together.

Our husbands had promised to be home for ushering in the New Year. That year, we were especially excited about spring cleaning and preparing the house for the New Year celebrations. Even though Dezfūl was in a war zone and was always on a red alert status, and the sounds of explosions could be heard every few hours near and far, we still felt good about the New Year

---

[82] The Iranian New Year is celebrated on the 21st of March (at the end of *Esfand*), on the Vernal Equinox.

despite all that. From early morning when we would wake up, we would start cleaning the house and scrubbing the walls and floors down and clean the windows so that they would sparkle and shine. We took out the carpeting onto the patio and washed the various pieces down with a broom and hose and washing detergent, and then hoisted them up to the roof with great difficulty to hang them to dry.

We washed the patio and the yard's walkways down and disinfected the WC in spite of all of the noise from the anti-aircraft machine-gun fire, and the bomb and rocket explosions. The house was filled with the smell of bleach and washing detergent; and there was not much time left before the New Year when the whole house became spic and span and smelled fresh.

When the spring-cleaning work was completed, I started arranging the *haft sīn*[83] spread. I laid the spread in the center of the living room, and would arrange any object that I thought was appropriate to the haft *sīn* spread on it: a Quran on its lectern, a timepiece, some coins, an apple, and so on. We didn't have any *sabzeh* or sprouted wheatgrass, despite looking to see if we could buy some somewhere within our development or even in Dezfūl proper. And so we thought to use some *sabzī* or aromatic herbs as a substitute.

---

[83] *Haft-sīn* is an arrangement of seven symbolic items whose names start with the letter *sīn* in the Persian alphabet. It is traditionally displayed at Nowruz, the Iranian New Year's Day, which is celebrated on the day of the vernal equinox, marking the beginning of spring in the northern hemisphere.

I took my shopping basket and stepped into our alley, but the greengrocers was closed, worse luck. And so, for the first time I took a stroll a few streets out. From a distance I saw a woman who was sitting in front of her door in front of a spread full of *sabzī*. I picked up my pace. She was an old woman wearing a black sleeved chādor and was wearing a black shawl in the Arab style. And she had a single blue dot tattooed in the center of her chin. I asked, "Is the *sabzī* for sale?"

She said, "Sure. How much do you want?"

"One kilo," I said, and held out my basket toward her.

She started to put her large and masculine hands under the herbs and bunched them together and placed them into my basket, filling it halfway. I said, "That's too much!"

The woman had a serious and fearless countenance. She held my basket toward me without looking up and said, "You can pay for a kilo's worth."

I didn't understand her meaning. I took some of the herbs that looked unfamiliar and said, "There are so many weeds mixed in it!"

The woman grabbed the leaves from my hand and, maintaining her serious frown, put them in her mouth and started to chew on them, saying, "*Parpīn* isn't a weed! *Parpīn* is good for stomach worms. It's a fever reducer and is effective against vomiting and nausea. It's good for the heart. It has a lot of good properties. And it is delicious with caramelized onions, dried mint leaves and fried eggs. Eat it and you'll see what it tastes like."

She spoke with a heavy provincial accent and I understood with difficulty that she was saying that these were not weeds but are herbs which have many medicinal properties. I later found out that the Hamedānīs call the same plant *khorfeh*. As I was counting out the money to pay her, the old woman kept on picking out the *khorfeh* and eating it! And so when I returned home, I gave an extended speech about the benefits of my new discovery.

But then Fātemeh said, "We Maryānjīs throw that stuff away, it's nothing but a weed!" And then she picked up some of it like the old woman but instead of putting it in her own mouth, she put it in mine! It was juicy and a little tart. It tasted new and different. I said, "It has a lot of medicinal properties. It's good for the heart, it's an anti-emetic, and a fever reducer. Who says it's a weed?!"

We had a good laugh and started to pick through and clean the *sabzī*. And contrary to our usual practice, instead of throwing the *khorfeh* away, we ate it with gusto both before and after having washed and disinfected it!

We placed the *sabzī* in a large platter and placed it on the *haft sīn* spread. Then we added the skins of some onions and some *sabzī* in two separate pots with a little water in each and let them come to a boil, and then placed a few eggs in each pot so that they would take on the color of the onion skins and *sabzī*. We didn't have any goldfish or any glass bowls to put them in. Nor did we find any in town. We had a glass saucer, in which we put some water and cut a red rose and placed it in it. We had bought a few sweets and chocolates and confectionary for the New Year, and we added these to the spread too.

We were very close to the New Year now. We put on fresh clothes. And we changed Zeynab into a nice set of new clothes, washed her hands and face, and tied her hair in two pigtails on either side of her face. She looked really cute. And then we sat next to the *haft sīn* spread and waited.

The more the moment of the new year's inauguration got closer, the more our worry and concern increased because we knew that from January onwards, the Karbala 4, 5 and 6 Operations would start. We were concerned for our husbands. We stood waiting behind the living room window until late. Fātemeh had pulled one side of the curtains aside and I had done the same on my side. We would get all excited when we saw a car coming into our street, but then when we saw it stop at another house and saw the wife of another commander open their front door with joy, we would let out a groan, let the curtain go, and slump back to our spot by the spread. But it would not be long before we both got up and repeated the same pattern over again.

The New Year was inaugurated and we were still standing behind the window, waiting. The lights of the neighboring houses started to go out one by one. We stayed up for a few hours past midnight, but our husbands didn't arrive. We left the lights on. We sat next to the *haft sīn* spread and waited for so long that our eyelids started to weigh down and close, and we gradually fell asleep right there.

It was Saturday, March 21st, 1987. We were half asleep when we heard the sound of the door opening. We got up and hurried to the window. They had come together, all dusty and disheveled and unkempt; but it was as if they had given us the world as a New Year's present.

Our first guests arrived all dusty and unkempt right with the dawning of the sun. They greeted us with smiles and *salāms* as soon as they entered the room. In a display of social ineptness, Ali Agha awkwardly put his hand in his pocket and took out a green colored bottle of perfume which he gave to me, saying, "Happy New Year!"

I was delighted with the gift as its timing couldn't have been better. We were all excited to be at home together; they even more than us. Seeing the *haft sīn* spread made them get all excited like little children. Ali Agha just stared at it for a long time. He was standing over it, counting the items one by one. "Ali Agha, too bad we couldn't find any goldfish," I pouted.

Ali Agha sucked in his cheeks, puckered his lips and started to open and close his lips like a fish. He said, "I'll play the part of the goldfish of the *haft sīn* spread. As a matter of fact, I just waded through a large fish farm on the way over here. So pardon me if I'm more of a smoked fish than a gold fish."

The two men sat down on the *haft sīn* spread with the same clothes that they had been wearing. We laughed and had fun as we caught up with each other's tales and thoughts, and had chocolates and sweets; and we sprinkled some rosewater on them too.

We went to the Imāmzādeh Sabzeh-Qobā shrine in the afternoon. The pilgrimage calmed us down and lifted our spirits at the same time. After that we went [on another pilgrimage] to

Shūsh, where the shrine of the prophet Daniel is located and felt even better when we were on our way back.

On Sunday, March 22st, 1987, we went to the Dez Dam – a wondrous and stunning dam set in a pristine part of nature with beautiful knolls and valleys. I was wearing blue and white sneakers with which I could climb the knolls quickly. Ali Agha enjoyed the spectacle; he said, "I always wanted my wife to be an outdoors type. I love the fact that you are active; don't change."

March finished and April arrived, bringing hot weather along with it. When the sun arose in the morning, it was as if the sun had fallen and landed on top of our roof. The sun came down very low so that it was very close to us and endowed the city with its abundant heat without a hint of parsimony. The walls radiated so much heat that it was as if they were on fire.

The swamp cooler banged away noisily from morning till night, but it was no match for the heat. The atmosphere was humid and suffocating. We hardly moved out of the living room, it was so hot. We had neighborly relations with our neighbors who were mostly like us in that they were from Hamedān and their husbands were also fighting on the warfront; but as soon as it got hot, we stopped visiting each other. I think everyone else had taken refuge under the registers at the ends of the ducts coming from their swamp coolers. And ultimately, each of these neighbors packed their belongings and went back to cooler climes.

Each day there would be some family who had packed all their belongings onto a moving van and who had come to bid us farewell. Zeynab had not been feeling well for a few days. She

Pink and Purple Curtains

was suffering from heatstroke and had bouts of vomiting and diarrhea. Nor was I in much better shape. I couldn't digest anything and could only take in water. Fātemeh had become a nurse to both of us, until the men arrived. As soon as Ali Agha saw the state I was in and as soon as Agha Hādī saw how weak and emaciated Zeynab had become, they both said, "Let's pack up and go to Hamedān."

I resisted because I didn't want to go back to Hamedān because I had come down to Dezfūl to be by my husband's side. I had come to live in Dezfūl. I said to Ali Agha: "This is where we live now. Where are we supposed to go to?

Ali Agha said, "You're not used to the weather here. It'll make you sick."

I said, "You will get sick too. And you are in the middle of the desert, whereas we at least have a swamp cooler."

Ali Agha was adamant about leaving. He said, "My conscience won't allow me to accept your suffering under this heat on our account. There's no telling where we will be posted next. In all likelihood, we will be posted to the western front, and if that happens, our minds will be much more at peace knowing you are in Hamedān rather than in Dezfūl."

I said with sadness, "What about *my* mind that will always be worrying about how *you* are doing? Won't you think of me too? What am I supposed to do? I've come here in order to fulfill what I consider to be my religious duty. I want to play a role in the war too."

Ali Agha smiled. "And you have fulfilled your duty admirably so far. You must forgive me, but in this way, our minds would be more at peace."

The more I insisted on staying, the more Ali Agha asserted his prerogative to move us back to Hamedān. I said, "At least let us stay here until you are posted to the western front." But he and Agha Hādī won out in the end, and so we packed up our belongings into moving cartons and loaded them onto a truck and returned the same way we had come down.

The day we left happened to be one of the days when the bombing of Dezfūl was at its worst. We passed a street and heard the sound of an explosion a little later, followed by a dense plume of smoke which rose up behind us. Ali Agha was flooring the gas pedal in an effort to get us out of the war zone as fast as possible. During the few times that I had come to Dezfūl, I had a good feeling about the place, and I was overtaken by a sense of worry and anxiety when we were leaving. I knew that being far from Ali Agha and having to wait in unfulfilled expectation for him meant that there were hard days ahead for me in Hamedān. I wanted to stay. And I thought that I should have resisted moving more than I had. My feelings only got worse when I heard Ali Agha and Agha Hādī talking about their return plans.

The eight-hour journey from Dezfūl to Hamedān went by for me like it was eight minutes. I didn't want to arrive at Hamedān, but we arrived there so fast this time.

It had rained in Hamedān prior to our arrival and the rain had cleaned the streets and the trees with their newly sprouted verdure. The air was fresh and the aroma of spring blossoms filled the air. The sky was covered with overlapping patches of cloud cover.

We unloaded our belongings and stored some of them in the small storage room at the top of the stairwell at roof level and the rest we stored in the small storage room in the corner of the front yard of my mother's house. Then we went to pay a visit to Mansūreh Khānum, who was not feeling well. Her kidneys were acting up again. At the same time, Ali Agha had been posted to the western front and had to be there on the fourth of Farvardīn (March/ April). The house was gloomy and did not have the same upbeat feeling that I felt in the past.

I could sense that Mansūreh Khānum had become more attached to Amīr Agha. Before Amīr Agha went to the warfront, he took care of all of my mother-in-law's needs and did all her shopping for her. But now that he had gone to the front, the house was quiet and eerily still and depressing.

Mansūreh Khānum missed Amīr Agha and complained about his absence. And she had a right to: Maryam was in Tehran busy with her new life and with raising her children. And Hājj Sādeq was occupied with the work at his office and with running his own life. And we were in the state that we were. Given these conditions, Amīr Agha's leaving for the front made things really difficult for Mansūreh Khānum. I felt sorry for Mansūreh Khānum and how lonely she had become. And so we decided that we should stay with her until we found a place of our own.

Ali Agha went back to the front on the following morning. The days rolled by one by one. I was not feeling well, and after some insistence on the part of Mansūreh Khānum, I went to the doctors. It was the ninth of Khordād. The doctor wrote up some lab work for me, the results of which I took to the doctor a few days later together with my mother.

Mother got excited when she heard the news. She took me to her own home so that she could "fortify me", as she put it. But I didn't stay for more than a few days at Mother's house because I had promised Ali Agha that I would stay with Mansūreh Khānūm. The night I went back to stay with Mansūreh Khānūm, Hājj Sādeq's family was visiting my mother-in-law's and the house was full of people. Ali Agha phoned that night too. I wanted to tell him the news before anyone else. I picked up the phone's earpiece and we greeted each other as usual. No matter how I tried, I couldn't get myself to break the news to him. Finally, I cupped my hands around the microphone and whispered, "Something important has happened. You put the questions to me about it and I will answer."

It seems as if Ali Agha was not in a situation where he could talk freely either. He dithered a little and then said, "Give me a hint."

I said, "It's something both of us like."

He said, "Hmmm... I don't know, give me another hint."

I said, "That's it; what else can I say? We talk about it together sometimes. It's something that you want..."

Agha Nāser cottoned on before Ali Agha did. He got up and said, "Let's go into the den and give Fereshteh Khānūm some privacy so that she can speak with her husband freely. Come on, let's go!"

I waited for everyone to leave the room, and then thought that I should give Ali Agha the news while my privacy lasts. I said cheerfully, "Ali Agha, you're going to be a father!"

I could hear Ali Agha's excitement over the phone. He paused for a short spell then said, "Seriously? That's great! It is a blessing. Is that why you were not feeling well, Fereshteh? Are you better now?"

I said, "I'm not feeling better, but its ok."

That night everyone heard the news. I think Agha Nāser had spread the word in a way that was appropriate to the situation. But no one mentioned anything to me about it. A few days later, I went to my mother's house and wrote a letter to Ali Agha. He responded to it quickly. He had told me to be sure and start a medical file for myself with a doctor.

I felt worse and worse with each passing day; and neither the visits to the doctor nor the medications which he prescribed did anything to relieve my condition. During this time, Ali Agha came to Hamedān a couple of times. He would stay for a few days, and then head back to the front.

Pink Lady

It was the 25th of June, 1987. I was staying at my mother's house, and I was not feeling well physically or emotionally. As usual, Mother spent her days in her sewing workshop with her activities in support of the soldiers on the warfront. Around noon, my cousin Vahīd came over to our house. He was clearly upset. Vahīd's coming over in that state of mind made all the bad thoughts and forebodings that existed in the world suddenly rush down into my head. I asked with great concern, "What's the matter, Vahīd? Has something happened? Tell me the truth! Has something bad happened to Ali Agha?"

Vahīd was so distraught, he couldn't speak. He said, "It's not good news, Fereshteh Khānūm. Ali Agha told me to break it to you gradually."

I said, "Hurry up and tell me. I can't take the suspense!"

He said, "Do you promise not to get upset?"

I said, "For the love of God, Vahīd, just spit it out!"

He said, "No one but Ali Agha knows. He said that you should go to your mother-in-law's house."

I said with concern and anxiety, "Are you going to tell me or not?! Please, Vahīd! Don't play around like this."

He said with tears in his eyes, "OK, I'll say it. Fereshteh Khānum, Amīr Agha has been martyred. Ali Agha told me to break it to you gently…"

He started crying before I did. I was just stunned. I didn't know what to do. I was in a state of shock. It was as if someone had hit my head with a sledge hammer. I felt dizzy and lost. What was Vahīd saying? Why was he crying? Why was it so hot in here?

I felt nauseous and ran to the bathroom. I vomited and kept thinking of Amīr, not being able to believe that he was gone. My head felt very heavy. I thought I must be dreaming. Could it be that Amīr was really dead despite his being so young?

The water from the faucet was cold. I bent over and held my face under the faucet. I needed to wake up from this dream, but I had never been so awake. I turned the faucet off and dried my face off. It had been about a month since Ali Agha had left for the front, but now he was back. And what a return it was! I dressed and left for my mother-in-law's house. Monīreh Khānum was there too. It was clear that she knew what had happened, but she didn't say anything. I greeted everyone in a state of emotional distress. Mansūreh Khānum was well; she was acting naturally, as if everything was normal. She obviously hadn't been given the news yet. Mansūreh Khānūm went into the kitchen to get me a sour cherry squash.

As she was preparing the squash, Ali Agha arrived with Agha Nāser and Hājj Sādeq. I had missed him. He went into the kitchen and kissed Mansūreh Khānūm. He had aged so much, and was hunched over with grief. Ali Agha and Hājj Sādeq both took their mother by her hand and went into her bedroom together with Agha Nāser. I could hear my heart beating. It was as if it had made its way up my throat. The atmosphere of the house was heavy and somber. I thought what a difficult task it was that Ali Agha had before him.

My heart went out to Mansūreh Khānūm. I was holding my breath and couldn't relax to let it out. I felt like getting up and leaving.

Suddenly the sound of Mansūreh Khānūm's wailing filled the room. She grieved and moaned and kept calling out to Amīr. Everyone knew that Amīr had a special place in her heart. Ali Agha came out of the bedroom. Mansūreh Khānūm's wailing got louder. She was saying things like, "My darling Amīr... my beautiful Amīr... Amīr, you were my heart and my soul, you were my life... All of my life went with you. My beautiful Amīr is gone! O God!!"

Mansūreh Khānūm's wailing broke everyone's heart. The depths of its sorrow seared my heart. I ran to Ali Agha with tears running down my face and asked, "Tell me the truth, Ali Agha, what happened?"

Ali Agha's eyes, face and throat had turned crimson, but he was not crying. He acted like he had just now seen me. He looked at me with a peculiar sadness and said, "My brother Amīr was martyred."

Mansūreh Khānūm ran out of the room and said, "Ali, Ali, wait. Tell me the truth. Where is my Amīr right now?"

Ali Agha was on the verge of tears. He opened his arms and embraced his mother. He caressed his mother's head and shoulders and whispered in her ear, "*Māmān*, be strong! Ask Her Eminence Lady Zeynab and Her Eminence Lady Zahrā for help. Implore God for His help and succor. You have to have forbearance, *Māmān*. Amīr is now next to the martyrs of the Plain of Karbalā, *Māmān*. Amīr pledged allegiance to Imam Hosayn and expressed his willingness to die in his cause. And we have to do the same. You, me, father, and everyone must pledge allegiance and express our willingness to die in Imam Hosayn's cause. Amīr has a high spiritual station with God; don't depreciate his achievement. Be as steady as a mountain. These are all nothing but tests. Don't cry for something which you gave up in God's cause. Be proud. Upon my word with God, today is the day that you become a true Moslem."

With those words, Mansūreh Khānūm calmed down a bit. Ali Agha faced us and said, "Try to quell your tears as much as possible. Hold your heads up high. Welcome Amīr's guests with dignity and pride. From this day forward, all of our actions are being carefully observed by the forces of the enemy. Do not show any weakness in yourselves."

Little by little, the rest of the family and friends and neighbors became aware of the news and started to come to my mother-in-law's house to pay their respects (both to offer their condolences as well as their congratulations on the occasion of Amīr's martyrdom). It never occurred to anyone that Amīr would be martyred so soon. Everyone was more concerned about Ali Agha who had been on the front from the beginning of the war. Mansūreh Khānūm was not well, but like the rest of the mothers of the martyrs, she tried to have forbearance and not to cry. Mother and Father and my sisters came over. Black banners were displayed on the walls of the apartment. A picture of Amīr was posted on the wall together with a black ribbon. Sorrow oozed from the walls of the house.

Some of the neighbors would go into the kitchen to help with making saffron squash with ice-water and to serve it with dates and *mishkā* halva. The house was filled with the aroma of pan-fried flour and halva. I was not feeling well; I felt delirious and weak. I wanted to retreat into a secluded place where I could sleep and have Amīr be back when I woke back up, so that I could see all of his kindness and verve for life once more. The Amīr I knew who used to wear the glasses with the black plastic rims and who used to smile every time he saw me and who never ceased calling me "Sister Fereshteh, Sister Fereshteh".

It was night by the time the Tehran contingent arrived and joined us in our tears: Maryam and her husband's family, Hājj Bābā and Khānūm Jān, Uncle Mohammad and Aunt Fātemeh. The way they wailed, one would have thought it was Āshūrā all over again. Amīr was dear to every member of the family, but was especially dear to Hājj Bābā and Khānūm Jān.

If it weren't for Ali Agha, all of us would have expired by the morning. He would occasionally take Mansūreh Khānūm's head into his arms and calm her down with his words, and occasionally he would sit next to Āghā Nāser and rest his head on his shoulders and give him heart and courage. He would then embrace Hājj Bābā and Khānūm Jān and pacify them with his words. But when he came to me, he would let out his mourning. He would say, "From the start of the war up to now, a whole battalion's worth of my friends and colleagues have been martyred; but I am still alive. It had been four months since Amīr had gone to the warfront. I have been on the front for seven years. This is not fair! What is it that I have done that God does not find me worthy [of martyrdom], and instead takes Amīr [to Himself] so soon? Why should Amīr attain to martyrdom so soon while I am still alive?"

I listened to him talk with a lump in my throat. I said, "Don't be ungrateful, Ali! As you say yourself, be content with that which God has ordained."

The following morning, our street was full of Land Rovers which belonged to the Construction Jehād Organization, the *Sepāh*'s Nissan Patrols, and of the buses and vans which were waiting in the street to take the people who had come to the house to pay their respects over to the Bāgh-e Behesht Martyr's Cemetery and back.

Ali Āghā was wearing a brown shirt which flailed in the wind against his body. It seemed as if it was only his shoulder-bones which held his shirt from flying away. His face was gaunt and had turned to the yellow color of jaundice; it was obvious that he had had a difficult night. None of us had had anything to eat for lunch, dinner, or breakfast from the previous day.

Ali Agha took Mansūreh Khānūm into his arms and was whispering in her ear: "*Māmān*, stay in control of your emotions. Have fortitude. Act like Zeynab acted. Always keep the enemy in mind."

Maryam couldn't keep her emotions in check. She wept like only a sister could weep. Ali Agha said to her, "Maryam Jān, it's ok to cry, but not at the top of your voice. Be sure that a *nāmahram*[84] person does not hear your crying."

I had started to feel worse ever since I heard the news of Amīr Agha's martyrdom. I was still vomiting. I was running toward the bathroom when Ali Agha saw me and asked, "What's the matter? Haven't you gotten better? Do you want me to have one of the guys take you to the hospital?"

I didn't think Ali Agha was paying any attention to me in the condition that he was in; much less his wanting to send me to the hospital. I said, "No, it's nothing. It'll pass."

The weather was warm, and I was more bothered by the heat than anything else. We all gradually came out of the apartment. Some of the neighbors stayed behind in order to help prepare lemonade and ice water and halva for those who were coming back from the cemetery.

I went downstairs with Father and Mother. The large crowd which had shown up for Amīr's funeral service boarded the buses or their own cars and started off toward the Bāgh-e Behesht Martyr's Cemetery. Our route to the cemetery was full of Land Rovers which belonged to the Construction Jehād

---

[84] See footnote 8.

Organization and the *Sepāh*'s Nissan Patrols, most of whose windows and side panels were covered with pictures of Amīr and flowers, or were draped in black cloth.

When we arrived at the Bāgh-e Behesht Cemetery, there was a military band playing, and there was a large number of soldiers from both the regular army as well as from the Sepāh or Revolutionary Guards standing at attention on two sides. Amīr's coffin was decorated with flowers and the flag and was on the floor in the middle of the gathering which had gathered outside of the building where they gave the bodies of the dead their final full body ritual purification or *ghosl*. The soldiers and Guards were standing to attention with their arms raised in a salute of respect and were mourning the loss of their colleague with their deep silence.

Seeing Amīr's coffin made my legs tremble. Mansūreh Khānūm, Agha Nāser, Hājj Sādeq and Ali Agha were standing under the balcony of the building where the ritual purifications were performed. Mansūreh Khānūm's and Maryam's faces were crimson, but they were not crying.

My legs were quivering. Mother held me by the arm. I was reminded of the day when we had come to Mosayyeb's wake. The music ended and the recitation of the Quran was amplified through loudspeakers. The *qārī* or reciter was reciting the Quran from the balcony. The crowd swelled and grew larger with each passing minute.

Agha Nāser, Hājj Sādeq and Ali Agha went up to the balcony together with the governor and the Friday congressional prayer leader and a few other dignitaries. When the recitation was concluded, the master of ceremony asked the Friday prayer leader to step up to the podium. The prayer leader and the governor each delivered a speech, after which it was Ali Agha's turn.

The weather in the cemetery was warm. I felt worse and worse by the minute. Ali Agha was speaking:

"*Salām bar Hosayn.* Peace be unto Hosayn. And peace be unto Hosayn's companions. I am grateful to the martyrdom-fostering people of the province of Hamedān for gracing us with their presence at the wake of Amīr Chītsāzīān. You have given freely of your time, for which I thank you… but the people have a greater request of you, and that is that you take the words of Imam [Khomeini] to heart. Three years ago, the imam asked us not to abandon the front lines of the war, stipulating the defense of the realm to be a religious duty. He stipulated that we were not to erect different fronts between ourselves; and that the only front was [to be] the front line [of the war], and that maintaining a presence on this front line was a duty which was generally incumbent on everyone. And so I say to you now that we should not act in a way that would compel the imam to go back to the podium and to implore us for the umpteenth time to be present on the front lines. If we are to be good soldiers, our dearly beloved imam has made this stipulation once, and once should be sufficient for us. We have to prove to the world that we are committed to the stipulations of our imam with heart and soul. And so, what I say to you now is to pick up a copy of the Quran in one hand, and a firearm in another, and march toward the front line of the battle of good versus evil, shouting: 'We shall fight, and fight again, until victory is ours'!"

The crowd chanted in unison, 'We shall fight and fight again until victory'!"

The Bāgh-e Behesht Cemetery had become so crowded that one could barely move. I had difficulty breathing and said, "Mother, I don't feel at all well." Mother took my hand in hers and forged a way out of the crowd and somehow got us to the Golzār-e Shohadā, or the martyr's section of the cemetery, where we found a spot to sit down under a tree. Mother had a bottle of water with her. She poured some water into her hand and washed my face over with it.

Ali Agha's voice could be heard on the speakers: "I thank God that my brother was martyred at the hands of God's enemies rather than at the hands of His false friends. With only four months of active duty on the front line, Amīr overtook us [in the race to gain spiritual propinquity to God]."

We were sitting under a weeping willow tree whose leaves were set in motion by a cool breeze. Mother was ambling around the martyr's section and would sit on a gravestone and recite the *Fāteha* or Opening chapter of the Quran. A little later, the loudspeakers went quiet. Mother came over to me and said, "I think they are performing the ritual supplications or *namāz*. Why don't you sit here while I go and offer my prayers as well. I'll be back soon."

A little while after Mother left, the crowd could be heard chanting:

> Come, O Mahdī; come, O Mahdī,
> In order to bury the body of the martyrs.

برای دفن شهدا مهدی، بیا! مهدی، بیا!

Amīr's casket was lifted onto the hands of the soldier pallbearers, who started moving, with the people following in tow. I got to my feet and looked to the crowd. I could see Ali Agha and Ḥājj Sādeq holding the casket up with their shoulders. I wanted to go closer, but I was suddenly surrounded by people who were rushing forward and chanting *lā ilāha illallāh* – there is no deity but Allāh. I was stuck in the middle of the crowd; I couldn't go forward any further, and the path of my retreat was closed behind me. Everywhere I looked there were men and women who were rushing toward Amīr's casket and chanting:

> Whither did this torn flower hail from?
> It came from the Journey to Karbalā.
> This is our torn flower;
> A present to our Leader.

این گلِ پرپر از کجا آمده؟ از سفرِ کربلا آمده
این گلِ پرپر ماست   هدیه به رهبرِ ماست

The heat and the density of the crowd made for a suffocating atmosphere for me. I was so weak I could barely breathe and my legs were quivering and could not support my weight. The thought of Amīr's body being in that casket made me feel nauseous. It was as if it was the end of the world. It was as if someone was driving me to my grave. I don't know how to describe how I felt that day, but what I do know is that in those moments, everything around me was dark, dead, lifeless and miserable. Everything before me was melancholy. Nothing had any importance for me; nothing had any value, nothing...

The people rushed forward without showing any consideration for their surroundings, reminding me [of the scenes depicted in the Quran] of the Day of Resurrection. There was an old Basījī[85] who washed our faces with rosewater which he had in a stainless-steel pressurized spray can [with a hose] which he carried in a shoulder harness.

The intensely radiated heat of the sun charred the earth. The sky was cloudless and the air was warm. Despite the large crowd that had gathered there, the cemetery made me feel lonesome and sad and filled me with a sense of anxiety. The sound of people's voices had merged into a single cacophony and out of that large crowd, no one's voice could be discerned. Nor was there any sign of a pleasant sound such as the sound of the breeze or some birdsong. Amīr had been freed and had departed on heavenly wings, leaving the sound of mourning behind him, which could be heard everywhere.

I sat down on an old grey tombstone.[86] Its inscriptions had been erased by wind and wuthering. An old pine tree which

---

[85] See footnote 26.
[86] Tombstones are laid flat in Iran, and are usually level with the ground or only slightly above ground level.

looked to be about forty or fifty years old had cast its shadow on the grave. Its pine needles had turned dull and dark from the heat and lack of water. I sat under the shade of the pine tree and all manner of thoughts raced through my mind.

A few hours must have passed before the crowd started to come apart like clouds dispersing, each in a different direction. The intense heat of the sun radiated down in waves and would send ripples of heat up from the tombstones like rising steam.

The buses were lined up in queues and people were hurrying back to their open doors. I made my way to one of them. As I did so, I could feel Amīr's kind and familiar spirit flying over me with a smile on his face.

The bus I boarded smelled of rose water. The women in the bus who were covered in black *chādors* would send *salawāts* to the pure spirits of the martyrs every now and again. There was an empty seat next to a woman in the second row, which I took. I felt dizzy and wanted to go to sleep.

As the bus started to move, the sound of the *salawāts* became louder. I stared at the crowd which was still gathered around the grave from behind the bus's window. I closed my eyes and opened them again. And then I closed them once more and whispered, "Fare well, dear Amīr; God be with you. I'm sorry that I was not able to do anything for you, but please do not forget to intercede on my behalf."

It was noon now and the house was filled with guests. I felt nauseous, but I contained myself. I felt embarrassed to run to the restroom every couple of minutes in front of so many people. I didn't feel good enough to get up and help out, nor was I able to sit still in one place. I had found a room whose window opened onto the street below and was lying down there with my *chādor* pulled up over my face. There were a few women in the room. I heard one of them say, "Did you see Ali Agha pull out one of Amīr's jacket buttons?"

Another woman replied, "No, I didn't. What was that about? As a ransom?"

I perked up my ears.

"Yes. They say he pulled out one of his brother's jacket buttons and swore him to take him up with him as soon as possible; to make him a martyr."

I sat up and stared at the women, bewildered. I recognized them; they were Mansūreh Khānūm's relatives. I could hear my heart beating up against my throat. I asked, "What happened?"

The women were taken aback as they had just noticed me; they said with embarrassment, "Oh, it's nothing."

The poor things didn't expect to see me. I got up and went into the den. The women were spreading the table spread on the floor, and the men were handing the catered lunch packs and bread and soft drinks into the house from the stairwell.

Mother was standing in front of the door and was busy helping out. I kept blacking out and everything swirled around me with the wooziness of vertigo. As soon as she saw me, she rushed toward me and said, "You made it back, Fereshteh Jān ... Where did you disappear to? Are you ok?"

Pink Lady

I opened the door to the restroom. Mother took me by the hand and together we went into the restroom that was adjacent to the front door. As soon as I smelled the smell of the kabābs, I felt like vomiting. Mother cooled my face down with a few handfuls of water and let me take whatever time I needed to throw up. After I started feeling better, I placed my head on her chest and took in her scents. She smelled so good. Her smell made me feel better. Mother smiled and said, "Don't go all lovey dovey on me; come on, let's go, girl!" Then she took my arm and walked me to the bedroom.

She brought a fan and placed it in front of me and turned it on. She opened the buttons of my *manteaux* and took off my *chādor*. I closed my eyes. I wanted to sleep so badly.

Ali Agha came into the room with great concern. He said, "How are you, my love? Are you ok? You want me to take you to the hospital?"

I raised my eyebrows in a negative response.

"Have you had lunch?" He asked.

Mother answered for me: "The smell of the food makes her nauseous."

Ali Agha said despondently, "We can't have that, my love. You have to have something eventually. What would you like me to bring for you?"

"Pink Lady apples," I said. That was the only thing I wanted to eat.

Ali Agha left right away. I could hear the sound of forks and spoons tapping against plates from the living room. The smell of the food and the kebab made me want to vomit. I said to Mother, "Mother, for the love of God, close the door!"

I suddenly became queasy and the room started to whirl around my head, like a spell of vertigo. My eyelids weighed down on me. Mother ran out of the room in a panic. I could hear her saying, "Ali Agha, call an ambulance. Fereshteh…"

Ali Agha came back into the room, together with a couple of men and a bag full of about five or six pounds of Pink Lady apples. The men were in navy colored army uniforms. One of the men was carrying a small briefcase. Mother was telling the man who was taking my blood pressure the history of my illness. The man fitted me with an IV drip and injected a few vials of liquid into the solution. It reminded me of Ali Agha's painting and the arrows which had pinned the butterfly's wings. The man said, "Her blood pressure is very low. She should get plenty of rest."

I closed my eyes. I felt like sleeping until the end of the world.

A Solution of Tears

The house was less busy in the second week. Other than the two of us, who didn't have a home of our own, the following were staying with Mansūreh Khānūm: Hājj BāBā and Khānūm Jān, Uncle Mohammad, Maryam, together with her six-month-old baby Monā, as well as Hāj Sādeq and his family.

One night I awoke in the middle of the night. Ali Agha got up and left the room very gingerly so as not to waken anyone. He passed us by slowly and set the curtain that was partitioning the living room from the den aside, and went into the den, and then to the restroom. I thought he'd come back soon. I waited for him for a long time, but he didn't come back. So I got up and went after him. He was in the den, praying. He was weeping with his forehead on the ground, in the prostrate position. His shoulders were shuddering. I sat behind him in a way that he wouldn't notice and leaned back against the wall. He was holding so many emotions in his heart, and he released them meekly and passionately. My heart went out to him. I had never seen Ali Agha like this before.

I saw how everyday he would look after Agha Nāser and Mansūreh Khānūm and how he tried to console them from morning till nightfall, talk to them, and try to bring smiles to their faces and make them laugh. I knew how much he loved Amīr. But during all this time, I had not seen him shed a single tear. Now this same Ali Agha was wailing like there was no tomorrow.

I waited until he finally came out of his prostration. Quietly, so that only he would hear, I said, "Ali Jān…"

He turned toward the sound of my voice. The den window was open and cast the light from a streetlight into the room. The room was lit such that we could see each other clearly. He was taken aback and said with surprise, "Fereshteh!"

I replied, "Yes, my dear."

He asked, "What are you doing here??"

"I couldn't sleep," I said.

"Are you not feeling well again?"

I was feeling fine.

He said, "I know you're not well. I know you're very weary. You are nearer to God than me right now. Pray for me."

I looked at him with surprise. His voice was still filled with the strain of lament. He said, "God has promised Heaven to those who take up arms in His cause. Blessed is Amīr's fate: he got his reward with [only] four months in this struggle. I think

I must have some sort of problem for me to be on the warfront for seven years and yet still be alive and kicking."

I said with a lump in my throat, "Ali, don't fall victim to ingratitude."

That got him to open up and start commiserating with me.

"I'm not kidding, Fereshteh. God knows Himself: I don't want to die in my sleep. I know that the war will end sooner or later and everyone will go back and resume their normal lives. But those of us who survive will die of envy a thousand times over every day."

I said, "Ali Agha, that's no way to talk. You should be content with what God has willed for you."

He said, "Are you?"

I said with assurance, "Of course I am."

He said with glee, "You mean to say that you would still be content if I am martyred? That you won't be upset?"

I paused a little, but answered eventually: "Of course I will be upset; I'll die from grief. You are my husband; the dearest person to me; and half of my being. We love each other. You are the father of my child. Just thinking about it is difficult for me. But if it is God's will, I will eventually find a way to come to terms with it and be content with it. I'll eventually be able to bear it."

He suddenly became very happy. He asked quickly, "Really?"

This conversation had made me want to cry. He didn't wait for my answer but continued, "Fereshteh, the life of this world, from the first year to the hundredth, will be over in something that will seem to be nothing more than a day. And we all will die eventually. But the opportunity to die the death of a martyr is just these few passing days."

He said this and then turned and faced the direction of prayer in Mecca. He raised his hands palms upward and at chest level in the way that is the custom for ritual supplications, and prayed, "O Lord, You are well aware of the needs of every one of Your devotees. You know that it would be a matter of deep shame for me to die in my sleep. Grant me the death of a martyr, dear Lord."

He never wept in front of anyone. His face turned crimson if he was upset or struck with grief, but he never wept. But this time he started to cry next to me and said with tears in his eyes, "I saw Mosayyeb in a dream once shortly after he was martyred. I took him by the hand and said, 'Mosayyeb, you and I had tried all of the solutions together before; so for the love of God, tell me [the secret to] this final solution.' Mosayyeb didn't answer. I held onto his hand fast. I knew that if you asked a question of someone who was deceased and didn't let go of his hand and swear him to answer you, he would answer whatever it was that you had asked. I said to him, 'I'm not going to let you go until you tell me the solution!' What do you think Mosayyeb said? He said, 'The solution is tears... only tears.' Fereshteh, the solution [of attaining] to martyrdom is tears."

He raised his hands up again in ritual supplication and said, "Dear Lord, if [the spiritual station of] martyrdom is granted on the basis of tears, then accept the tears and lamentation of this wretched and blameworthy servant of yours."

Ali Agha changed a lot after Amīr's martyrdom. The 'solution of tears' was a new addition to his list of characteristics. He was more inward and taciturn and didn't talk much. He was no longer be seen being rowdy and making fun and raising up a ruckus. He didn't eat much and had become emaciated. But at the same time, he had become kinder and more considerate. Often, he was seen with tears welling up in his eyes. He spent his nights in prayer and supplication and tears. He would sleep less and less with each passing day.

After Amīr's *chehellom*[87] passed, he arranged to take Mansūreh Khānūm and Agha Nāser on a pilgrimage to Mashhad in order to elevate their spirits. There were a few people on that trip who were close relatives of people who had been martyred. There was a family by the name of Toranjīān who had struck up a conversation with Mansūreh Khānūm and Agha Nāser and were trying to lighten their spirits.

Ali Agha went back to the front as soon as we returned. Mansūreh Khānūm couldn't stand to be alone in her apartment, and so she went to stay with Hājj Sādeq. I perforce followed them.

[The Islamic lunar month of] Moharram fell on September that year. As Ali Agha himself put it, he had come back to Hamedān for the first ten days of Moharram after being

---

[87] See footnote 19.

away for these somber days of mourning[88] for seven years. Each night he would go to different places in order to perform ritual mourning ceremonies (*azādārī*) and would return after midnight. In the past, my mother and sisters and I would go to the *Sepāh* each year for these mourning rituals. The *Sepāh* had a good *hey'at* or religious community group and their *azādārī* program was better than other places. One-night Ali Agha said, "Fereshteh, I want to go to the *Sepāh*. Do you want to come along?"

I thought of the memories of bygone years and the spiritually uplifting experiences which were still lodged in my memory, and happily accepted his invitation. That year, Hamedān's weather had started to get cold from the beginning of September; and the nights were colder still, of course. As we didn't have a permanent home, and I wasn't sure where I had stored my winter clothes, Monīreh Khānūm had a thick black jacket which she gave me to wear. We got in the car and left with Ali Agha driving.

Everyone in the city was wearing black. Black and red banners were draped on walls throughout the city. Ali Agha parked the car close to Bābā Tāher Square, and as always, we set

---

[88] The Mourning of Moharram is a set of rituals associated with both Shia and Sunni Islam. The commemoration falls in Muharram, the first month of the Islamic calendar. The event marks the anniversary of the Battle of Karbalā, when Imam Hosayn, the grandson of the Prophet Mohammad, was martyred by the forces of the accursed Omayyad caliph Yazīd. The commemoration of this event during the yearly mourning season, with the Day of Āshūrā as the focal date, serves to define Shia communal identity.

the time and place for our return, because we still did not walk together in Hamedān. And this was a particularly relevant precaution tonight that we were going to the *Sepāh* as there was bound to be many friends and acquaintances which we might come across on our way over and back. Before we got out, Ali Agha said, "Fereshteh, pray for me."

I said, "I always pray for you."

He said, "No, don't pray for my health and well-being. Pray that I should be martyred as soon as possible."

I looked at him irately.

He said with sadness, "You're about to go to a *majles* or ritual mourning ceremony for Imam Hosayn. He has been my role model from the beginning of the war, which is why I have gone to fight on the warfront. I want to get my bill of exchange tonight. I have come to ask him to pronounce me worthy of martyrdom. But I know that if your heart is not at one with mine, and if you do not pray for me, that I will not get anywhere. So pray for me, my love."

I lowered my head and said nothing. It was only natural that I didn't take these words of his very seriously at the time, although my heart quivered each time the subject of martyrdom came up between us.

Ali continued in a peculiar and very strange way: "Fereshteh Khānūm, do you remember when you said that I should be content with what God has willed? Well, I have become contented. And so, I ask that you pray God that He should be content with me also. For if God is not content with what we do in His Way, and our efforts (*jehād*) are not acceptable to Him, then we are indeed at a great loss. I don't know at all whether or not I will ultimately be able to discharge myself honorably before God. But I have grown weary of this *donyā* or lower realm of existence, which has become like a cage to me. Tonight, pray to Imam Hosayn to help me break out of this cage, like the other martyrs who were able to make their escape and leave; like Shahīd Shāh-Hosaynī, like Imam Hosayn himself. I will be going there tonight to renew my pledge of allegiance to Imam Hosayn so that I can live my life until its final moment just as he did. As you say, the rest of it lies in God's hands, and I am content with what He wills for me."

After he said these words, Ali Agha took in a deep breath. We got out of the car and he locked the car doors. It was as if he was flying. He overtook me quickly and walked so fast that I couldn't catch up to him no matter how fast I walked. A cold wind was blowing. Ali Agha was ahead of me, far ahead.

There was a large crowd gathered on the sidewalk, but I could see Ali Agha between them all, wading ahead in a black shirt covering his strong shoulders.

Knitting

The Hamedān autumn arrived that year with the gusts of a cold front which arrived in the middle of September. Ali Agha returned to the front after Āshūrā. I stayed at Mansūreh Khānum's house. We closed the windows very quickly. We took out our winter clothes from the bundles in which they had been wrapped. The wind unjustly tore green leaves from their trees. The leaves fell before they had a chance to turn color, leaving the trees stripped and bare. We all knew that we had a long and hard autumn and winter in store.

I spent the long autumn nights knitting clothes for the baby I was expecting. Mansūreh Khānum had taken out her wool and knitting needles from a drawer. She was wearing a beautiful blouse and was busy knitting while muttering elegies and laments. She had taught Monīreh Khānum how to knit as well.

An Altar of Roses

We all knitted several sets of sweaters and trousers for the newborn we were expecting together.

Split Pomegranates

It was the middle of November. Ali Agha had come to Hamedān for a few days and was planning on going back to the warfront that same evening. I had done my best to attend to Mansūreh Khānūm and Agha Nāser as much as possible during the few days of Ali Agha's sojourn in Hamedān. Mansūreh Khānūm's illness had taken a turn for the worse after Amīr's martyrdom, affecting different parts of her body each day. But the worst problem which she had to deal with was the problem with her kidneys which got worse with every passing day. Ali Agha took her to the hospital a few times in order to consult with several seasoned specialists concerning her condition, but he didn't get anywhere.

We were sitting in the den. Ali Agha got up, rolled up his sleeves and his trouser cuffs and went to make his *wūzū* or ritual ablutions. He always used to make his *wūzū* in the kitchen. I got up and followed him; it was as if someone was telling me, "Fereshteh, look at him carefully and take all of him in." I looked at his tall and muscular sportsman-like body and at his large and broad shoulders. He had a thick and strong neck which came together with his head in the back. His beefy and pale calf muscles could be seen together with his pink ankles which landed steadily on the floor as he walked in the house. He ran his wet fingers over his head and feet. He thought I had gotten up to make my ablution too. He moved to one side, away from the kitchen sink. I was monitoring his every move with precision so that I wouldn't forget anything. He left the kitchen for the living room, took out a *mohr* or a small cake of clay[89] from his shirt pocket and started reciting the *azān* or call to prayer. I had followed him out of the kitchen and was sitting behind him, looking at him with a lump in my throat. His head was leaning downward in a gesture of humility and supplication as he offered his ritual devotions to his Maker. When he reached the *qunūt* [phase of the ritual devotions in which supplications are made in a standing position with the forehands touching and raised

---

[89] Following a hadīth report from the Prophet of Islam in which the Prophet is authoritatively reported to have said that he only lowers his forehead on the earth, the Shi'a use a small cake of clay (usually but not necessarily baked from the earth of the Plain of Karbalā, where Imam Hosayn was martyred) to lower their foreheads onto, so that their foreheads do not touch anything but the earth, in obeisance to the exemplary model of the Prophet of God, unto whom be God's peace and blessings.

heavenward at chest level], he repeated three times: "Lord, grant me [the honor of attaining to the spiritual station of] martyrdom in Your Way."

When his *namāz* or ritual devotions were completed, he came and sat next to Agha Nāser and started to stipulate certain things to him: "Agha Jān, this time around, my return will take longer; maybe a couple of months. I might not even be able to come back if Fereshteh needs me. I have asked one of the guys to bring some clarified butter for Fereshteh from the countryside. I told him to bring a live sheep as well. If I am not able to make it back in time, offer it as a sacrifice for her."

When he finished making his requests, he came over to me and said, "Fereshteh, would you go and get my photo album please?"

I got up to go and get it, but bumped into him in the doorway as I was on my way back with it. He smiled and said, "Let's sit and look at the pictures right here."

We sat down and Ali Agha opened the album and started leafing through its pages. He would see the pictures of his friends who had been martyred and let out deep sighs. At times he would say something like, "Where is Shahīd Nazarī now? Or Shahīd Takrānī? May your memories last!"

His face had turned crimson and his eyes sparkled with fresh tears. I took the album and wanted to put it aside, but he took it back and said, "Let it go, my love. This album contains the entirety of my life. It is what motivates me to continue to stay on the front lines and fight."

I said, "You get yourself all worked up and upset."

His tears had started to fall on his cheeks one by one.

He said, "Fereshteh, these guys all loved Agha Abā Abdollāh.⁹⁰ They shed a lot of blood, sweat and tears for his sake. They sustained a lot of injuries, lost a lot of sleep, went without food and water, and suffered under the scorching sun... but never once did they say that they had grown weary, or that they were hungry or thirsty, or needed to get some rest. I look at these pictures so that if I start to feel tired or weary, I will be reminded of the fact that instead of sleeping at night, Shahīd Qaragozlū would stay up half the night and devote himself to prayer and supplication, and to the recitation of the Zīārat Āshūrā,⁹¹ and

---

⁹⁰ Abā Abdollāh is one of the titles conferred on Imam Hosayn by the faithful. It means 'Father of the Devotees of Allāh', and it is so chosen because it is believed that Imam Hosayn's exemplary model and sacrifice on the Plain of Karbalā was a seminal event in the history of Islam, without which the continuation of true Islam would not have been possible.

⁹¹ *Zīārat*: 1. The act of making pilgrimage to a pilgrimage site, usually a shrine of a prophet, imam or *imamzāda* (the progeny of an imam); 2. A liturgical form of supplication or ritual prayer recited specifically during one's pilgrimage to a sacred shrine or location. The second meaning is that which is intended here, and the Āshūrā Zīārat is a leading case in point. Ziyarat Ashura is attributed to Muhammad al-Baqir, the fifth Shia Imam. It is a Shia salutatory prayer to Hosayn ibn Ali and the martyrs of the Battle of Karbala. The prayer is part of the liturgy used in pilgrimages to the shrine of Hosayn in Karbala. Imam Baqir recommended reciting Ziyarat Ashura on Ashura while facing Karbala, as a symbolic visit to the shrine. The prayer is found in sacred

would wail out loud. I look at these pictures so that if I ever wish I had a homestead and a [settled] life, I will be reminded of what Mosayyeb used to say, which was that one should not dwell too much on wishes because death will make a mockery of all one dreams and wishes for. I look at these pictures so that I would be reminded that now is not the time for wishful thinking; it is not the time for talk, but for taking action. Anyone who has a good head on his shoulders must offer it as a gift. Anyone who has a strong arm must offer it as a gift. And if someone is old and cannot come to the front, then he should act in a supporting capacity to the forces on the warfront."

I knew he was tired and weary and that he was grieving the loss of his brother. As he used to say himself, from the time of the beginning of the war until the present, a whole battalion's worth of his friends had been martyred. So, I sat next to him and we looked at the pictures of the martyrs together. He shed tears in front of me without compunction, and his weeping gave me a lump in my throat and made me cry with him.

He had a small dinner that night, after which he said, "I want to get some sleep, my love. Will you wake me at 2:30 in the morning?"

I would always be overtaken with melancholy on the eve of his departures. I could become restless and fretful and wouldn't have the patience to stick to any given task. I spread his bedding out for him, switched the light off and let him sleep. I knew that

---

hadith narrated in particular by Shaykh Tusi in *Misbah al-Mutahajjid* and by Ibn Qulawayh in *Kamil al-Ziyarat*.

he would not be able to get any sleep in the car. I left the room. Mansūreh Khānūm and Agha Nāser were watching a program on TV; it was a documentary about Shahīd Kharrāzī. The camera had focused on the face of his younger son, Mahdī. His wife was talking about her memories of him. My heart quivered. I thought what if – God forbid – Ali is martyred and our child becomes like this one. I got up and went back to the bedroom. I turned the light on. Sleep had overcome Ali Agha very quickly. His sleep was so deep that he was not disturbed in the least by the strong rays of the lamp. I sat next to his head. I recalled the moments of the evening when he had wept at the memory of his martyred friends. He looked so innocent in his sleep. It was again as if someone was telling me to take a good look at him and to take in all the details of his face and to vouchsafe them to my memory for a whole lifetime. I stared at his face and all of the lines on his forehead and around his eyes. He was only twenty-five, yet he had so many wrinkles on his forehead! His feet were sticking out from under the blanket. I thought I should take a good look at them too so that I don't forget them either. His feet were so pale that it was as if a white sheet had been drawn over his veins – strong and numerous veins, like the root of a stout tree. I wanted to memorize all the details of his body. I needed to commit all of his details to memory: his muscular biceps, his tall frame, his long and light brown beard, his blue eyes, his bushy brows and his straight hair which was never combed properly. Why did his eyebrows grow so much? Sometimes I would chase him with a pair of scissors in my hands, asking him to let me trim his eyebrows. But he would not let me. After my insistence, the best that he would concede was to wet his fingers with his mouth and run them over his eyebrows to wet them down! Those blue eyes of his never once got a full night's rest; he always slept with "one eye open", as they say. But that night was different. What a deep sleep he was in! I sat over his head for a long time, but then I got up and came back out. I packed his duffel bag. Pomegranates and tangerines were in season. I put two large pomegranates that had split open in his duffel bag for him. Hājj Sādeq and Monīreh Khānūm and the kids were in their own bedroom, and Agha Nāser and Mansūreh Khānūm were sleeping in the den.

I went into the kitchen, washed the dishes, and then started to cry. I wiped the counters down. I wasn't sleepy. I wasn't feeling well. I felt nauseous again; I felt like I wanted to vomit. Despite my nausea and pregnancy, I took up the hose and hosed down the kitchen floor and did a good job of cleaning the tiles. How I wanted us to have a house of our own. I had grown weary of imposing on other people so much. Then I thought that No, I'm not tired, nor do I have any complaints; and that if I have Ali Agha by my side, I would happily live like this for my whole life with him.

I dried the dishes and placed them in the cabinets. I wasn't sleepy and I didn't want to go to sleep. I kept looking at the clock in the kitchen with ever increasing anxiety. I put my *chādor* on and went out to the patio. A vicious wind was blowing by. The lights of the surrounding apartments were switched off. I thought of how fortunate those who were sound asleep were. The weather was very cold, and I couldn't stand it so I came back inside. I would roam around the living room, den, and kitchen, not knowing what else to do. I went back to our room and sat back down above his head. The light was off and the room was dark. Just knowing that he was there in the room breathing with me was enough to calm me down. I wanted time to stand still with us in that state and never to move forward again; never...

But the hands of the clock disagreed with me and kept turning around and around and around. It was now a quarter past two in the morning. I placed my hand on his shoulder and gently rocked him.

"Ali, Ali dear, wake up."

He awoke immediately. He sat up in his bed and asked anxiously, "What time is it?"

I said gently, "Don't worry, it's a quarter past two."

He went and made his ritual ablutions and dressed. I gave him his duffle bag.

I said, "I put two pomegranates in there for you, one for each of us. Remember me with each aril that you eat. And for the love of God, please come back soon this time."

He looked at me and said, "I'll be back, and very soon. But don't tell *Māmān*."

I asked, "Like how soon?"

He said, "Soon, like in a few days. But keep it between the two of us; don't tell anyone. It will be a week at the latest."

These words of his made me happy. Mansūreh Khānūm woke up too. Ali Agha said with distress, "*Māmān*, why did you get up? I could have gone without putting you to the trouble..."

Ali Agha bent down and kissed his mother's face. Mansūreh Khānūm put her hand around Ali Agha's neck, put his head on her chest and said, Ali Jān, *Mādar*, take care of yourself. Go safely and may God be with you."

Ali Agha said, "Take very good care of yourself, *Māmān*."

Agha Nāser had woken up as well. Ali Agha kissed him too and said, "Agha, you be sure and take care of everything. Don't forget my requests. And look after *Māmān* for all of us."

Ali Agha caressed his mother's shoulders and kissed her face again, then looked at his watch and quickly tied his boot laces. He turned to me and Mansūreh Khānūm and said, "Go back inside now; its cold out." But we followed him out.

It was cold and I was only wearing something thin. I was shivering and my teeth had started to chatter with the cold. His car was parked in our alley. I could feel a lump forming in my throat. I felt like yelling, "Don't go, Ali! Don't go, Ali Agha, for my sake and for the sake of our child!"

I felt like yelling at the top of my voice, "Wake up! Wake up, O neighbors! Don't let my husband, the love of my life, leave me! For the love of God, someone stop him!!"

But instead of all that, I said with a lump in my throat what I always would say: "Ali Jān, don't forget to intercede on my behalf for the sake of…"

But I was too embarrassed to say anything about the child in front of Mansūreh Khānūm, so I whispered, "Come back soon!"

Ali Agha smiled and looked deeply into my eyes and said, "Fereshteh Jān, my love, *halālam kon* – forgive me any trespass that I might have committed against you."

Mansūreh Khānūm opened her arms again and held Ali Agha in a tight embrace. She kissed him and took in his scent ten times over. I was just standing there and taking in the sight. Ali Agha had placed his mother's head on his chest and was whispering something into her ear, but he was looking at me. His eyes were transfixed on my belly. Was he worried about me and his baby? Was he talking to his mother about us? I couldn't hear anything. Ali Agha then quickly sat in the car and started it up, put his foot on the pedal and took off in the "Deer of the Desert". We had so many fond memories with that Deer. The Deer moved forward and Ali Agha waved at me. But then he suddenly made a U-turn and came back. He came back and slowed as he passed us. He rolled down his window and said, "Go inside, it's cold out!"

We stayed until the car disappeared around the corner of our alley. I could see Ali Agha waving his hand at me in the darkness of the night. Mansūreh Khānūm and I went back inside the house. It seemed like ages before we got from the door of the front yard to the house itself. Neither of us spoke. We switched the lights off one by one in a deep and sad silence. I got in the bed I had made for Ali Agha and pulled the blanket over my head. The blanket and bedding carried his scent. I no longer got nauseous from the smell of men and sweat. I inhaled his scent deeply and wailed out loud until I cried myself to sleep.

Living with a Real Man for One Night

It was the end of November. We were still living in Hājj Sādeq's apartment. Ali Agha had said, "When I'm not there, stay with my mother, because when you are there, it is as if I am there for her." But because he had said that he would be back within a week, I stayed where I was and preferred not to move back yet.

I was worried and couldn't sleep. There was a bookcase in the living room. I picked out one of Ayatollah Motahharī's books and read a few pages, but my mind wasn't on what I was reading, but didn't take any of it in. No matter what I did, I couldn't concentrate. I would turn a page every half hour. My eyes were on the words, but my mind was everywhere else. I picked up my diary and amused myself by transcribing some of the passages from the book. I thought of last night and Ali

Agha's deep gazes into my eyes, and my heart quivered. Why had I tried to vouchsafe all of his physical features to the safekeeping of my memory? Had I perchance been inspired to do so? But then I thought to myself that, "No, I should dismiss such negative thoughts"; after all, he had said that he would be back soon this time. But then, if he is to return, then why can't I let sleep overtake me? Why am I filled with such a sense of anxiety and foreboding? I gave myself a pep talk: "Fereshteh, you should not think bad thoughts; it's not good for the baby. This anxiety must be just another normal symptom of the pregnancy process. And my sleeplessness must also be due to my pregnancy. All pregnant women go through this…"

Agha Nāser noticed my fatigue and grogginess over breakfast and asked me how I was feeling. I replied, "I couldn't sleep last night; I was worried."

Agha Nāser consoled me in his usual fatherly manner. I tried to change my own mood as well, but the phone's ringer kept on intervening. It kept ringing off the hook from the early hours of the morning.

Hājj Sādeq had not gone to work. I comforted myself with the thought that the callers' business was with Hājj Sādeq. But one cannot fool oneself indefinitely! My whole being had been overtaken by pandemonium. I told myself, "It's nothing, Hājj Sādeq's work is complex… This is what responsibility entails: if he doesn't go to work for a single day, everything will fall apart unless his people call and consult him about what to do." But there was another voice in my heart which asked, "Hmm, whatever has prevented Hājj Sādeq from going to work

Living with a Real Man for One Night

in the first place?" I argued with myself: "What's it to you? So what if he hasn't gone to work! What are you, his *moftī*[92]?? Maybe he just didn't feel like going and felt like staying at home and getting some rest." But these arguments notwithstanding, I wished that the blasted phone would stop ringing. I had one eye on the front door and another on Hājj Sādeq's mouth which was carrying on a conversation over the phone in a way that was peculiarly out of everyone's eyesight and earshot.

Why didn't anyone open the door and come in? Why didn't Ali Agha appear? He had told me himself that he would be back within a week. What an arduous Wednesday it was turning out to be!

On Thursday morning, my whole attention was fixed on the front door and the doorbell. Ali Agha had promised me that he would come back soon. Seven days had passed. I had never heard him say that he would be coming back soon with such certainty. My sense of foreboding was very strange. Why had he told me not to tell his mother?!

Hājj Sādeq left the apartment first thing in the morning. Agha Nāser was restless and couldn't sit still. His mind was preoccupied and distraught. The phone was quiet and did not ring. That same voice that agitated for bad news from deep within my heart averred that something bad had happened; but I ignored it. I feigned ignorance, ignoring the odd behavior of others which I well knew to be suspect in my heart of hearts. I was on the edge of despair with worry, and the lump that had

---

[92] A religious authority.

formed in my throat prevented me from being able to breathe properly. I was hoping that someone would give me an excuse so that I could start bawling; but everyone had withdrawn into their own shells. Everyone minded their own business. What a miserable and difficult Thursday!

My father came for me Friday morning. The sight of my father filled me with a sense of dread because there had never been an occasion for a member of my family to come to Hājj Sādeq's apartment in the past. So I thought that something bad must have happened. My father tried to act normal, but anxiety and concern radiated in waves from the back of his ever-kind eyes. He was standing before the front door. He said, "Fereshteh, we have guests. Your uncle has come to visit. Your mother said that you should join us for lunch today, so that we can all be together."

There was a white Renault parked in front of the door with a man waiting behind the wheel whom I didn't recognize. I went and put on my outerwear with an increased sense of foreboding and took a seat in the back of the car. I said, "Father, Ali Agha is supposed to come back today. I have to get back soon."

Father didn't even turn to look at me. The stranger put his foot on the accelerator and drove us through the cold and deserted streets toward our home. The barren trees were frozen under a thin layer of snow.

When we got home, there was no sign of any guests or of Uncle Mahmoud. Mother was pacing back and forth in our small front yard. She rushed toward me as soon as she saw me.

Before she had a chance to say anything I asked, "What's happened, Mother? Tell me the truth!"

Mother looked at Father and said with difficulty, "Nothing. It's nothing! Only... Only..."

I couldn't take it anymore and yelled, "Only what??!"

Mother's face had become ashen. Royā and Nafiseh had drawn the curtain back and were looking at us with concern.

Mother said gently, "Don't panic, ok? It's nothing; it's just that Ali Agha has sustained a slight injury."

I don't know why I had become like this, but I lashed out, saying: "So what if he's injured. It wouldn't be the first time. So why all the theatrics and secrecy? It's not like it's the first time he's been injured. He's been injured a hundred times before!"

The words came out of Mother's mouth with difficulty. She talked in spurts and spasms: "Because... because it's different this time. He lost... he lost... one of his arms."

Suddenly I thought that this was not important. I said, "Well, ok. So what? He's lost an arm, but at least he's alive. So that's fine."

Mother looked to father for help with desperation and despair. Father said, "But Fereshteh Jān, if only it was just his arm that he had lost. One of his legs has been severed too."

At that moment, the thought that occurred to me was that everything would be just fine even if all of Ali Agha's limbs had been cut up into little pieces as long as he was alive; I just wanted him to be alive, so I answered quickly, "That's not a problem!"

And then I started bawling.

"I swear to God, it's fine. Even if both his arms and both his legs are gone, it's still fine. Just tell me that he's alive! For the love of God, Father, tell me he's alive!"

Father turned away from me so that I wouldn't see his tears. He said with a lump in his throat, "Bābā Jān, Fereshteh, do you know what happened?"

I lost it. My heart had become hardened. I looked heavenward and said, "O God! Why won't anyone tell me the truth?! I know it myself; I know that Ali Agha has become martyred! O God!!! What am I to do now?!"

I lowered my face back down and looked to Father and Mother and implored them, begged them, "Isn't that so, Mother? Am I right, Father? Has Ali Agha been martyred? *Has he??*"

Mother started crying; and Father went to a corner of the front yard and leaned his forehead against the wall; and Royā and Nafiseh let the curtain go and slouched back into their room.

I sat down on the cold ground. I felt like clawing the earth and throwing handfuls of soil on my head. But my fingertips were confronted with the cold and hard surface of mosaic tiles. I leaned forward toward the soil of the garden, which was covered with a thin layer of ice. My hands moved around haphazardly looking for something to hold on to. I didn't want to cry if I could help it. With despondency I said, "I knew it. Ali Agha was never one to go against his word; his word was his bond. But Ali Jān, waiting for you is killing me; I've been waiting for you since Tuesday night. You had promised me you'd be back within a week. But in all fairness, Ali Jān, it's Friday now;

didn't you think to yourself that I would be beside myself with worry? Didn't you think to yourself that I would not be able to endure such a great stress? Didn't you take into consideration the fact that I am not well? Did you not think that all this stress and anxiety would not be good for me? And now... what am I to do without you?"

Mother came toward me and took me by the arm. Her face was hidden behind a veil of tears. She uttered with difficulty: "Get up, my love. Would that I was sacrificed for you sake... Come on, get up, dearest, as the ground is cold. You'll catch a cold, *Mādar Jān*."

I had no peace or tranquility. I felt like heading out of the house. I felt like going somewhere far away; somewhere where I wouldn't have to hear this kind of news. What was I supposed to do? I got up off the ground. I asked, "Does Mansūreh Khānūm know?"

Mother raised her shoulders.

I said, "Let's go and see her."

Father came over. His eyes were red. I hadn't seen him like this ever before. Mother dusted off my *chādor* and kissed me, wetting my face in the process with her tears. I asked, "Bābā, do you remember what you told me on the night of the wedding?"

Father wept and shook his head. "You said it is better if my daughter lives with a real man for a single night than for her to live her whole life with one who is merely posing as a man."

Mother said through her tears, "It seems everyone knew from the very beginning that your life would turn out like this. You knew it yourself too, didn't you? We all knew it."

I remembered the day when Ali Agha and his parents had come as suitors to ask for my hand in marriage, and the things that I had said to him. I had told him that I wanted to have a part in the war and in the Islamic Revolution, and that I wanted my husband to be a *pāsdār* or Revolutionary Guard, and for him to be a true believer and a revolutionary.

I thought of the *pāsdārs* as people who were righteous and God-fearing. Ali Agha had said, "It is possible that I might be taken as a prisoner of war, or be wounded or martyred."

And I had smiled and said, "Don't worry; it is not as if all three are going to happen at the same time."

I knew that Ali Agha would never be taken prisoner. But at the same time, I knew in my heart of hearts that just as there was the possibility of being wounded in this path, there was also the possibility of martyrdom.

Mother wiped my tears away with the wing of her *chādor* rapidly and supplicated to Lady Zahra,[93] "*Yā Hazrat-e Zahrā!* O, Your Eminence, Lady Zahrā: give my daughter forbearance and longanimity! *Yā Hazrat-e Zeynab!* O, Lady Zeynab! Please help her!"

---

[93] Her Eminence Lady Fātema' oz-Zahrā (Fātema, the Luminous One), the daughter of the Prophet of Islam and one of the "Fourteen Immaculates" (the Prophet, Lady Fātema, and the Twelve Imams), who are believed by the Shī'a to be sinless and inerrant exemplary models commissioned by Almighty God to act as guides and leaders for mankind. The tee in Fātema' oz-Zahrā is pronounced when the name is followed by the title (*oz-Zahrā*), but is not pronounced when the name appears on its own, in which case the tee is silent.

My shoulders were shaking uncontrollably. The Renault was still parked in front of the door to the front yard. The driver had gotten out and was looking upon us with sadness and sorrow.

I lamented, "Upon my word with God, it was only one night! I only lived for one night!"

I felt like wandering around in the streets aimlessly. I felt like going somewhere far away, to the summit of a mountain, to the middle of the ocean, or up there in the heavens. I wanted to go where no one else could be seen. I felt like screaming and crying aloud for as long as I could. I couldn't see anywhere or anything; it was only Ali Agha's image that was before my eyes.

There was pandemonium in front of Block No. 6, which was Mansūreh Khānūm's apartment building. There was a number of young men dressed in black standing in front of my mother-in-law's building and weeping silently. Mother and Father took me by the arms and we climbed the fifty-four steps with difficulty.

The door to the apartment was open. Mansūreh Khānūm was sitting in the middle of the den. She got up and came over to me as soon as she saw me and embraced me in her arms. Mansūreh Khānūm cried and whispered in my ear: "See what happened, Fereshteh Jān? Ali left us. We lost Ali from our midst! Ali didn't live to see his child. Ali left without that satisfaction. Oh, Ali Jān! Oh, Ali Jān! Would that your mother had died in your stead, my beautiful groom! My groom didn't live the full life that is worthy of a groom! O God!!!"

I felt a hand on my shoulder. The hand held Mansūreh Khānūm and me in its embrace and placed his head between both our shoulders and cried out, "Dear Lord, Dear God, forbearance! Grant us forbearance and strength! Praise be unto You, dear Lord. Ali Jān... Ali! Ali, my son, where did you leave to, *Bābā*?!"

It was Agha Nāser. He cried out loud along with the two of us. And his laments and bawling set off the crowd around us, all of whom started to sob and wail also.

Mother was standing to the side somewhere, but I recognized her voice: "Send *salawāts*. *Yā Hazrat-e Zahrā!* O, Your Eminence, Lady Zahrā: give them longanimity and forbearance! *Yā Hazrat-e Zeynab!* O, Lady Zeynab! Please help them!"

A little later, the three of us separated from each other. Agha Nāser sat in a corner on the floor, raised his knees up to his chest and placed his forehead on his knees. Mansūreh Khānūm moved to and fro, moaning: "Ali! Whose shoulder am I supposed to rest my head on now? Ali Agha, who do I have now to console my heart and to give me comfort and courage? Come back, Ali, and tell me it's a lie. Come and tell me that you haven't left me alone to myself! Oh, Ali Jān! Oh, Ali Agha! O God! My whole life left me! He was my everything... Oh, Ali Jān! Ali Agha left me! ..."

I snuggled up to Mother's breast and asked, "Where is Ali? Let's go and see him."

Mother whispered in my ear, "He's not back yet. He's with his friends."

I asked, "Where was he martyred?"

She said, "In Māwūt, In Iraq. He stepped on a mine." She continued, sobbing, "He's been in the western front line for a few days now. His friends had said their goodbyes to him."

Friends, family and acquaintances all came to pay their respects. No one could believe it; everyone looked at us in shock. It had only been five months since Amīr was martyred.

That night, Maryam and Khānūm Jān and Hājj Bābā and the Tehranī part of the family arrived. What a bitter moment that was! What heart-wrenching cries were heard that night! Maryam's terrible bawling and Mansūreh Khānūm's and Agha Nāser's painful laments were so piteous and doleful. What an endless night; what a long and black Friday!

On Saturday morning, one of Ali Agha's friends brought the news that Ali Agha's body had been brought to Hamedān the previous night and taken to Maryānaj, where they held an all-night vigil and observance for him.

I was completely restless and couldn't stand still for a minute. Everyone had put on their outerwear clothing and was ready to go. I said, "I want to come too."

They said, "No, that's not possible right now."

"I want to come too," I repeated.

They said, "It is ill-advised [according to the sacred law of Islam]. It's not good for your baby."

I cried. I promised that I would be ok. I said, "I swear I won't cry. Please take me along too."

I beseeched Hājj Sādeq: "For the love of God, let me come along too."

An Altar of Roses

I said to Mother, "I miss him, Mother!"

But all of it was to no avail. I begged Agha Nāser. "For the love of God, Agha Nāser, take me along with you."

Agha Nāser pleaded with Mansūreh Khānūm on my behalf: "Let us take Fereshteh along with us too."

I grabbed my mother's hand. "Mother, for God's sake, *you* say something! Do something so that I can come too. I swear to God I won't break down and cry."

Mother made a few calls and put the question to a few people. But they said that it is religiously not advised for a pregnant woman to look upon the body of a *meyyet* or a dead person.

I said, "Ali Agha is not a *meyyet*; he is a *shahīd* (martyr)!"

They finally took mercy on me and said, "It's ok, come along then."

I lowered my head and quietly followed the crowd out. They had taken Ali Agha's casket at night and in secret to a secluded place in a military hospital which was five kilometers out on the road to Kermānshāh in order to ensure that no problems would arise with the *monāfeqīn*.[94] And entry of unauthorized personnel was forbidden at that hospital. Our group had fit in only two cars. We entered the hospital grounds and paused for a little while once we were within the hospital campus. Eventually one of the hospital ambulances led the way and our two cars followed in tow. There was a long and seemingly endless narrow road that wound its way along the hospital

---

[94] See footnote 20.

grounds. The grounds all around the hospital were landscaped like a beautiful garden. The street that we passed was lined on both sides with ancient weeping willow trees. They were dry and bare of any foliage and were covered with a thin layer of snow. There was more snow in the surrounding hills and mountains and prairies, which were all white with a covering of snow.

We covered the seemingly endless road at speed. Everyone was quiet and didn't speak. We all looked at the snow-covered grounds of the hospital through the car windows in bewilderment.

A little later, at the end of that road, a container came into view that was hidden behind a large truck. There were a few Nissan Patrol SUV's parked around the container which belonged to the *Sepāh* or Revolutionary Guards. A few people got out of the ambulance and went toward the container. We got out too. They opened the door of the refrigerated container and lowered the casket to the ground. Hājj Sādeq stepped forward with a broken posture and shoulders which were slouched forward. Agha Nāser rushed forward and embraced the casket. Mother was holding me by the forearm. They opened the casket. Mansūreh Khānūm let out a cry, "Would that I was sacrificed for you sake. Would that your mother died in your stead, Ali! Is this where you spent the night last night, my love?"

Everyone started crying. Mother started to sob; and I bawled without any consideration of the people standing around me.

Mother's hands shook as she caressed my shoulders. The casket was surrounded by people. I made my way to Ali Agha.

My heart was racing. My feet were aquiver. A few people stepped aside.

I sat by the casket. Hajj Sādeq was holding Ali Agha's head in his hands. Agha Nāser and Mansūreh Khānūm were holding his right hand. I was seated to his left. I moved the plastic sheeting to one side, exposing his left hand. It was cold and bloody. The shrapnel from the mine had injured and bloodied the left side of his body and a part of his head. I squeezed his hand. I remembered how much I had stared at these hands the last night we were together, and how I had told myself that I needed to vouchsafe the shape of his hands to my memory, and that I was not to forget the shape and form of his hands and fingers.

No matter what I did, his hands remained cold. Hājj Sādeq got up and gave his place to me. Ali Agha was reposing peaceably and comfortably with a pale face, as if lit by moonlight.

His friends had tied a green headband around his forehead and over his light brown hair. His beard and brows had been combed and were tidy, and his hair was neatly trimmed.

Mother bent over and took me by the hand. "Get up, Fereshteh Jān; come on, get up now."

I said with a lump in my throat, "I won't cry; I'm ok." Mansūreh Khānūm turned to Ali Agha's friends and said, "Is this how you looked out for Ali? My boy caught the death of cold last night! …"

Everyone started to cry. Mother put her hand under my arm. "Get up, Fereshteh Jān; come on, get up now. It's cold; you'll catch a cold."

Everyone was crying except Ali Agha. I said, "Ali Jān, you've found your peace now. Go to sleep, my love. You need to catch up on seven years' lack of sleep. Now it's over. Now you can relax. Sleep. Rest easy. I'm only sorry that you were not able to see your baby. I wish that you had seen your child before you left."

I don't know why but the thought of the pomegranates came into my mind. I wished I could know whether he'd been able to have his split pomegranates, or whether he'd given them away like everything else he possessed.

Mother placed her hands under my arm and helped me up. My legs were slack and lifeless. My teeth were chattering. My hands were still cold from holding Ali Agha's icy cold hands. Everyone was standing around the casket in the black clothing of mourning, weeping for their loss. Again, I couldn't see anywhere or anything. I didn't recognize anyone. Mother and I slowly walked away. I wanted to leave just like that: to leave and go away. I didn't want to believe that I won't be seeing Ali Agha ever again. For me, Ali was alive: in the summit of that mountain, in the sky… he was sitting in the middle of the clouds and was looking down on us; looking out for us; making sure I didn't fall down; making sure nothing bad happened to his child.

I said, "Let's go", and Mother and I strolled away all the way to close to the mountain's outskirts without speaking a word.

I didn't want to believe that Ali Agha had been martyred, but that night the local Hamedān TV network announced the news: "Tomorrow, the eighth of Āzar, has been declared a holiday in commemoration of the martyrdom of the courageous

Commander of Islam, Ali Chītsāzīān. Three days of public mourning have been declared for the province of Hamedān."

The family was gathered together and was talking about tomorrow's funeral and wake ceremonies. It was decided that Hājj Sādeq would give a speech. Agha Nāser shied away from speaking. I determined that I was not among those who were going to speak.

On Sunday morning, there was bedlam in front of my mother-in-law's house. People had gathered in droves in the public thoroughfares of the apartment buildings of the Honarestān housing development with placards and flags of mourning. I was standing behind the window, looking at the gathered crowd. Someone said from within the room, "They've brought Ali Agha." An ambulance entered the alley. The casket was wrapped in the tri-colored flag of the Islamic Republic of Iran and it was being carried on the roof of the ambulance. My legs quivered. I held onto the wall to keep myself from falling down. The lump in my throat broke out into a flood of tears. After a year and eight months of married life, Ali Agha still didn't have a home he could call his own. I thought of our belongings, each of which were stored in a different place: half in Mother's storage room and half in Hājj Sādeq's house; with my bag of clothes in a corner of a room in Mansūreh Khānūm's apartment.

In the street below, the people were shouting:

Woe! Ali has been slain!

The Lion of God[95] has been slain!

وای علی کشته شد! شیرِ خدا کشته شد!

These voices made my body quiver. They lowered the casket from the roof of the ambulance. The neighbors in the opposite apartment blocks were standing behind their windows, weeping. The streets were completely packed with people. The huge crowd was like the body of a hydra, one of whose heads was in the apartment of my mother in law, and whose other heads were in the various alleys and walkways which lead away from the center of the body where Ali Agha's casket lay. The crowd was so thick that they were not able to navigate through it to bring the casket upstairs. They put it back on the roof of the ambulance instead. When the ambulance started to move, the crowd chased after it, continuing to chant their elegiac slogans and couplets.

The mood in the house was somber and sad and the atmosphere weighed heavily on everyone. The streets and environs of the Honarestān housing development had never seen such a crowd before. The people chanted, "Yā Hosayn! Yā Hosayn!" "O Hosayn! O Hosayn!"

It tore my heart to pieces. I felt like opening the window and flying out like a bird and leaving. Leaving for the distant climes where Ali Agha now resided; where Ali Agha and his martyr friends talked and laughed.

The people had created quite a pandemonium around the casket. They beat their chests and heads and faces in

---

[95] The Lion of God is one of the honorifics of Imam Ali.

mourning and commiseration, and shouted, "Yā Hosayn!" Many of the mourners had shown up barefoot in the ice and snow for this funeral ceremony.

Mother stood beside me. There were a few cars waiting outside to take us to the Bāgh-e Behesht cemetery. The street was still crowded. They forged a path for us and we got in a Nissan Patrol. The area by the front door of the apartment had been covered in black banners and placards.

When we entered the street, we saw Ali Agha's picture on the walls and behind shop windows. The following inscription was written on the black banners: "Congratulations on your martyrdom, Ali Jān." Black flags were hanging over the doors of office buildings, on rooftops, and over windows and doors. Mother constantly whispered in my ear: "Fereshteh Jān, hold yourself together. The situation is going to be very different when we get to the cemetery. There will be all sorts of people there. It will be a mixed crowd of friends and foe alike. Be strong, *Mādar*; don't show any weakness."

Ali Agha's picture smiled at me from the rear window of the cars in the traffic which we had to work our way through on the way there. His picture was everywhere; any direction that one cared to turn one's head, one could see a picture of him. I had never seen the route from our house to the cemetery be this crowded and to take so long.

The driver took an alternate route and said, "The people have gathered in the Imam Square and they plan to carry Ali

Agha's casket from the square to the cemetery in a formal procession."

The alternate route was about five kilometers. When we reached the cemetery, we heard Ali Agha's voice being broadcast from the speakers. I didn't feel well. How was I supposed to believe that the owner of that voice was no longer with us? I could not accept the fact that I was never going to see him again. No, no; I missed him already. I wanted to be with him, and had become like a child who kept making some impossible request from her mother. Hearing Ali Agha's voice had affected Maryam and she had started to shed tears involuntarily, but she did so silently. I saw Ali Agha in front of me; as always, he walked with square shoulders and a strong gait.

I thought to myself, "Where are you going, Ali Agha? Weren't we supposed to save our earnings so that we could have a house of our own after two years and start our life together? So, is this what the dodging of buying a house was all about? You were looking for real estate in a better neighborhood, huh?" I started to cry. I thought that Ali Agha really believed death [in God's cause] to be more beautiful than life. I whispered, "Is martyrdom so sweet and desirable that you courted it like a suitor and preferred it to me and to your unborn child and to your mother and father, all of whom you loved so much? How did you come to such an understanding of the sweetness of its taste? How did you attain to such wisdom? After all, you were only in your mid-twenties! And what feelings do you have now that you have accomplished your objective? Joy? Freedom? Release? And if this is your emotional state, then why am I feeling so miserable? Why is there a tempest raging in my heart? Why can't I swallow the lump in my throat? Why can't I breakdown and cry? Why am I so restless?" And these words broke my heart. In those moments, I came to feel with all my being what it truly meant when one said that one's heart was broken.

A large crowd had come to the Bāgh-e Behesht cemetery. The place was packed and there was hardly any room to move. A young man got out of a Nissan Patrol SUV and came over and started to talk to our driver. Then a few others opened a path between the crowd, and our car waded through the crowd inside the cemetery to where the crowd was making ritual supplications in congregation for those who have passed (*namāz-e meyyet*). To the right of the area, there was the building where they gave the body its final full body ritual purification or *ghosl*, which was divided into a male and female area. Between these two areas there was a staircase to the second floor. The same few people opened up a path for us, and we went upstairs.

There were two rooms on the second floor. The menfolk were sitting inside one of the two rooms: the commanders of the *Sepāh*, the Army, and the Air Force; the Governor of the province, the Friday Prayer Leader, and other high provincial officials and dignitaries. There was a long and narrow balcony at the front of the building which was used for various funeral ceremonies. When we entered the room where the womenfolk were gathered, I started to feel ill. I cursed myself for having to be there. Mansūreh Khānum and Khānum Jān and Aunt Fātemeh had arrived there before us. Mother went and fetched me a glass of water.

Maryam had come with our car, and she now went and took a seat next to her mother. After about an hour, the sound of people could be heard chanting slogans outside:

> Don the dress of mourning,
> For Ali has been slain.
> Woe, Ali has been slain!
> The Lion of God has been slain!

رخت عزا به تن کنید   که علی کشته شد!
وای علی کشته شد!   شیرِ خدا کشته شد!

A young woman entered the room who was holding her *chādor* very close around her face and body, such that it covered her forehead right above her eyebrows; as well as her chin and the greater part of her face. She said, "Excuse me, where is the martyr's wife sitting?"

Mother pointed to me, and I said, "Can I help you?"

The young lady came over. I could only see her eyes and nose. She said, "It is arranged that you are to be one of the speakers, sister."

Hearing this made me panic. I said, "What?? A speech!? No, no such thing has been arranged with me!"

The woman said, "Your name is on the list. Your turn comes after the martyr's brother." I mumbled something under my breath. "Why was I not informed earlier? You could have at least told me last night."

The woman didn't say anything and just left.

The room in which we were seated didn't have any windows, but the sounds from outside could be heard clearly. Suddenly I heard Ali Agha's voice. They were playing a tape of one of his speeches. Everyone came to attention, and Mansūreh Khānūm started to cry.

Ali Agha was saying, "All of our values are [personified] in the martyr. Happy is the destiny of the martyrs, for they are the flagrant flowers which God picks for Himself. They are [the ones who are] chosen by Almighty God. The martyrs are alive... for those who continue on their path. Be worthy trustees of the path that they have left in trust to you..."

Mansūreh Khānūm was lamenting her loss, saying things like, "Would that I was sacrificed for you, who was a flower which God picked. Would that God had taken your mother instead of you, who always used to say 'happy is the destiny of the martyrs'. Now it is our turn to say 'happy is your destiny', Ali Jān! ..."

Mansūreh Khānūm said these words and sobbed. I thought, "Ali Jān, I can't speak as well as you; I'm afraid I'll say something and embarrass you."

Mother brought me a pen and some paper and said, "Here, take this, Fereshteh Jān. Write it down so you won't forget."

I took the pen and paper. It was the first time I was going to make a speech; and I had to deliver it to such a large crowd. What did I, who had not even gotten my high school diploma [yet], have to say to these people? What was I supposed to write down?

I said, "Ali Jān, you said it yourself, that martyrs are alive. That they are alive for those who continue on their path. And so, if you are here with me, help me."

When I put my pen to paper, the words started to stream through my mind. I started writing the words and I had the feeling that he was standing next to me. I could hear his voice; it was as if he was dictating the words and I was writing them down. I wanted to just continue writing like that so that I would continue to hear his voice uninterrupted. Eventually Ali said *wa salāmū alaykom wa rahmatollahī wa barakātū*.[96] I could still feel his presence after I wrote those closing words and placed the pen down on the paper. I felt he was still talking to me, saying, "Fereshteh Jān, stand strong, like Zeynab did; be just like Zeynab!"

My tears started to flow down my cheeks.

I said, "Help me. Help me to read it without making any mistakes."

Ali Agha smiled, and his smile brought peace and tranquility to every inch of my being. The people's voices could be heard from outside:

> For the burial of the martyrs,
> Come, O Universal Savior,
> Come, O Mahdi!

---

[96] This is the traditional formulaic way in which religious people and the clergy in Islamic countries end a speech or sermon, after the example of the Prophet. The literal meaning of the words is: May God's peace and mercy and blessings be with you.

برای دفن شهدا   مهدی، بیا! مهدی، بیا!

Maryam and Mansūreh Khānum and Khānum Jān started to weep when they heard these words. Mother was stronger and held her own. A little later the chanting stopped and the sound of a funeral dirge could be heard. After that, someone started a Quranic recitation with a peculiar elegiac tone.

Maryam and Khānum Jān and Aunt Fātemeh were trying to raise Mansūreh Khānum's spirits. Her condition had worsened these last few days and her kidneys were giving her a lot of trouble. Maryam said, "*Mamān*, if you cry, your condition will only get worse. Did you forget what the doctor said? Grieving and crying are like poison for your condition!" Mansūreh Khānum replied impatiently, "Well, then, poison it is! I don't even want to live, with Ali gone!"

After the Quranic recitation, the sound of the crowd chanting shook the room:

> Mourning and lament!
> Today is a day for mourning and lament!
> Mahdi, the Lord of the Age,
> Is the lord of mourning and lament today!

عزا، عزاست امروز   روز عزاست امروز
مهدیِ صاحبِ زمان   صاحبِ عزاست امروز

That same young lady entered the room and said, "Mrs. Panāhī, be on the ready. It will be your turn after the martyr's brother's speech."

All of a sudden, my hands froze. I could hear my heart beating. I talked myself up and gave myself courage.

After Hājj Sādeq's speech, the people shouted, "*Allāho akbar! Allāho akbar!* God is greater! God overcomes [all adversity]! Khomeinī is our leader! Down with the Hypocrites and Saddām! Hail to the Soldiers of Islam! Peace and blessings unto the martyrs!"

I got up onto my feet. The woman appeared in the doorway. Mother got up and accompanied me up to the balcony door, sending *salawāts* for me in rapid succession. A *pāsdār* or Revolutionary Guard stepped aside from the balcony door and said, "This way please, Mrs. Chītsāzīān."

The crowd continued their chanting:

Woe! Ali has been slain!
The Lion of God has been slain!
O Hosayn!

وای علی کشته شد! شیرِ خدا کشته شد!

The balcony was full of dignitaries and high officials who were standing in line in front of the crowd. The *pāsdār* who had been guarding the door forged ahead and lead the way all the way to the podium, where he started to adjust the height of the microphone. When I stood behind the podium, I was able to see the whole crowd who had gathered in the cemetery grounds. There were also some people standing on the roof of the mosque which was opposite the building where they gave the bodies their final full-body ritual purification rites. There were two soldiers holding each end of a placard on the top left corner of which was Ali Agha's picture, and on which it was written in large lettering, "Congratulations on your martyrdom, Ali Jān."

There was a large crowd gathered to the right, at the grave site of Āyatollāh Ākhūnd Mollā Alī Ma'sūmī-e Hamedānī. To the left there was nothing but a large throng of people to be seen, all the way back to the entrance gate to the cemetery and even beyond it. It was a sea of people wearing the black clothing of mourning for as long as the eye could see who had shown up to witness the funeral ceremony of their beloved commander. I had never seen such a large crowd in the Bāgh-e Behesht cemetery before. The *pāsdār* who had adjusted the microphone for me indicated that it was ready for me to begin.

"In the name of God, the *pāsdār* (or Guardian) of the dignity and honor of the shed blood of the martyrs, and the Helper of the oppressed…"

I felt my voice was quivering. I screamed inside: "Ali, Ali Jān, help!!!"

"I do not consider myself to be worthy of being able to stand before you in this sacred station and deliver a speech. I just wanted to make a brief appearance as a sign of respect before all of you dearly beloved friends and acquaintances who have honored us and gone to the trouble of being present at the funeral of the courageous Commander of Islam, Ali Chītsāzīān."

I drew in a deep breath. The crowd was completely silent. I raised my head. Ali was smiling at me in the picture on the placard opposite me. I continued:

"And similarly, I do not consider myself worthy of being the wife of such a personality: someone who was so God-fearing, so pious, so courageous, and so full of selflessness and self-sacrifice."

At the same time that I was stating these words, I recalled each of these attributes in Ali Agha, and examples of each of these characteristics of his came to my mind. I said, "Ali Agha was the boon companion and helper of the orphans." And I remembered that in these last few days one of his friends related that whenever Ali and his friends came on leave to Hamedān, they would fill a pickup truck full of food and clothing and other necessities and would go to the Sang-e Sefid neighborhood and distribute everything to addresses which they had determined beforehand. They would leave the goods outside the doors and honk their horn a couple of times to let the recipients know someone was outside. The families in need had come to recognize these sounds for what they were. Ali Agha and his friends would step on the gas and leave, followed by the families who would come to their front doors to collect their rations and take them inside.

I said, "Ali is the kind of person whose memory is still alive in all of the fronts of the war and in the hearts and minds of all of our dear brothers and courageous and honorable soldiers who are present in the field of battle."

Suddenly the sound of the crowd breaking down in tears could be heard. I resisted [the urge to do the same] and pulled myself together.

"This humble servant humbly requests all of the mothers, wives and sisters here present to abide by the wishes and order of our beloved *imam* [Imam Khomeini], and to send their men to the fronts in the war of the forces of good against the forces of evil."

In a split second I remembered that Ali Agha had stood behind this same podium on the day the martyrdom of Amīr Agha was being commemorated, and that he had made a similar appeal to the people not to abandon the war fronts.

I could hear Ali Agha's voice reverberating in my ears: "And so I say to you now that we should not act in a way that would compel the *imam* to go back to the podium and to implore us for the umpteenth time to go to the front lines…"

I said, "God willing, your presence in the warfronts will cause the enemy to be defeated and bring the army of Islam to victory all the sooner. I again thank you all from the bottom of my heart, and I pray that you will all continue on the path of the martyrs, and especially of this great martyr. *Wa salāmū alaykom wa rahmatollahī wa barakātū.*"

When I said these words, I saw that Mansūreh Khānūm was standing beside me, and that the same *pāsdār* was presenting her and me with a few stems of white gladiolas. We took the flowers and threw them onto the crowd below. The crowd's chanting of *allāho akbar!* shook the cemetery once again. Among that cacophony of sound, I made out the lamentations of a few people moaning Ali Agha's name and sobbing, and their voices touched the depths of my heart.

Mansūreh Khānūm and I went back inside. The people continued their laments and the beating of their chests in a ritual of redemptive suffering (*sīneh-zanī*) unabated. That same woman who had told me to be prepared to make my speech came into the room and said, "Thank you very much, Mrs. Chītsāzīān. It was a great speech!"

I said, "Please take me downstairs. I want to be at Ali Agha's side when they start the procession to the grave."

The woman glanced over at Mansūreh Khānūm and toward Mother and said, "The crowd is so thick that even the dignitaries and high officials will not be able to make it through to the burial. His friends erected a fence around the gravesite last night to keep people away, but I heard that this didn't stop the crowd. I hear its pandemonium over there. One of his comrades in arms, Mr. Elāhī, who is a man of the cloth, has been inside his grave since early morning, reciting the Quran and the Zīārat Āshūrā.[97] I don't think you'll be able to get close to there."

Mansūreh Khānūm said, "If only they would have buried Ali next to his brother."

The young lady said, "Hājj Khānūm, the adjacent grave belongs to someone who is Missing in Action. And the father of the MIA soldier has placed a tombstone over the grave as a way to reconcile his wife with the loss of her son, on which the name of their martyr has been engraved. They come to the grave on

---

[97] See note 90.

Thursday nights and recite a prayer. They gave the grave as a gift to your Ali Agha. They said that it would be an honor if our son's grave would belong to Ali Agha. They said that they would be happier this way, and their son would be more contented too. Pray that Hājj Khānūm's son is not martyred so that he returns [in good alive and in good health]."

Mansūreh Khānūm raised her hands heavenward in the ritual formation of supplication and prayer. "*Āmīn, rabbī*. Amen, my Lord. Pray God that He will make it so that their hopes will not be frustrated. Pray God that their hearts will be full of joy. O Lord, I beseech you on the right that our broken hearts have, to make it so that their hearts will be joyous, and that their hopes will not be dashed. O Lord, I beseech you on the right that the broken ribs of her Eminence Lady Fātema^t oz-Zahrā have, to make it so that they no longer have to wait in suspense for their missing son. *Āmīn*."

Then Mansūreh Khānūm sobbed, "Happy your fortune, Amīr! Get up! You have a guest tonight. Ali Agha has come to visit. Your brother has come to see you."

Hearing these words made everyone break down and cry. Mansūreh Khānūm and Maryam and Khānūm Jān and Aunt Fātemeh insisted on going to the gravesite, and they started to make their way toward it, but no matter what I did, I was not given permission to go along, [because of my pregnancy]. And so, Mother and I stayed behind and waited in the room.

Time dragged and moved with difficulty. The next two or three hours passed for me like they were two or three days. I begged and pleaded with Mother to take me to the gravesite so that I could say my last goodbye. But instead, Mother took my hands in hers and kept on reciting verses and short chapters from the Quran. And sometimes she would put her hand on my heart and recite the *tasbīhāt* of Her Eminence Lady Zahrā.[98] I had peeled my ears in an effort to figure out what was going on outside. I felt that my heart had stopped beating for a few minutes. Something inside me imploded. I stood up and ran toward the door. Mother grabbed hold of my arm and I started to weep. I sat down on the floor and sobbed: "Mother, Ali Agha's soul departed! I'm sure he just left from our midst."

Mother started to weep too. I put my head on her breast and said, "Mother, I'm never going to see him again. I'm sure he has been buried by now. I saw him. He came to bid me farewell."

Mother, who had controlled herself in front of me, started to bawl.

"Ali Agha Jān, *khodā hāfez*, fare thee well and may God protect you."

Mother's breast was a suitable place for my sobbing. A little later, Hājj Sādeq and Agha Nāser and a few other people entered the room. Their black clothes were streaked with soil and they were unkempt and disheveled. We went down the stairs. The crowd had thinned around the environs of the building, but the cemetery itself was still swarming with people. But it had thinned enough to allow us to make our way on foot between the

---

[98] These are *zekrs* or ritual invocations of blessings and grace which consist of the repetition of the following three formulas thirty-three times each: *allāhū akbar, sobhān allāh*, and *alhamdolellāh*: God is greater, Glory be to God, and God be praised.

crowds, even though my legs wobbled and I could barely walk. They said that two or three of Ali Agha's fellow soldiers passed out and had to be taken to the hospital.

The gravesite was still very crowded. I didn't feel like fighting the crowd. I whispered under my breath: "Ali Agha, you got your wish, but I don't have the strength to withstand so much sorrow and a lifetime of loneliness without you."

A few people saw us, and as soon as they did, they shouted, "Make way for the martyr's mother and family." A path parted before us. Hājj Sādeq was holding his mother by the arm. Hamīd Agha, Maryam's husband, held her hand. Mother and Father were walking ahead of me, talking to Agha Nāser. I said, "Ali Jān, who is going to hold my hand? Whose shoulder am I to rest my head on? How soon you left me on my own, Ali! How soon have I become alone! I'm still only nineteen!"

I couldn't sit cross-legged. I picked a spot and stood there. His grave was full of white gladiolas. I pulled my *chādor* over my face. The smell of rose water filled the air. I didn't want to think about the fact that Ali was buried under there; under all that earth. No, Ali wasn't there; Ali was up there in the heavens. I set my *chādor* aside and raised my head upward. Even though the sky was clear and sunny, the air had a cold nip in it. I said, "Ali Jān, where are you? Up in the sky! I turned up, but he wasn't there. I couldn't see him.

"Where am I supposed to look for you, my love?"

I felt a warmth next to me and thought it was my mother. I looked but it wasn't her. There was nobody there. So where did this warmth come from? Ali Agha's image resolved before my eyes, with his light brown hair, blue eyes, and haggard beard. I kept saying, "Ali Jān, trim your beard!" And he would say, "No, it's too soon." And I would respond, "Ali Jān, had you let your beard grow in anticipation of today?"

With this thought I started to cry again, but I felt Ali was standing next to me. I leaned into the warmth and at that moment heard Ali Agha's voice in his thick Hamedānī accent: "Fereshteh, *halālam kon*, forgive me any trespass that I might have committed against you. Stay strong like Zeynab, my love; live strong like Zeynab!"

Mansūreh Khānum and Maryam had thrown themselves on the flowers which were over the grave. Their shoulders trembled with their silent weeping. I had a strange feeling. I thought that if I were to live like Zeynab, how was I supposed to behave at this very moment?

A vicious lump was clawing the back of my throat. I bit my lower lip with my upper teeth. I went and sat down next to Amīr's grave with difficulty. I made my hands into a hemisphere on the gravestone and recited the *fāteha*.[99] I whispered, "Amīr Jān, take care of my Ali for me." A Nissan Patrol cruised by; it was carrying a large picture of Ali. Ali passed us by quickly. He left... a cold wind blew us by. Agha Nāser bent over and helped Mansūreh Khānum get up. And Maryam's husband stepped forward too and peeled her away from the flowers on the grave. Mother and Father each took one of my arms gently. I felt like

---

[99] The opening chapter of the Quran.

crying again. I didn't want to leave. I didn't want to part from Ali so soon! I said, "Mother, let's not go yet."

Mother was crying. I said, "Bābā, let's stay a while longer."

Father's strong shoulders were shaking. My legs were quivering. My hands were frozen. I missed Ali already. Just then I wanted everyone to leave so that I could be alone with him. I wanted Ali to stand beside me like he had done a few minutes ago so that I could ask him, "Ali Agha, what does Zeynab-like mean?" I wanted the cemetery to be completely secluded so that I could cry at the top of my lungs.

When we sat in the car, the driver turned on the tape recorder. The tape consisted of a series of heart-wrenching elegies. I remember the elegy that was playing was about the trials and difficulties Her Eminence Lady Zeynab suffered in the cause of her brother Imam Hosayn. It brought tears to my eyes. I placed my head on Mother's shoulders and covered my face with my *chādor* and wept silently. I wept, and wept, all the way home.

Father's Star

The commemoration ceremonies were held for Agha Ali throughout the province, and these lasted until the fortieth day of his martyrdom, and even until its fiftieth day. I participated in the family's commemoration ceremonies during the first few days. But from the second week on, it was only Agha Nāser and Hājj Sādeq who would attend, after which point it became a matter of taking turns: either one or the other of them would go, but not both.

Gradually the phase of strange dreams started. The family and even the neighbors would dream of Ali Agha and relate their dreams to us with passion. Hearing the dreams being recounted made us miss him all the more, but at the same time they brought a certain peace and tranquility to our hearts. Everyone saw Ali Agha in their dreams in the best of places and dressed in the best of clothes. The dreams spoke of the fact that he had attained to a high spiritual station in the hereafter, and that he was contented. But he was worried; worried about us Earthlings, and especially worried about his mother.

Mansūreh Khānūm's illness peaked with Ali Agha's martyrdom, to the point where Agha Nāser and Hājj Sādeq had to take her to Tehran to see specialists a few days after the fortieth day of Ali Agha's passing. Those days coincided with the height of the Hamedān winter as well. Snow and ice prevented people from leaving their homes except to take care of unavoidable business. But notwithstanding these conditions, after Mansūreh Khānūm left for Tehran, I packed what little belongings I had and having wrapped Mohammad Ali safely in a blanket, moved back to my mother's home.

Mother and Father accepted me into their open arms as usual. I started to feel better once I moved back there. It felt like Ali Agha was still on the front lines and would be back to visit before too long. The cold days of winter passed by very slowly. The news that we got from Tehran was not good. Mansūreh Khānūm's kidneys were not functioning properly and the cysts had grown larger. The doctors recommended dialysis. And so it was that Mansūreh Khānūm's unpleasant dialysis sessions started.

One evening I was sitting with Mother and Father at home; we were looking out the window at an unceasing snow storm. Mother was sewing clothes for Mohammad Ali. Father asked, "Fereshteh, have you decided what you want to do?"

I was surprised at this question of my father's. I said, "Well, isn't it obvious? I want to raise Mohammad Ali."

Father asked, "And that's all?"

I said, "Raising Mohammad Ali is a lifetime's work!"

Mother interrupted Father, "Additionally, Fereshteh needs to continue and finish her studies."

I had no patience for classes and homework. "When am I going to have time to study when I have a baby to take care of??"

Mother said, "We'll help you. You have to continue your studies!"

Father faced Mother and I, and said, "OK, let's assume you continue and finish your studies. Then what??"

I knew what Father was getting at with these questions of his. I couldn't stand it anymore and started to cry. Mohammad Ali was sleeping in a corner of the room. I crawled on my hands and knees over to him and told him quietly so as not to wake him, "I guess that's it; my life is over."

Mother came over to me, concerned. I got up; I wanted to leave the room. I said to Father, "Bābā, Do you remember what you said to Ali Agha on the night of the wedding? You said 'it is better if my daughter lives with a real man for a single night than for her to live her whole life with one who is merely posing as a man'. The last year and eight months went by like lightning. For me it was like a night. I lived with a man for a single night, and that's that; I don't think there will be anyone else like him to be found." Then I looked at my wedding ring through my tears and said, "Have you seen anyone who is more of a man than Ali, Father?"

Father got up and came and stood next to me. His eyes were red and full of tears. I hadn't seen him like this before. He embraced me and kissed me and said, "No, Bābā Jān; no. I don't know of any such man; I swear it. Ali Agha was truly a great man. He was unique: there's no one else like him."

Father placed his head on my shoulder. I was staring at my wedding ring and was thinking about the day we went and bought it on the day we were betrothed. Father said, "Fereshteh, your mother and I are here for you and your son. If you deem us to be worthy, you and your son are welcome to stay with us for as long as you want."

I started crying again. Mother started crying too. The sound of our sobs woke Mohammad Ali up. Mother picked him up and kissed him. Father went and stood behind the window. The snowfall had covered the front yard with a white blanket. He said, "Come the spring, we'll build an addition on the roof. You need to have a place of your own. You need to have your independence. Whatever you need, you just tell me, Bābā Jān, and I'll buy it for you, Bābā. Don't you worry about a thing. You and Ali Agha and his son have a claim over us, and we are very much in your debt."

The following spring, as soon as the weather started to warm up a little, Father brought over a couple of masons and ironworkers and some laborers and building materials and started building an addition up on the roof which consisted of a room, a kitchen, and a bathroom, with the rest of the roof area serving as our 'front yard'. When Mohammad Ali grew up a little, we used to spend our summer nights on the roof in our 'front yard'.

Mohammad Ali missed his father: "Where is my father?"

"He's next to God."

"Why doesn't he come next to me?"

"Because he is looking out for us from up there."

"But didn't you say that God is looking out for us? Besides, Mādar Jūn and Bābā Jūn and you are looking out for me."

I would be lost for words with which to reply to him.

"Do you see that star?"

"Sure!" Mohammad Ali replied with glee.

"That is your dear father's star."

That made Mohammad Ali happy. He would stretch his arm out so that he could hug his father, but he couldn't reach it. And then he would start to cry. And I couldn't calm him down no matter what trick I tried. I would pick him up and hug him and kiss him. He smelled just like Ali Agha. I would address him as "Ali Jān" as a reminder of how I used to talk to Ali Agha. Everyone used to refer to him as "Ali" in honor of his father's memory. Ali Jān, my son, usually cried himself to sleep.

The Parent-Student

I started to go back to school. I had to take the tenth grade over again, because I was not able to sit the tenth-grade finals in 1987 due to my engagement and marriage commitments, after which we left for Dezfūl of course. But with the encouragement and upon the insistence of my mother, I registered to attend the tenth grade for the third time in the 1989-90 academic year. Mother had reduced her workload at her sewing workshop. She would come upstairs in the mornings and take care of 'Ali Jān'. A year went by in this fashion. The principal of the Tahzīb School had set aside and equipped one of the rooms of the school as a makeshift day care center in order to help teachers who had young kids.

I would get to school before everyone else and entrust Ali to the daycare manager; and I would go and fetch him later than everyone else in the afternoon so that no one would become aware of the fact that I was married and had a child. But in the following year I registered Ali in another daycare center so as to avoid the possibility of such entanglements altogether.

And so, these were the kinds of conditions in which I was finally able to get my high school diploma. Ali was four years old by then. Mother insisted that I participate in the test which the Ministry of Education carried out each year for hiring teachers. I took the test and was accepted and started work as a teacher in the Twenty-Second of Bahman[100] Elementary School for Boys, which is located in the Manūchehrī district, which is the district where Hamedān's leatherworkers are located.

---

[100] The Twenty-Second of Bahman is the anniversary of the triumph of the Islamic Revolution of Iran.

Behind the Row of Trees

It was the 16th of August, 1995. Mansūreh Khānūm had been hospitalized for a few days in the Ekbātān Hospital after having had a heart attack. She had had a successful kidney transplant operation, but this time it was her heart which was giving her trouble and had made her bedridden.

Mother and I went to visit her that day. Maryam was there too, worried and restless. She started to weep as soon as she saw us.

"Fereshteh Jān, Vajīheh Khānūm, *Māmān* is not at all well," she said. She then turned to Mother and pleaded, "Please pray for her, Vajīheh Khānūm!"

With Maryam's intervening on our behalf, we were let into the CCU ward in lieu of Maryam, who waited outside. Mansūreh Khānūm was lying on the bed and looked emaciated and as white as a ghost. There was a whole bunch of tubes and hoses attached to her arm and nose. And there was a small screen next to her which monitored her pulse and blood pressure. Her heart rate was very erratic: 105, 180, 100, 120, 200, and so on. I took her hand in mine; it was cold. I looked at Mother with concern. She shook her head with sadness and took out her copy of the Quran which was leather-bound and zippered – the one which she always had with her – and said, "Go and get a glass of water, Fereshteh."

She then said in a kind voice, "How are you feeling, Mansūreh Khānūm Jān? Are you well?"

I started looking for a glass. There was a pitcher and a glass on the small refrigerator by the window. I filled the glass with cold water from the fridge and brought it back to the bedside. Mansūreh Khānūm opened her eyes slowly and as soon as she saw me asked, "Fereshteh Jān, how are you? How is Ali Jān? Is he well? Where is he? Did you bring him?"

I responded clumsily, "*Salām*. Are you well, God grant? I wanted to bring Ali Jān, but I was concerned they might not let him in. I'll talk to the administrators and will be sure to bring him tomorrow."

Mansūreh Khānūm closed her eyes. A few tears slid from her cheek onto her pillow. Then she opened her eyes again and said with a lump in her throat, "Vajīheh Khānūm, if I die, then I will see Amīr and Ali again…"

Mother responded gently as if there was no problem and she was happy about the current state of affairs, "God forbid, Mansūreh Khānūm! Rest assured that they are both here right now, right next to you. One of them is standing to your right and the other to your left. They are helping you to recover ever faster. And Ali Jān will be grown up before you know it and will buy a car and come and pick us up and take us for rides. And so, you still have to hold on for some years to come! May God grant you long life!"

Mansūreh Khānūm let out a deep sigh and said, "No, Vajīheh Khānūm Jān, it's all but over now. I can't stand being away from my boys any longer. It's been eight years since I saw my boys. I want to leave. I miss them terribly."

She was visibly distraught. She closed her eyes and let them stay closed. Mother quickly dipped each of the four corners of her Quran in the glass of water which she then gave me, saying, "Wet her lips with a tissue."

I pulled out a tissue from the steel stand next to the bed, wet it with the water from the glass and gently moistened Mansūreh Khānūm's lips with it. Mansūreh Khānūm slowly opened her eyelids halfway. She looked at me lifelessly and then closed her eyelids again. Mother pointed to Mansūreh Khānūm's feet. I pulled out another tissue, wet it, and drew the sheet aside. I placed my hand on Mansūreh Khānūm's feet. They were as cold as ice. Concerned, I said to Mother, "*Mādar*, her feet are ice cold!"

Acting like she knew exactly what was going on, Mother opened the Quran. She placed her hand on Mansūreh Khānūm's heart and began reciting the Quran. I looked at the monitor: 30, 25, 20, 32… The spikes on the cardiopulmonary monitor's rhythm strip had started to flatten. I grabbed Mansūreh

Khānūm's hands and they were ice cold too. I could see beads of sweat on her forehead and upper lip. She was wheezing. I looked at Mother with concern and ran out to the nurse's station. A nurse was entering the room at the same time. I said, "Nurse, Mrs. Altāfi... my mother-in-law... is feeling very poorly..."

The nurse rushed in. A few other nurses rushed in and gathered around Mansūreh Khānūm's bed. Mother was sitting on the chair beside the bed and was calmly continuing her Quranic recitation. As for me, it was as if someone had placed both their hands around my throat and was busy strangling me. Something or someone was clawing at my heart. Everything smelled of sorrow. The world had become petty and worthless for me. O God! You mean to say that Mansūreh Khānūm left us, just as simple as that? The room was closing in on me and I couldn't see the nurses. I spied something beyond the window. Behind the row of tall green trees, Ali Agha and Amīr were standing far away, in the heart of the sky. The room had taken on a dolorous odor. I had had enough of the life of the *donyā*, of this lower world and domain of existence. I couldn't believe that Mansūreh Khānūm had left us so soon.

The nurses asked us to leave the room and brought in a defibrillator and delivered electric shocks to Mansūreh Khānūm. A couple of doctors ran into the room, but a little later I looked with incredulity as the nurses decoupled the hoses and monitor wires from Mansūreh Khānūm's body.

A Miraculous Sign

The days pass by like lightning now, but those days were the hardest days of my life and each of their moments pass by with difficulty. After Mansūreh Khānūm's passing, life turned even harder. I became more isolated.

After Ali Agha was martyred, Agha Nāser and Hājj Sādeq had bought an apartment and lived together. And Ali Jān and I would always go and visit them on the weekends. This arrangement continued after Mansūreh Khānūm's passing. What made these visits especially necessary was the fact that Hājj Sādeq also had had to have a kidney transplant due to the genetic ailment which he had inherited from his mother. And so, we would pay them a visit to see how they were doing; but with Mansūreh Khānūm's passing, I had lost a strong buttress of support. But life went on, with difficulty, accompanied by the pain of loss and loneliness.

Ali Jān had turned eleven in 1998 and was in the fifth grade. He had been ill for several months with stomach troubles and nausea. Thus, Mother and I were busy in those days, occupied with taking him from one specialist to another each afternoon. After having run the whole gamut of tests and sonography and endoscopy and color imagery, the diagnosis of several doctors was that he had a duodenal ulcer.

Hearing this diagnosis made no sense to me. Mother and I had raised this child in a bed of goose down, so to speak; we were so careful to ensure that all his needs were met. So then why did it have to turn out like this?!

The anniversary of Ali Agha's martyrdom was approaching. He had been martyred on the fourth of Āzar, and buried on the eighth. Each year, we held commemoration events on and in between those days. And if either of those two days fell on a weekend, then the commemoration ceremonies were all the more resplendent.

Mother was busy with the commemoration arrangements. She was giving the house a thorough going over in anticipation, and had taken the couch and armchairs out of the way and put them into temporary storage. She washed the crockery and glassware that was used to serve fruit and halva and tea to the guests, and she polished the salt shakers that the guests used to sprinkle salt on the delicate and fragrant Persian cucumbers, which they peeled and ate as a fruit. And she had invited a large number of guests and ordered copious amounts of fruit and halva for them.

Those days coincided with the peak of Ali Jān's illness. His illness had become so bad that he could barely take in a glass of water. We therefore postponed the major commemoration of the anniversary from the fourth of Āzar to the eighth. We had no choice. The last doctor whom we had seen had looked at the various test results and lab imagery and said, "A small duodenal ulcer can be seen in the picture. You need to take the patient to Tehran immediately."

On the sixth of Āzar, we eventually found one of the best specialist physicians for duodenal ulcers after much asking around, managed to get an appointment, and headed out for Tehran on an overnight bus.

In those days, not everyone had cell phones. One of my friends lent me her cell phone for the occasion. Ali Jān had stopped eating. All he did was throw up whatever he ate. He was feeling so poorly on the bus that the passengers who were seated in the adjacent front and back rows tried to help us in any way they could. But despite this, Ali Jān would say, "There's nothing wrong with me, *Mādar*; I'm feeling better."

I had taken an overnight bag with me. Ali would throw up and I would wipe his mouth and face with a flask of water and a handkerchief, and change his clothes. Oh, how difficult that night passed for me! It seemed that the six-hour journey to Tehran would never end.

We finally arrived, a few hours past midnight. We had been able to reserve a room in a hospice that was used exclusively by teachers. There was a hospital close by, and I took Ali to its emergency room. They examined him and wrote him a prescription. Father went to have the pharmacy fill the prescription; and Ali and I went back to the teacher's hospice.

Ali was running a fever that bordered on 109 degrees (43 Celsius), and we couldn't get it to come down no matter what we did. We were completely helpless, and father was gone without a trace, and it seemed that he would never come back. I started to weep involuntarily. My son was no longer talking and trying to cheer me up. His eyes were closed. He was burning up with fever. I took whatever bedsheets I had and wetted them down and placed them on his upper body, forehead and legs. I called 911. They asked, "What are his symptoms?"

"He has a high fever," I said.

The operator responded, "Put his feet in a tub of ice-water. This is not a 911 case."

I pleaded and cried over the phone until the operator finally agreed to send an ambulance. But when the paramedics arrived, they were not able to do anything for him either. All they did was give him a sedative injection and tell me to take him to the hospital as he needed to be hospitalized.

After they left, we put his feet back in ice-water and washed his legs down again. My beloved son wouldn't get better, and there was nothing that I could do about it. Nor had Father come back yet. No one had heard a word of complaint leave my lips throughout all these years, but now I cried in a plaintive voice, "Where did you run off to, Ali Agha?! After all, you are his father! Do something! I swear you to whatever you hold dear; to

Her Eminence Lady Zahrā, whom you love so dearly!! You are a martyr now, you are way up there [in the spiritual hierarchy], looking down on us. You know that I am not worthy, so please intercede on my behalf and ask God to bring our child back to health. Do you remember how you wanted him to be born as soon as possible? And when he was born, do you remember how you wanted to name him? We named him after you so that you would always be with us. Now we are losing our child, Ali Agha! For the love of God, do something!! Your son is dying!! You were known for your knowledge and wisdom, and you were concerned for the well-being of everyone under the sun; you treated your prisoners of war as if they were members of your own forces. From the moment our son was able to distinguish his left hand from his right one, his only joy has been to wait for nightfall so that he can find you between the stars of the night sky. Ali Agha, for my sake, and for the sake of your beloved Lady Zahrā, descend from your heavenly perch. Come to the aid of your wife and son this one night! Come and make an appearance for the sake of your son this one night! Forsake the comforts of Heaven just this once. Help us, Ali Agha, for the love of God. Ali, Ali Agha: I want you to bring back my Ali Jān! For the love of God, Ali Agha!!! …"

      I didn't know what else to do and I didn't know what I was saying. My hands were raised heavenward, and I was wailing and shedding tears as wide as my face, and kept repeating, 'Ali… Ali…' I don't know how much time went by, but when I turned my head, I saw that I was sitting next to Ali Jān's bed and my head was resting on his pillow, holding his hand in my own. The pillow was soaked with my tears. And Ali Jān was sleeping restfully. I put my hand on his forehead and saw that his fever had come down. But I was not going to leave it at that. I went and made my ritual ablutions and prepared myself for prayer by putting on the *chādor* which I used especially for making my prayers, and stood and made my ritual devotions and supplications. I don't know how many cycles (*rak'ats*) I made that night, or how many *Tawassol* supplications and Āshūrā Ziārats[101] I recited, but I remember well that after each cycle of my devotions, I would enter into the position of full prostration and would beg and beseech Ali Agha as follows: "Ali, you told me to continue your path like Zeynab would have done. I swear upon my word with God, I swear upon your soul, that I have lived my life with forbearance and strength, as Zeynab would have lived hers if she was in my place. No matter what calamities befell us, and no matter who or how much people talked behind our backs, I let it ride and didn't complain. I'm still in love with you and with our life. I am happy with the memories I have of you, and I have not opened my heart to anyone else, nor will I ever do so. In this *donyā*, my only consolation other than my memories of you is our son. He is a part of your being and your memento, and I have taken good care of your memento up to now. Besides your and God's protective shade, I have not let anyone else's umbra cast a shadow over him. Ali Jān, put in a good word for him with God. Return him to me. I know that nobody loves us like you do. Listen to my request just this one night, and I will be at your beck

---

[101] See footnote 91.

A Miraculous Sign

and call for the rest of my life. I promise. I beg you, Ali Jān, not to send me back down empty-handed. For the love of God, Ali Jān, do not disregard my entreaty. If there is something that you can do, do it. Show me that loving, helping hand of yours, Ali Jān! I miss you... I miss you. Caress me with that loving helping hand of yours. Help me, Ali. Help me! ..."

That night I cried to make up for a lifetime's worth of loneliness and loss. My mourning and laments were truly endless.

After all of those ritual devotions and supplications, I went to check on my son. He was in a deep sleep and was breathing easily and peacefully. I kissed his forehead. The poor thing had been suffering for two months and his malady had been so bad that it had prevented him from attending school for that whole time. I placed my hand on his belly. It was hollow and concave. I kissed his belly and said with a lump in my throat, "Ali Jān, I know you're here. I entrust our son to you. Keep an eye out for him. I know that if you were here physically, you would love your son like all good fathers. But I also know that you are more alive and attentive than all other fathers despite your physical absence."

The following day we took Ali to the doctor with whom we had made the appointment. We had been told [by another doctor] that we needed to have a CT scan made and to bring the results with us. They wouldn't let me go in with him, preferring to take him into the room alone. A little later, a nurse rushed out and called for me. I died of freight a hundred times over by the time I reached the room. My son had vomited over all of his clothes. I changed his clothes quickly and comforted him, "Ali Jān, don't worry, dear; you're going to get better now."

My son comforted me despite his condition too. He said, "I'm fine, *Mādar Jān*. I'm feeling much better. I have less pain."

After we had the CT scan performed, we were to go to Dr. Malek-Zādeh's office at noon on the following day. It so happened that this was the day of the anniversary of Ali Agha's martyrdom. Mother kept calling the cell phone I had borrowed and asking how Ali was doing and giving us reports and up to the minute updates about the commemoration ceremony: "The guests have all arrived... They have filled the seats wall to wall... We are reciting the *Tawassol* supplication for Ali Jān... Here, take a listen (and she held up her earpiece to the crowd)."

My belly was aflutter with butterflies. I felt Ali Agha's presence more than ever. He was sitting next to me, between me and my son; and I talked to him constantly while we were waiting for our turn to come.

The phone rang again. I could hear the voices of the womenfolk reciting the Āshūrā *ziārat*. Our turn finally arrived. Dr. Malek-Zādeh, who was a gastro-intestinal specialist, had a very somber and honorable character. He spoke formally and courteously. I placed Ali Agha's thick medical folder on his table. He examined the pictures, lab results and the endoscopy findings, and examined Ali Jān. He said, "I don't know what to make of these tests and findings. Please prepare the patient; he will have to have another endoscopy performed in the other room."

In those days, fifty thousand Toumans was a lot of money. But I had no choice and so I paid the price. Then a couple

A Miraculous Sign

of nurses came over and took my son by the hand and took him away. A little later, a nurse called out, "Would the person accompanying Mohammad Ali Chītsāzīān kindly step up?"

He had thrown up again. I took out a clean change of clothes out of my bag. I cried as I was changing his clothes, and talked with Ali: "Ali Agha, Ali Jān. I begged and pleaded with you so much last night… OK, so does this mean you don't feel sorry for me? But back then you felt so sorry for the Iraqi prisoners of war that you would take off your jacket and have one of them wear it instead. Now take a look at me and your child! Look at the kind of misery we have to suffer through. Take a good look, because we are losing your son! Yes, you are right, Ali Agha. You are nice and comfortable up there; why ever would you want to think of us poor mortals?"

I stopped the tears from welling up in my eyes with difficulty. I changed Ali Jān's clothes in that miserable emotional state and started to cry as soon as I was able to leave that room and go back to the waiting room. A nurse who had a petite frame and a likeable face followed me out. It seems she took pity on me. She said, "Mrs. Chītsāzīān, don't worry so much. It's not anything serious. He'll be better soon."

She had a high-pitched voice that had a friendly tone. I went and sat next to Father. Mother phoned: "Fereshteh, we are reciting the *Jowshan-e Kabīr du'ā* (or supplication). You should recite it along with us too." I could hear the sound of a chorus of female voices reciting the powerful supplication in the background.

I abruptly started to cry. I missed Ali Agha and needed him to be by my side so badly. His broad shoulders were stronger than mine. His heart was greater than mine and he was always sprithelier than me; his faith in and recourse to God was stronger, and his heart was calmer and more at peace. His presence was such a blessing and his absence... his absence... I whispered: "Ali, you left me on my own so soon. If you were by my side, I would surely be at ease now. You would have taught me how to put my trust in God. You are still present, Ali; I know you are here. So if you are present, give me a sign, somehow. Tell me that you are here with me, that you are looking out for me, like you used to when we were together. Tell me that I have not yet become a widow. Tell me that you are covering me with your protective shade. I am certain the martyrs are alive, and have great standing with God, and are honored by Him. Tell me so that I believe in you even more. Tell me that you will always be by my side, by our side, and that you will never leave us alone to fend for ourselves. Tell me that you are concerned for the well-being of your son, like every other father. Tell me that you love your son. Tell me that you love us. For the love of God, Ali, let me know where I stand one way or the other this day! Ali Jān, appear before me! ..."

The friendly nurse opened the endoscopy procedure room and indicated that I should go inside. My son was lying down on a table. The doctor was sitting upright and erect behind his desk. He indicated that I should take a seat. Then he said with a serious and confident voice, "Mrs. Chītsāzīān, there is nothing wrong with your boy. He has a very minor inflammation of the intestine which can be remedied with a simple dietary change which I will write up for you. And he is to strictly avoid all uncooked fruit for several months. And for the time being, he is to avoid all beans and pulses, soups and stews, aromatic herbs, spices, pepper and soda pop."

The doctor wrote these things down as he spoke out the words, and all I could do is to look at him in disbelief.

"There are also some drugs which he should take for a course of two months."

I said, "Doctor, forgive me, but the results of the endoscopy which was performed in Hamedān has been examined by several other specialists and they all agreed that it indicated a duodenal ulcer which had to be operated on!"

The doctor picked up the thick medical file that was compiled in Hamedān and gave it back to me respectfully and said, "Yes, it is true, Mrs. Chītsāzīān, that these results confirm the diagnosis of a duodenal ulcer; but I have complete faith in the findings of my own endoscopy. Now you tell me: should I trust what I have seen with my own eyes, or put my trust in this file?!"

Father spoke up slowly and skeptically: "Doctor, are you saying that the doctors in Hamedān all came up with the wrong diagnosis, or that the test results and endoscopy findings have been switched somehow?"

The doctor shook his head and said confidently, "No. By no means. I do not make any such pronouncements. But we have faith in the veracity of our work, and the endoscopy which we just performed does not confirm the results of last month's procedure."

There was nothing more to say. And I didn't *want* there to be anything more to say; I wanted with all my heart to believe and accept Dr. Malek-Zādeh's words and prognosis. And the joy that his diagnosis and prognosis brought overtook my whole being. I stood up and hugged and kissed my son who was lying down on the examination table. The findings of the Hamedān endoscopy were no longer important to me. What was important was that Dr. Malek-Zādeh had said that my son didn't have a problem. What was important was that my son had recovered. What was important was that Ali Agha listened to and heard what I had to say. What was important was that Ali Agha was looking out for us. What was important was that Ali Agha was standing beside us as solid as a great mountain. What was important was that I was not a widow and Ali Agha was still my husband. What was important was that my son had a kind and loving father who always kept a constant vigil over him. What was important was that Ali Jān was not an orphan. What was important was that Ali Agha's [spiritual] presence and lack of physical presence was a bounty and blessing for us both. I was overcome with a strange divine bliss. Ali Agha had answered me. He had let me know where I stand and where my duty lay. I kissed Ali Jān, but this time with tears of joy. He had taken on Ali Agha's scent in a strange and wondrous way. I placed my head on his chest and took in his scent. I remembered my wedding ring, which I was still wearing. I brought it to my lips. I closed my eyes and kissed it intensely. The perfume of wheat fields filled my senses.

The End.

وَلَا تَقُولُوا لِمَن يُقْتَلُ فِي سَبِيلِ اللَّهِ أَمْوَاتٌ ۚ بَلْ أَحْيَاءٌ وَلَٰكِن لَّا تَشْعُرُونَ

[2:154] And say not of those who are slain in God's cause, "They are dead": nay, they are alive, but you perceive it not.

An Altar of Roses

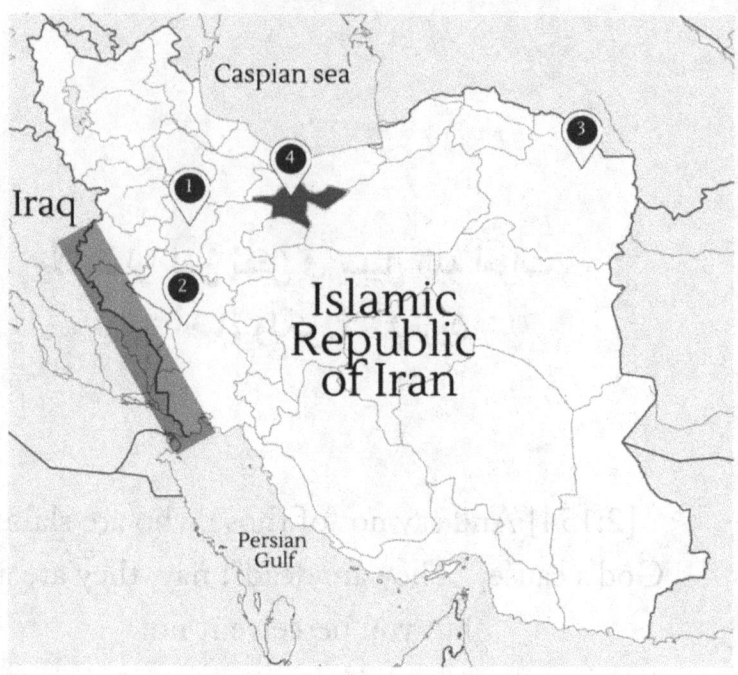

Map of Iran showing:
1- Hamedān
2- Dezfūl
3- Mashhad
4- Tehran province

The western front during the Iran-Iraq war is shown in the shaded area.

Shahīd Ali Chītsāzīān pictured with his parents.

Shahīd Ali Chītsāzīān pictured with is his brother Shahīd Amir.

Commander Ali Chītsāzīān pictured on the front lines.

The intelligence and operations unit of the 32nd Ansar al-Husain Division. The martyrs in the picture, respectively * Standing from the right: Didar Kordestani, Saeed Shali, Ali Chītsāzīān (Commander) * Sitting from the right: Jalal Eskandari, Hassan Tork, Mehdi Bahramji, Hossein Samavat, Mohammad Fathi.

www.ingramcontent.com/pod-product-compliance
Lightning Source LLC
Chambersburg PA
CBHW010244010526
44107CB00063B/2677